Scottish and Border
Battles and Ballads

By the same author:

OF SCOTTISH INTEREST: Travel & Historical:
Ho for the Borders
Over the Lowlands
Around the Highlands
A Hunt Around the Highlands: Standfast Press
The Scottish Highlanders & Their Regiments: Seeley Service & Co. Ltd.
Scottish Crafts & Craftsmen: Johnston & Bacon
A Guide to Scotch Whisky: Johnston & Bacon
The Original Scotch: A History of Scotch Whisky: Hutchinson Benham

HISTORICAL:
The Hunting Instinct
Hunting & Shooting: A History of Field Sports: Weidenfeld & Nicolson
The Life & Sport of the Inn: Gentry Books
The Georgian Gentleman: Saxon House
The Tenth Royal Hussars: Leo Cooper

SPORTING:
A Dictionary of Sporting Terms: A. & C. Black
Gundogs: Their Care & Training: A. & C. Black
The Gameshot's Vade Mecum: A. & C. Black
The Horseman's Vade Mecum: A. & C. Black
Roughshooter's Dog: Gentry Books

Scottish and Border Battles and Ballads

Michael Brander

Musical Arrangements by

Jimmie Macgregor

SEELEY SERVICE & CO. LTD.
LONDON

First published in Great Britain 1975
by Seeley Service & Co. Ltd.
196 Shaftesbury Avenue, London WC2H 8JL
Copyright © 1975 Michael Brander
ISBN 0 85422 105 0
Printed in Great Britain
by Ebenezer Baylis and Son Limited,
The Trinity Press, Worcester, and London

Contents

Foreword		11
Chronology		15
1	Largs	21
2	Bannockburn	27
3	Otterburn	36
4	Harlaw	48
5	William Dunbar	55
6	Flodden Field	60
7	Johnnie Armstrong	72
8	Elliot of Larriston: Musselburgh Field	79
9	Corichie	85
10	Raid of the Reidswire	90
11	Bonny Earl of Murray; Parcy Reed	95
12	Kinmont Willie: Jock o' the Side	106
13	Bonny John Seton: Bonnie House o' Airlie	123
14	Alford	134
15	Kilsyth: Philiphaugh	149
16	Montrose	156
17	Dunbar: Rullion Green	160
18	Loudon Hill: Bothwell Bridge	168
19	Killicrankie: Haughs o' Cromdale	177
20	Sheriffmuir	190
21	Prestonpans	200
22	Falkirk: Culloden	209
	Ballads	219
	Appendix: The Battlefields	279
	Bibliography	291
	Index	293

Maps

1 Sites of Battles and Ballads   20
2 Bannockburn   31
3 Flodden   65
4 Aberdeen   137
5 Auldearn   143
6 Alford   145
7 Kilsyth   150
8 Dunbar   162
9 Prestonpans   203
10 Falkirk   211
11 Culloden   216

Musical Settings
Arranged by Jimmie Macgregor

1	Bruce's Address to his Army	34
2	The Battle of Otterburn (1)	43
3	The Battle of Otterbourne (2)	43
4	The Battle of Harlaw (1)	51
5	The Battle of Harlaw (2)	51
6	The Flowers of the Forest	70
7	Johnnie Armstrong	74
8	Lock the Door, Larriston	81
9	The Bonny Earl of Murray	97
10	The Bonnie House o' Airlie (1)	129
11	The Bonnie House o' Airlie (2)	129
12	The Bonnie House o' Airlie (3)	130
13	The Battle of Loudon Hill	171
14	The Braes o' Killicrankie	183
15	The Haws o' Cromdale	187
16	The Field of Bannockburn	231

TO HELEN

Preface

I must acknowledge with thanks the assistance of many people on this book. Colonel Iain B. Cameron Taylor, historian to the National Trust for Scotland, was very helpful concerning battlefields in the care of the Trust. The Dowager Countess of Airlie was most helpful in connection with Airlie Castle. I must also thank the ever helpful staff of the National Library of Scotland, who were tirelessly patient. The late Mr William Leslie and the staff of the East Lothian County Library once again helped in every way possible. My son, Andrew Michael, took over a great deal of the drudgery of copying out ballads and proof reading for errors as well as criticizing ably. My wife, Evelyn, was long suffering and put up with a great deal, including proof reading and criticism while my daughter Kathleen produced the index. Without the help of all the above the book could not have been written in the form it now appears. This does not mean to say that for any faults or omissions I am not entirely responsible. I am conscious of many, but I hope that readers will get enjoyment from the result just the same.

Finally I must acknowledge with grateful thanks my collaborator Jimmie Macgregor's assistance. Not only has he produced the music and an excellent long playing record, but he has also advised me soundly at intervals throughout the writing of the book. Without their music the ballads are without life.

Readers will appreciate that, due to lack of space, variants on the ballads could only be included when of special interest; hence in some cases the words set to music differ slightly from those in the text. Likewise, there occurs a very wide variation in the spelling of proper names. I have not attempted to impose an arbitrary standardization, since, in most cases, it would be presumptuous to say that one spelling was right and all the others wrong.

MICHAEL BRANDER

Foreword

As the title suggests this is a book about Scottish and Border ballads of battle and strife. Since the battle inevitably came first it is necessary to know something about the action before the ballad can be fully understood and appreciated. Logically it is desirable to set the battles and their accompanying ballads down in historical sequence. Both battles and ballads can be seen more clearly set against a brief outline of Scottish history. So that the ballads may be sung as was originally intended, musical scores for the major ballads have been included. To gain a fuller understanding of the ballads it is worth visiting the battlefields themselves, but for those unable to do so descriptions of the major battlefields as they were and as they are today have been included in the appendix.

Although, strangely enough, this is the first time ballads have been presented chronologically with their historical background, their setting in the countryside and their music included, this is not, strictly speaking, a pure ballad collection. Where neither traditional nor more modern ballads have been available to illustrate a point either verse or song have sometimes been used instead. Thus it would perhaps be as well to start by explaining the difference between traditional and modern ballads for the benefit of those who do not know.

Professor F. J. Child's view was that the early traditional ballads may be regarded as a primitive art form, the product of a homogeneous people, prior to the development of poetry as we recognize it. That their authorship is long lost may be considered unimportant compared with the fact that they have been passed down the generations verbally, artless, unpolished and inimitable. He put these views forward forcibly in his *English & Scottish Popular Ballads* (1882–98) which remains the definitive work on the subject, the sum of all collections made before that date. Yet in his earlier work of 1849, also a notable collection,

11

Professor Child included many ballads of which the authorship was known and acknowledged. Even if he later rejected such ballads as modern and not traditional, it is only reasonable to accept them when considering periods, such as the eighteenth century, beyond the scope of the traditional ballad.

It might be thought that Child and others, by limiting their collections solely to traditional ballads, would be restricting the subject matter too greatly. Unfortunately this is only too clearly not the case. The principal difficulty facing anyone interested in ballads, whether traditional or modern, is the vast mass of material involved. Undoubtedly we owe a great deal to the early ballad collectors such as Bishop Percy, David Herd, Allan Ramsay, James Hogg and Sir Walter Scott, to name only a few of the eighteenth- and nineteenth-century collectors of note. Yet all their collections, even Child's own monumental and scholarly work, are curiously unsatisfactory in that the enormous scope of the subject obscures the content. There are just too many ballads. Thus, even where the collector knows his subject perfectly, as Child undoubtedly did, suitable presentation of them is so difficult that too often the reader is left floundering.

It was Mrs Hogg, mother of the 'Ettrick Shepherd', James Hogg, who highlighted another of the essential weaknesses of ballad collections. She warned Scott prophetically that as soon as he printed the old ballads which she was repeating for him to include in his *Minstrelsy of the Scottish Border*, they would cease to be sung. The point she was trying to make was that they were essentially verbal communications, passed down through families in the long winter evenings and intended to be sung or chanted, but above all spoken rather than printed. Once in print the necessity to learn them no longer existed and, more important, their essential impact was lost. True, they were not forgotten and lost to future generations as many ballads must have been in the past, but without their music they were without their most important dimension.

If printing the ballads without their music was one great weakness of many ballad collections, another undoubtedly was a total failure to classify the ballads according to content and period, thus losing all direction and cohesion. Even where explanations of each ballad are provided the reader is likely to find himself daunted by the seeming lack of relationship between them. Romance and tragedy, battles and bawdiness, jostle with each other uneasily. One ballad may belong to the south country whereas the next as clearly has its origins in the north, and there may be centuries between ballads set side by side. Such a mixture

12

of content, place and period makes for considerable confusion even with a full background knowledge of the history of each ballad and of the ground over which the events related in it took place.

The ballads in this book relate solely to battles or affrays fought in Scotland and the Border country. The Scots have long been recognized as a warlike race and they have also long been given to expressing their feelings in verse and song. The Highland Gaels, the Lowlanders and Borderers have all produced much in this form. Like the Norse with their sagas, scarcely a battle seems to have passed without becoming the inspiration for a ballad. Such ballads have the advantage over the romantic ballads to the historian, or student, that they can more easily be dated and the contents checked for accuracy more readily. Where there are gaps the historical background is available to fill them and provide chronological cohesion.

Against the background sweep of history the ballads can be seen as the vivid reportage of the day. With a description of the ground over which the battle was fought, as well as a clear idea of the course of the battle itself, the reader can obtain a real identification with the ballad. Above all, when the music is to hand and the ballads can be sung as was originally intended, he can feel entirely at one with them.

The fact that the ballads were intended to be sung or chanted cannot be over-emphasized, for it is their oral significance which chiefly differentiates them from poetry and song. The expert ballad singer could readily produce a ballad on any event, often using similar phrases in each. It follows that no two recitations would be exactly the same, hence various forms of the same ballad might be current in different parts of the country. With the development of poetry and more stylized forms of verse, which were both printed and recited, more sophisticated forms of song developed. Thus from the time of William Dunbar in Scotland the traditional ballad gradually evolved into more modern form, being slowly transmuted into verse and song.

It will be appreciated that, as well as traditional and modern ballads, there are two types of modern ballad, namely those which are contemporary, as for instance 'Hey Johnnie Cope' in the '45, and those which purport to describe events which took place much earlier, as for instance 'The Haughs o' Cromdale'. Where possible examples of each have been included, but obviously in order to give a balanced effect some battles and some ballads have not received as detailed treatment as others. Conversely some battles and some ballads, or on occasions even songs, have been deliberately brought in to fill a gap, or make a point

13

clear. For instance Robert Burns's famous 'Scots wha hae' has been included in the case of Bannockburn, where no contemporary ballad remains extant, and details of Montrose's famous campaign are included though not specifically covered in ballad.

Wherever possible, however, the traditional ballads have been used and the major battles and ballads have been included, even on occasion alternative versions noted in the appendix. Thus the period between the Battle of Largs in 1263 and the Battle of Culloden in 1746, the last battle fought on British soil, is comprehensively covered, providing in the process a fresh angle on Scotland, on Scottish history and on the Scottish and Border battles and ballads themselves. In this way it is hoped these ballads have been restored to life from the haphazard graveyards of print to which they have been too long condemned.

Chronology

Ballad	Battle	Date	Century (of ballad)	Victor	Area
Largs		1263	18th	Scots	Ayr
	Dunbar	1296		English	East Lothian
	Stirling Bridge	1297		Scots	Stirling
	Falkirk	1298		English	Stirling
	Loudon Hill	1307		Scots	Lanark
Bannockburn		1314	18th	Scots	Stirling
	Dupplin Moor	1332		English	Perth
	Halidon Hill	1333		English	Berwick
	Neville's Cross	1346		English	Durham
Otterburn (& Chevy Chase)		1388	15th	Scots	Northumberland
	Nisbet Moor	1402		English	Northumberland
	Homildon Hill	1402		English	Northumberland
Harlaw		1411	19th	Internal	Aberdeen
	Gretna	1488		Scots	Dumfries
	Sauchie Burn	1400		Internal	Stirling
Flodden Field		1513	16th	English	Northumberland
Johnnie Armstrong		1530	16th	Internal	Roxburgh
	Solway Moss	1542		English	Dumfries
Elliot of Lariston			18th	Scots	Roxburgh

Ballad	Battle	Date	Century (of ballad)	Victor	Area
Pinkie, or Mus'burgh Field		1547	16th	English	Midlothian
Corichie, or Hill of Fare		1562	18th	Internal	Aberdeen
	Langside	1568		Internal	Lanark
Raid of the Reidswire		1575	18th	Scots	Roxburgh
Bonny Earl of Murray		1592	17th	Internal	Fife
	Dryfe Sands	1593		Internal	Dumfries
Glenlivet, or Balrinnes		1594	18th	Internal	Banff
Kinmont Willie		1596	16th	Scots	Cumberland
Jock o' the Side				Scots	Northumberland
Archie o' Cawfield				Internal	Dumfries
Death o' Parcy Reed				Internal	Northumberland
Bonnie House o' Airlie		1640	17th	Internal	Angus
	Tippermuir	1644		Royalist	Perth
	Aberdeen	1644		Royalist	Aberdeen
	Inverlochy	1645		Royalist	Inverness
	Auldearn	1645		Royalist	Nairn
Alford		1645	17th	Royalist	Aberdeen
	Kilsyth	1645		Royalist	Stirling
Philiphaugh		1645	17th	Covenanter	Selkirk
	Carbisdale	1650		Covenanter	Ross & Cromarty
	Dunbar	1650		Cromwell	East Lothian
	Inverkeithing	1651		Cromwell	Midlothian
Rullion Green, or					

Ballad	Battle	Date	Century (of ballad)	Victor	Area
Pentland Hills		1666	17th	Crown	Midlothian
Drumclog, or Loudon Hill		1679	17th	Covenanter	Lanark
Bothwell Brig		1679	17th	Crown	Lanark
	Airds Moss	1680		Crown	Ayr
Killiecrankie		1689	17th	Stuart	Perth
Haughs o' Cromdale		1645 & 1690	18th	Crown	Moray
Sheriffmuir		1715	18th		Perth
	Glenshiel	1719		Hanover	Ross & Cromarty
Prestonpans		1745	18th	Stuart	East Lothian
Falkirk		1746		Stuart	Stirling
Culloden		1746	18th	Hanover	Inverness/Nairn

Scottish and Border Battles and Ballads

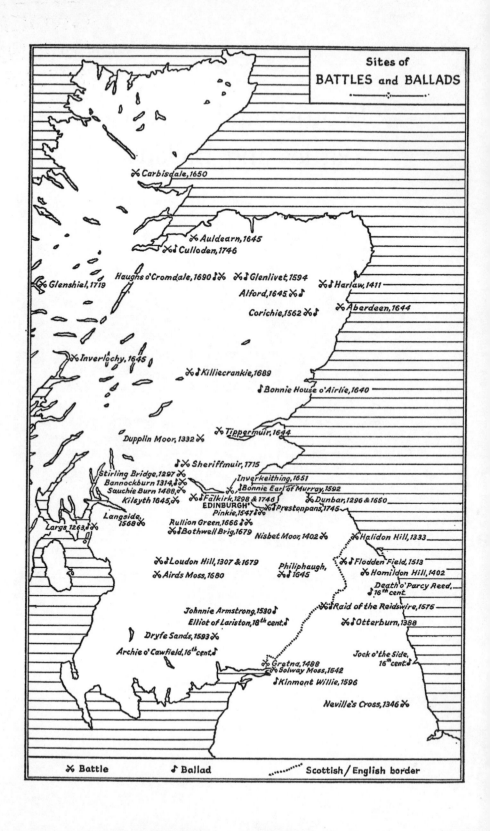

Sites of
BATTLES and BALLADS

Carbisdale, 1650

Auldearn, 1645
Culloden, 1746

Haughs o'Cromdale, 1690   Glenlivet, 1594
Glenshiel, 1719   Harlaw, 1411
                    Alford, 1645
                                        Aberdeen, 1644
                    Corichie, 1562

Inverlochy, 1645

        Killiecrankie, 1689

            Bonnie House o'Airlie, 1640

                Tippermuir, 1644

Dupplin Moor, 1332

        Sheriffmuir, 1715

Stirling Bridge, 1297   Inverkeithing, 1651
Bannockburn 1314,   Bonnie Earl of Murray, 1592
Sauchie Burn 1488,
Kilsyth 1645,   Falkirk, 1298 & 1746   Dunbar, 1296 & 1650
                EDINBURGH   Prestonpans, 1745
Langside,   Pinkie, 1547
1568   Rullion Green, 1666
Largs 1263,   Bothwell Brig, 1679   Nisbet Moor, 1402   Halidon Hill, 1333

        Loudon Hill, 1307 & 1679   Flodden Field, 1513
        Airds Moss, 1680   Philiphaugh,   Homildon Hill, 1402
                        1645   Death o' Parcy Reed,
                                            16th cent.
                                        Raid of the Reidswire, 1575
        Johnnie Armstrong, 1530
            Elliot of Lariston, 18th cent.   Otterburn, 1388
        Dryfe Sands, 1593
        Archie o' Cawfield, 16th cent.   Jock o' the Side,
                                            16th cent.
                    Gretna, 1488
                    Solway Moss, 1542
                    Kinmont Willie, 1596

                            Neville's Cross, 1346

Battle   Ballad   Scottish / English border

Largs

One of the earliest battles referred to in ballad form is the Battle of Largs, which was fought on the plain of Haylie close by Largs on 3 October, 1263. The battle was an attempt on the part of King Hakon of Norway to assert his overlordship of the Western Isles. These had been under Norwegian suzerainty since 1102, despite an abortive effort by Alexander II of Scotland to regain them in 1249 during which he was taken ill and died. Since then they had remained a continual source of contention between Scotland and Norway.

In 1262 the Earl of Ross, one of Alexander III's principal advisers, attacked some of the islands' chieftains who promptly appealed to King Hakon for assistance. In August, 1263, taking advantage of a famine in Scotland and intent on reasserting his authority, the Norwegian king assembled a fleet of 160 ships and a mixed force of Norwegians and Danes estimated at over 20,000. His own ship was noted as being over a hundred feet in length, larger than any other ship then built. With this impressive war fleet he sailed round the north of Scotland and in late August anchored in the Firth of Clyde off Arran in comparatively sheltered waters, but with plenty of room to manoeuvre where he wished.

Largs itself lies well inside the Firth of Clyde opposite the island of Bute, with the smaller islands of Great and Little Cumbrae little more than a couple of miles offshore. The high ground above Largs provides a fine vantage point to see right down the Clyde and over to Bute and Arran; almost certainly it was from here that the Scots kept watch on the enemy. The narrows between the Cumbraes and the shore, known as Fairlie Roads, extend from Largs to Hunterston, with an unwelcoming shoreline for ships. Only in dire circumstances would anyone attempt to anchor in Fairlie Roads. Nor would this normally be considered a suitable place for a landing by hostile troops. All the odds would be in favour of the defenders.

Although the Norwegian invasion must have had an element of surprise there seems to have been sufficient advance notice to gather a hastily summoned army to oppose it. When King Hakon's fleet arrived off the Ayrshire coast they found the Scots drawn up on the shore. For the moment therefore the Norwegians were content to sack Arran and Bute unopposed. Meanwhile Alexander temporized, sending messengers to discuss terms and gain time while he recruited further forces from as far east as Dunbar and as far north as Inverness, until eventually his army was estimated at 40,000, almost double that of the Norwegians.

In the end it was the arrival of the autumnal gales which decided the matter. Towards the end of September the Norwegian fleet was forced to anchor offshore in the Fairlie Roads in the shelter of Great and Little Cumbrae. As the weather worsened on 1 and 2 October anchors began to drag and with a full-scale gale many of the boats were soon out of control. Those who were driven ashore were mercilessly attacked by the waiting Scots army and slaughtered to a man. Finally the Norwegians made a determined assault on 3 October, but were repelled by the Scots with heavy casualties.

The remainder of the Norwegian forces were forced to withdraw to their ships in disorder and set to sea again. Scattered by the gale they then had to make their own individual way back to Norway as well as they could in the circumstances. King Hakon himself died in Orkney on his way home. From the Norwegian viewpoint it was an unmitigated disaster. Although undoubtedly aided very considerably by the elements, the Scots had achieved a notable victory. From then onwards the Norwegian hold on the Scottish islands began to weaken.

In 1266 by the Treaty of Perth the Western Isles and the Isle of Man, together known as the Sudreys, were formally ceded to Scotland. The Nordreys, or Orkney and Shetland, remained under Norwegian domination until 1468–9 when they were ceded as the dowry of Margaret of Denmark on her marriage to James III of Scotland, but the battle of Largs had already effectively broken the Norwegian grip on the West of Scotland. Thereafter Alexander III continued to reign successfully for a further twenty-three years until 1286.

Unfortunately the ballad tells us nothing of all this, because, quite simply, it is a very obvious fake. Its authoress was Elizabeth Halket, Lady Wardlaw, who was born in 1677 and died in 1727, the wife of Sir Henry Wardlaw of Pitrearie near Dunfermline. The ballad of *Hardyknute*, or the Battle of Largs, was, she claimed, mysteriously discovered in a vault near Dunfermline, but no original manuscript was ever produced and the 1767 edition of Percy's *Reliques* ascribes the ballad to her, almost certainly correctly. She certainly lived during a period when forging 'ancient' ballads was becoming regarded almost as an accepted intellectual amusement in Scottish literary circles.

The finished version as given by Child in his 1856 collection is a long and rather excruciating production which has little merit.* The start is perhaps typical of the whole; it refers to the improbably named Scots hero, Hardyknute:

> Stately stapt he east the wa,
> And stately stapt he west;
> Full seventy zeirs he now had sene,
> With skers seven zeirs of rest,
> He livit quhen Britons breach of faith,
> Wroucht Scotland meikle wae;
> And by his sword tauld to their skaith,
> He was their deadly fae . . .

A few further brief extracts will suffice to exemplify the style and content:

> Lang did they rage and ficht full feirs,
> With little skaith to man,
> But bludy bludy was the field,
> Or that lang day was done . . .
> In thrawis of death with wallowit cheik,
> All panting on the plain,
> The fainting corps of warriors lay,
> Neir to aryse again: . . .
> On Norways coast the widowit dame,
> May wash the rocks with teirs,
> May lang luke owre the schiples seis,
> Befoir hir mate appeirs . . .

So it drags on interminably for page after page with no relation to the truth unless by accident. Almost the only point corresponding with the known facts is the assessment of the Norwegian force at twenty thousand strong. It is only necessary to compare it with a traditional

* See Appendix p. 221 for a more readable version in full taken from *The Border Minstrelsy of Scotland* by Alexander Gardner, 1893.

ballad such as the Battle of Otterburn, or Harlaw, to see at once the very noticeable difference in quality and content. This is a palpably poor imitation, although it was enthusiastically acclaimed in its day as a lost original, an authentic near-contemporary account of the battle. It seems to have escaped the attention of all but a discerning few at the time that there is little relating to the actual battle or the circumstances surrounding it in the entire ballad.

Yet even Child included this in his first ballad collection and it emphasizes the difficulties facing all ballad collectors in striving to contain their collections within reasonable limits. Should such a 'false' ballad be included at all? If it is, should it be inserted around the thirteenth century where it is reputed to belong, or around the seventeenth/eighteenth century where it undoubtedly does belong? In this instance it forms a useful introduction.

As we have seen, the Battle of Largs was the turning point in Scotland's relations with Norway; it was also the turning point in relations with Scandinavia in general. From this stage onwards there was to be a steady decrease in Scandinavian influence in Scotland. With the beginning of the 'auld alliance' with France before the end of the thirteenth century Scotland was henceforward to be orientated towards Europe rather than Scandinavia.

This steady weakening of Scandinavian influence was not immediately apparent when Alexander III died in 1286 without a son to succeed him. His three-year-old granddaughter Margaret, the 'Maid of Norway', daughter of King Eric of Norway, became his heir and during her minority Guardians were appointed to govern the realm. When Edward I of England proposed her marriage to his son there was general approval, but her premature death at the age of seven in 1290 ended these plans. There were then thirteen claimants to the Scots throne and the Guardians appealed to Edward to make a choice for them. On the condition that he swore fealty to him, Edward chose John Baliol. However, in 1294, when charged by Edward to raise taxes to finance the English war with France, Baliol's Council urged him to make a stand. In 1295 he made the historic treaty of alliance with France which was to influence Anglo/Scottish relations for more than four hundred years.

Unfortunately the Scots were divided amongst themselves and Baliol was unable to unite them. In 1296 Edward I led the siege of Berwick, in person and followed this success by winning the Battle of Dunbar, when the Scots army impetuously left their strong position on the hill above the town and were summarily defeated. Finally Baliol surrendered, to be borne away captive to England after the enforced humiliation of a public penitence. Understandably Edward thought he had successfully conquered Scotland. Then the leader the Scots had hitherto lacked appeared in the person of William Wallace, who with Andrew Murray led a guerrilla force to defeat a considerable English army at the Battle of Stirling Bridge in 1297.

Following this success, Wallace led his forces on plundering raids into England. Throughout Cumberland and Northumberland the country was laid waste. Whole villages were put to fire and sword in retaliation for the English treatment of the Scots. It was bitter and merciless fighting which welded his small guerrilla force into an efficient fighting unit.

His bowmen from the forests of Ettrick and Selkirk armed with long bows and quivers of twenty-four arrows were able marksmen and sturdy fighters with their short swords when their arrows were exhausted. His spearmen were second to none. Armed with shields, or targes, mail gloves, helmets and padded coats as protection against arrows, their principal weapon was the twelve-foot spear. In formations known as *schiltrons*, or shield troops, some five hundred strong, close-packed, they would advance steadily by weight of numbers, or in defence form a circle with those behind projecting their spears over the shoulders of the kneeling front rank. In this fashion they presented an impenetrable hedge of steel against which even knights in full armour were powerless.

Only Wallace's cavalry, for the main part light horse, was inferior to that of the English. The heavily armoured English knights wore chain mail under emblazoned surcoats and carried twelve-foot lances, with battle axes, or maces, for close-quarter combat. Their heavy horses were often lightly armoured, or blanketed with flowing coverings known as 'trappets' designed to entangle sword or spear thrusts. Their superiority was painfully demonstrated when Edward I invaded Scotland once again in 1298 with a powerful army of knights in armour, foreign crossbowmen and Welsh archers, in search of Wallace and his supporters.

The English army finally caught up with the elusive Scots outside Falkirk. Wallace's strength was estimated at between 1,500 and 2,000, whereas that of the English was around 6,000. A master of guerrilla warfare, Wallace had been deliberately avoiding a confrontation, but his small force was skilfully deployed in a strategic position north-east of Falkirk close to Torwood, part of the old Caledonian

Forest. His spearmen were in four large *schiltrons* and between these he lined up his archers some six feet apart. In reserve at the rear were his small force of light horse.

Whether from treachery, as was suggested, or from panic, the Scots horse fled at the first attack, leaving their archers unprotected against the attacks of the English knights. Inevitably they were unable to withstand the unequal contest, although they fought magnificently to the last man. Though the armoured knights were unable to penetrate the spear-tipped *schiltrons*, the English archers were able to shoot at them unmolested and they were forced to give way as gaps began to appear in their close-packed ranks. In the end only a small portion of the Scots force escaped. By this decisive victory it seemed as if Edward had once again crushed the Scots' resistance completely.

Yet despite this defeat, Wallace continued to organize guerrilla actions, although on a much reduced scale. Eventually came the day when he was betrayed and captured, to be condemned and executed in 1305. By this time, however, the spark that he had fanned was in full flame. In 1306 Robert Bruce was crowned King of Scots at Scone, but soon afterwards his forces were surprised by the English and defeated at the Battle of Methven near Perth. Although forced to fly the country, he returned in 1307 to win a victory over the English at Loudon Hill.

Grimly determined to crush all Scots resistance, despite his failing health, Edward once more led an army north. He died at Burgh Sands on the Solway Firth as he prepared to cross the Border yet again. The 'Hammer of the Scots' was silenced at last and the news brought fresh support for Bruce, but Scotland was still an occupied country with English garrisons in every major town and castle.

Chapter 2

Bannockburn

While Edward II was occupied principally with his friend Piers Gaveston and events in the south, Bruce was able to range the country almost at will, retaking town after town. Soon he was raiding over the border into England. Eventually he was pillaging as far south as Richmond and Ripon and systematically reducing the English-held castles in Scotland. Roxburgh was captured by Sir James Douglas and Edinburgh was surprised and taken in a daring assault by Thomas Randolph, Earl of Moray. Finally the only castle remaining in English hands was Stirling. Hard-pressed by Edward Bruce, Robert Bruce's brother, Sir Philip Moubray, commander of Stirling, agreed to surrender this last stronghold if it was not relieved before Midsummer Day, 24 June, 1314.

The disadvantage of this agreement from the Scots viewpoint was that it almost certainly meant that the English would bring north a large army to relieve the castle. Bruce's forces were as yet more accustomed to guerrilla warfare than to set battles and his light horse were no match for knights in armour. On two previous occasions, in 1310 and 1312, when the English had invaded Scotland in strength, Bruce had carefully avoided a pitched battle. No doubt the memory of Wallace's defeat at Falkirk still lingered, but on this occasion the rewards of victory made the risks seem worthwhile. With an English garrison in Stirling Castle Scotland could not claim to be an independent nation.

Like a mailed fist upthrust from the plain, Stirling Castle, on its granite base, guards the heart of Scotland. It is no accident that so many battles have been fought nearby, for control of Stirling ultimately implied control of movement north or south. Here at the headwaters of the Forth a strong well-trained garrison could deny passage to any but the most powerful invading force from whichever side it might come.

It was March of 1314 before Bruce learned definitely of the English

King's intention to raise an army for the relief of Stirling. By then Edward had sent commands to all the northern English counties to raise levies to assemble at Wark on Tweed near Berwick by early June. From there he planned to advance by Lauder and Soutra Hill to Edinburgh and thence by Linlithgow and Falkirk. It was an ominously similar plan to that followed by his father Edward I before his victory at the Battle of Falkirk.

When the English army assembled on 10 June it proved an impressive array. There were between 2,000 and 3,000 armoured knights, whose charge Edward relied on to win the day. As well as English knights there were many from the Continent attracted by adventure or possible gain. There were also about 17,000 foot soldiers composed of the formidable Welsh archers, spearmen and others. In addition there were those Scots opposed to Bruce, notably the Comyns, or Cummings, whose chieftain, the Red Comyn, Bruce had killed in his bid for the Crown, also the MacNabs and the MacDougals. Finally there was an unwieldy and lengthy baggage train of over 200 wagons drawn by oxen and horses.

Against this powerful army Bruce had only about 5,000 foot and 500 light horse under Sir Robert Keith. His foot were divided roughly by area, or clans, into four divisions, or *batals*, each of which probably formed four *schiltrons*. Thus Sir James Douglas commanded the Borderers and the men from Dumfries, Lanark and Renfrew. Randolph, Earl of Moray, commanded the men from Ross and Moray, including the burghers of the principal towns of Moray, Inverness, Nairn, Forres and Elgin. Edward Bruce commanded the men from Angus, the Mearns, Strathearn, Menteith, Mar, Buchan and Lennox. Bruce himself commanded the strongest *batal* of clansmen from the West under Angus Og, MacDonald of the Isles, and the men from Kintyre, Argyll and Bute, also from Carrick, Kyle and Cunningham.

At this time the greater part of Scotland was still divided by clans and was mostly Gaelic-speaking. Over twenty clans took part, mostly under their own clan chiefs. Noblemen and knights, clansmen and burghers, Highlanders, Lowlanders and Borderers alike fought side by side for freedom setting a high standard of courage and discipline.

Bruce's chief weakness was lack of bowmen, so many from Ettrick Forest had been killed sixteen years previously at Falkirk, but as a form of reserve he gradually accumulated some 2,000 late arrivals and poorly armed volunteers without sufficient training, whom he wisely held in the rear. His army, though small, was composed of seasoned fighters

28

who needed little training, but, forewarned by the failure of the *schiltrons* at Falkirk, Bruce determined to achieve greater mobility, even to the extent of avoiding full-scale battle and relying solely on guerrilla tactics if necessary. With time to make his choice of battlefield he decided against going south to meet the English on the border. Instead he set about preparing the approach to Stirling itself.

Taking a knoll of high ground on the Coxett Hill above St Ninians as his headquarters and the Bannock burn as his chief line of defence, Bruce strengthened his position astride the old Roman road, the principal approach to Stirling, by digging rows of pits and strewing the ground with calthrops, a four-spiked iron device for laming cavalry, so constructed that when thrown down they always landed with spike pointing upwards. His right flank was covered by a thick wood unsuitable for cavalry; his front was protected by bogs, rows of pits and calthrops as well as the Bannock burn, and his left flank was along the line of the escarpment overlooking the track to St Ninians and the Carse, the flat ground where he hoped to have the opportunity of attacking the English. By his skilful preparation of the ground he engineered a trap for the English army, utilizing the irregular line of the Bannock burn and its associated bogs. He then sent his light horse on to Torwood to report on the enemy's movements and patiently awaited their approach.

The English army left Wark on 17 June and marched by Lauder and Soutra to Edinburgh, where they halted for supplies which had been sent by sea. On 22 June they marched twenty-two miles to Falkirk on a hot sunny day. On the 23rd they advanced from Falkirk directly towards Stirling, a long, impressive and glittering column with a small patrol of armoured knights in the lead. They approached the Bannock burn about midday.

When the first English knights came into view Bruce was still with his forward troops supervising last minute preparations. He had not yet put on his armour and was riding a small garron, or Highland pony, probably in order to keep his charger fresh for battle. One of the leading English knights, Sir Henry de Bohun, recognizing Bruce by his gold coronet, couched his lance and charged. Although armed only with a battle axe, Bruce calmly avoided the lance and rising in his stirrups as the impetuous knight thundered past he dealt him a blow which split his helm and skull in two and broke the shaft of the axe.

The English attack was not long delayed. Edward was confident that the small Scots army would never withstand a direct charge from his heavy armour. He therefore sent a small force of between five and eight hundred knights in armour along the edge of the Carse take up to a position in the rear of the Scots to cut off their escape. The main body of his armoured knights he sent forward directly against Bruce's *batal* awaiting them behind the Bannock burn.

As soon as the advance parties had crossed the Bannock burn with some difficulty, Bruce's *batal* advanced in *schiltrons* and sent them staggering back over the burn in disorder into the midst of the main body which was in trouble among the pits and calthrops. On the left flank of the Scots the Earl of Moray, advancing downhill with his *schiltrons*, was likewise successful and effectively annihilated the force of English knights detached to cut off the Scots retreat. Not unnaturally these successes induced a high state of morale in the Scots army.

Despite these reverses, Edward and his advisers were convinced that the Scots would never dare to attack such superior numbers. They decided therefore to by-pass the Scots position and press on towards Stirling across the low-lying Carse. This, however, was a great deal easier proposed than executed. The steep-sided tidal Bannock burn, as well as other tidal tributaries of the Forth and deep ditches, which also required to be bridged, ensured that progress was painfully slow and difficult. They also ensured that no supplies of food reached the English that night. On reaching the Carse there was no alternative but to spend the night huddled together in the open and the last of the army was not across that 'evil, very deep tidal stream' until dawn was breaking. The English morale was at very low ebb as a result.

Even then Bruce was uncertain whether to attack, but it was at this stage that Sir Alexander Seton slipped away from the Scots attached to the English army and, arriving at Bruce's headquarters, is said to have exclaimed: 'Now's the time and now's the hour'. Whoever said those famous words, and it seems certain someone must have done, Bruce saw that the English were in no position to manœuvre in their cramped situation. Soon after sunrise he gave orders for the attack.

Edward Bruce was in the lead with the Earl of Moray and Douglas on his left. In reserve behind them was Robert the Bruce. Hepburn's horse were held back out of sight, as were the 2,000 latecomers and poorly armed volunteers at the edge of the escarpment, by way of a final reserve. After kneeling in prayer the Scots advanced to the attack.

The English armour charged as soon as the alarm was given but, met by Edward Bruce's *schiltrons*, was halted and the armies became locked in combat. Moray and Douglas came up to Bruce's assistance and the three Scots *batals* pressed steadily forward against the entire English

30

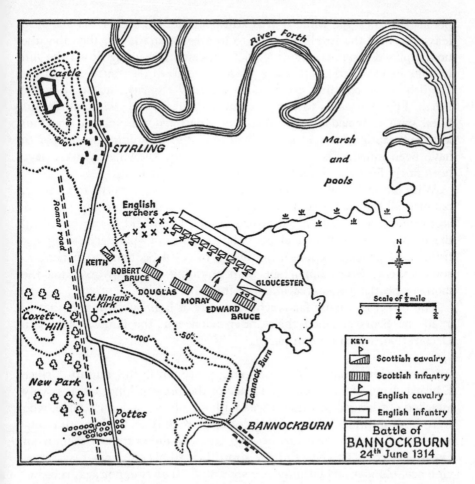

Battle of
BANNOCKBURN
24th June 1314

army, which was unable to present more than a narrow front due to the nature of the ground. From this stage onwards the battle seems to have become a vast armed scrum with the Scots, pressing forward inexorably in their massed *schiltrons*, presenting a formidable and almost impenetrable hedge of steel.

At one point the English successfully detached some archers on the flank to attack the Scots, but Keith's horse charged and dispersed them effectively, thus saving the day. Bruce then brought his own *batal* into the fray, sensing that the crisis of the battle was approaching. With this extra weight against them the English began to give ground. As their own men being driven back added to the chaos there must have been total confusion on the English side. At this stage Edward was

31

persuaded to escape while it was still possible. On seeing his standard leave the field the English began to lose heart and it was then that the undisciplined reserves, scenting victory, came streaming down the hill to join in the battle. Thinking these were fresh, seasoned troops the English broke and fled, to be drowned in the burns, the bogs or the Forth. Few were able to escape capture or death and the Bannock was filled with drowned horses and men. Apart from almost all the foot killed or captured nearly seven hundred English knights were said to have been killed. The Scots casualties are not known, but must have been fairly heavy, although nothing by comparison.

With his small but devoted escort Edward fled eastwards to Dunbar, pursued all the way. From thence he took a small boat to Berwick and so to safety. Sufficient knights were captured and held to ransom to fill the empty Scots coffers and provide magnificent spoil. The baggage train itself provided enough for every town in Scotland to benefit to some extent. More important than anything else, however, for the moment Scotland was secure and united once again.

The direct and most far-reaching result of Bannockburn was that in 1320 the Scots affirmed their independence in the famous Arbroath Declaration, which runs in part:

'Our nation lived in freedom and peace until the mighty Prince Edward, King of England, the father of the present king, aggressively attacked our kingdom, while it was without a head, and our people, who were both guiltless of any wrongdoing or perfidy and at that time unaccustomed to wars or invasions. No one who did not know them from experience could describe or fully appreciate all his outrages, massacres, violence, plunder and burning . . . sparing neither age, nor sex, religion or order . . . But we have been liberated from these countless evils by our valiant Prince and Sovereign Lord Robert (Bruce) . . . To him as the author of our people's deliverance we are bound . . . and are determined to be loyal to him in everything. But if he were to abandon our cause by being ready to make us or our kingdom subject to the king of England or the English we should at once do our utmost to expel him as our enemy . . . and should choose some other man to be our king, who would be ready to defend us. For so long as a hundred of us remain alive we are resolved never to submit to the domination of the English. It is not for glory, wealth or honour that we are fighting, but for freedom, and freedom only, which no true man ever surrenders except with his life.'

Here was the true sum of the wars of Independence. This hatred and distrust of the English was to last for over four hundred years. The Scots were unable and unwilling to forget the treatment they had suffered at the hands of Edward I, but his harsh tactics had ultimately recoiled on the nation he led. The 'Hammer of the Scots' had unwittingly forged an independent nation on the anvil of tyranny.

Unfortunately all the contemporary ballads of the battle have been long lost, although a chant was still believed extant as late as the nineteenth century. Burns composed his famous ode entitled 'Scots wha hae wi' Wallace bled' in 1793 and the tune to which it is sung is traditionally supposed to have been the tune of Bruce's battle march. (Hey tuttie taitie.) Some idea of how deeply Burns felt on the subject may be had from his notes on a visit to the battlefield in 1787:

'Came to Bannockburn; the hole in the stone where glorious Bruce set his standard. Here no Scot can pass uninterested. I fancy to myself I see my gallant, heroic countrymen coming o'er the hill and down upon the plunderers of their country, the murderers of their fathers; noble revenge and just hate glowing in every vein, striding more and more eagerly as they approach the oppressive, insulting and bloodthirsty foe! I see them in gloriously triumphant congratulation on the victorious field, exulting in their heroic royal leader and rescued liberty and independence.'

After composing his famous ode in 1793 he noted:

'I am delighted with many little melodies which the learned musician despises . . . I do not know whether the old air *Hey tuttie taitie* may rank among the number . . . it has often filled my eyes with tears. There is a tradition which I have met with in many places in Scotland that it was Robert Bruce's march at the battle of Bannockburn. This thought in my yester-night's evening-walk, warmed me to a pitch of enthusiasm on the theme of liberty and independence, which I threw into a kind of Scottish ode fitted to the air, that one might suppose to be the gallant royal Scot's address to his heroic followers on that eventful morning.'

Another song on Bannockburn, which was extremely popular, principally because of its rousing tune, is included in the appendix. The style is typically late Victorian and the words by Mr MacGregor Simpson were written around 1875. By contrast Burns's genius and inspiration stand out even more clearly.

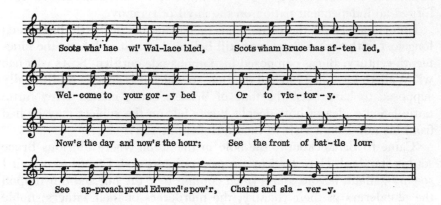

Scots wha' hae wi' Wallace bled, Scots wham Bruce has aften led,

Welcome to your gory bed Or to victory.

Now's the day and now's the hour; See the front of battle lour

See approach proud Edward's pow'r, Chains and slavery.

SCOTS WHA HAE

Scots, wha hae wi' Wallace bled,
Scots, wham Bruce has aften led!
Welcome to your gory bed,
Or to victorie!
Now's the day an' now's the hour;
See the front of battle lour —
See approach proud Edward's power,
Chains and slaverie!

Wha will be a traitor knave?
Wha will fill a coward's grave?
Wha sae base as be a slave?
Let him turn and flee!
Wha, for Scotland's king and law,
Freedom's sword will strongly draw,
Freeman stand, or freeman fa',
Let him follow me!

By oppression's woes and pains,
By your sons in servile chains,
We will drain our dearest veins,
But they shall be free.
Lay the proud usurpers low!
Tyrants fall in every foe!
Liberty's in every blow!
Let us do or die!

Chapter 3

Otterburn

Bruce's reign ended triumphantly with recognition of Scotland as a separate nation by Edward III in 1328, but further wars with England lay ahead. The Scots might hate and distrust the English as a result of their sufferings during their struggle to attain nationhood and independence, but this hate and distrust was matched in full measure by the English, especially in the northern counties where they had suffered continual raiding by marauding Scots. Intermittent warfare between England and Scotland persisted until well into the sixteenth century as a direct result of the deep animosity engendered between the nations during the wars of Independence.

Unfortunately it was to be Scotland's fate, time after time, to have a minor succeed to the throne at critical periods in her history. She was further fated all too often to have weak rulers when the need for a strong king was paramount. For much of the next three hundred years there was also to be an intermittent struggle for power among the more prominent noble families in Scotland. The Earls of Douglas, the Black Douglases, and the Earls of Angus, the Red Douglases, the Hamiltons and the Lennox Stewarts were all related to the Scottish Crown by marriage, as well as frequently being inter-related among themselves. There were other powerful noble families related to them. In the circumstances it is scarcely surprising that Scotland's history is tumultuous and even chaotic at times.

On Bruce's death in 1329 he was succeeded by his five-year-old son David II, who was ultimately to prove, though not lacking in personal courage, a weak and unworthy offspring of so famous a father. The 'auld enemy', England, lost little time in taking advantage of the presence of a minor on the Scots throne. With Edward III's active support and encouragement Edward Baliol, son of John Baliol, claimed the Scots throne. In 1332 he invaded the country with a mainly English force and was crowned King at Scone after routing a much larger Scots army under Donald, Earl of Mar, as Guardian at Dupplin Moor near Perth.

There were three contributory reasons for Baliol's victory. The first was the aid of a guide with local knowledge, said to have been a Murray of Tullibardine and a Baliol supporter, secondly the military incompetence of Mar in failing to post sufficient sentries or to ensure that they remained awake, and finally the deadly accuracy of the English archers soon to be demonstrated to all the world at Crecy. Thanks to their guide the English were able to cross a ford of the River Earn in darkness and approach the Scots camp at dawn while they were still asleep. Due to the lack of alert sentries the English archers were able to take up their positions on either flank before the Scots became aware of their presence. Inevitably, despite a gallant attempt to rally and charge the enemy, the murderous hail of arrows proved too much for the Scots. Mar himself was killed and the entire army routed in a very short time.

In the following year, 1333, the Scots suffered an even more disastrous defeat at Halidon Hill near Berwick in an effort to raise the siege of the town by the English. Led by Sir Archibald Douglas, who had succeeded Mar as Guardian, they ignored all the rules of war and the tactics so deftly demonstrated by Bruce. They advanced across a bog against a strongly held position on Halidon Hill under heavy fire from the English archers with their deadly longbows. As might have been anticipated they suffered enormous casualties and failed even to get to grips with the English. Douglas and most of the other leading Scots nobles and fighting men were left dead on the field.

In 1334 Baliol acknowledged Edward III's overlordship and ceded the southern half of Scotland from East Lothian to Dumfries to England, an act which was to mean over a hundred years of warfare before they were recovered. It seemed as if Edward III and Baliol were utterly triumphant. Yet so strong was the feeling against Baliol that he was unable to live anywhere in Scotland in safety without Edward's support. Meanwhile Sir Andrew Moray of Bothwell, as Guardian, continued to keep guerrilla resistance alive, though discreetly sending the young king for safety to France. In the south Black Agnes, daughter of the great Randolph, Earl of Moray, who had fought beside Bruce, successfully held her castle at Dunbar against the besieging force of the Earl of Salisbury for over five months. This was celebrated in the derisive jingle attributed to Salisbury:

> Came I early, came I late,
> I met Black Agnes at the gate.

When the English turned their attentions to France in 1338 at the start of the Hundred Years War the pressure on Scotland was greatly reduced. By 1341 the castles of Perth and Edinburgh had been recaptured, Baliol had been driven south to England and it was considered safe for David II to return. Unfortunately the young king soon proved himself incompetent as a ruler and even more useless as a general.

In 1346, aged 22, David invaded England with a strong army, partly in response to an appeal from the French and partly in search of military renown. At Neville's Cross near Durham he encountered an English force and as a strategist proved himself disastrous. Instead of emulating his father at Bannockburn he committed most of the mistakes that had been made by Edward II. He chose his ground badly, allowing little room for manœuvre and failed to send his horse to attack the English archers. Once again it was their accuracy which decided the day and although David fought with courage his army was defeated and he was taken prisoner.

Negotiations regarding the ransom required for his release dragged on interminably. When all seemed settled in 1354 the French persuaded the Scots to renew hostilities. Then in 1356 Baliol resigned all claims to the Scots throne, passing them to Edward, who decided on a final foray into Scotland in an attempt to impose his own rule. The Earl of Douglas as Guardian replied with the old form of 'scorched earth' guerrilla warfare recommended by Bruce. The small wooden villages and dwellings of the Scots were burned and the livestock driven off at the approach of the enemy. The Scots, carrying their provisions with them in the shape of meal, were unencumbered by heavy baggage trains. Whether on horseback or on foot they were thus able to move much faster than the English, who were unable to bring them to battle.

Edward invaded the country on 2 February, the feast of Candlemas, finding nothing but burned villages with no one to be seen. Throughout February, with steadily decreasing supplies, constantly harassed at night, or ambushed by day if they were rash enough to leave the main force, the English army searched for their elusive enemies. Eventually they retired thwarted to Carlisle, after what was termed understandably the 'Burnt Candlemas', and it was perhaps as a result of this experience as much as anything that David II was allowed to return on payment of a vast ransom. Thereafter an uneasy peace ensued until

David's death in 1371, when he was succeeded by his nephew Robert II, the first of the Stuarts.

Robert's principal policy was to strengthen the bonds of the auld alliance. Despite the uneasy truce with England, border warfare continued almost without check. In 1385 a force of some 2,000 French came over to fight the English with the Scots, but found the methods of guerrilla warfare employed little to their liking. Encountering Richard II's army they expected to do battle, but the Scots merely retreated. When the English burned Dryburgh and Melrose and sacked Edinburgh they still refused direct action, but when Richard's forces withdrew the Scots followed and plundered Cumberland at their leisure.

In the late 1380s Richard quarrelled with his uncles and as a result the two noble families, the Percys and Nevilles, who controlled the north of England, were soon at daggers drawn. With such prominent English noblemen at loggerheads the way seemed open for a successful invasion by the Scots. To this end the Scottish barons met in Aberdeen, ostensibly on the pretext of a banquet. During the feasting and drinking they prepared their plans, agreeing to meet in August, 1388, near Jedburgh, with all the forces they could gather. Their intention was a full-scale invasion of England. In the event they mustered 40,000 fighting men and 1,200 lances.

While these preparations were taking place the Percys, at least, were not unaware of what was afoot. Their spies, in the guise of minstrels and packmen, had learned of the Scots plans, but it was agreed that it was best not to show themselves aware of these hostile developments. Since they felt themselves incapable of opposing such a powerful attacking force they decided that their best plan was to mount a counter-raid, either against the east or the west, depending on which side the Scots attacked. By this means they hoped to draw them off, or at least gain some measure of spoils and satisfaction from the retaliatory raid.

It is said that while the Scottish leaders were discussing their plans for invading England at Southdean Church near Carter Bar they were overheard by an English spy disguised as packman. Some of the Scots, however, became suspicious of him and he was captured before he could get away with the news. Under cross-questioning he revealed the English plans for a counter-invasion. Thereupon the Scots decided to divide their forces. The main body continued towards Carlisle and the west under Archibald Douglas, Earl of Fife. A smaller force of three or four hundred picked men at arms and two thousand good archers, all well mounted, was detached under the command of James Douglas,

Earl Douglas, who was accompanied by the Earl of March and Dunbar and the Earl of Murray. Their intention was to ravage the country towards Newcastle in the east and as far south as Durham, taking what spoils they could in the process.

This smaller force under Earl Douglas acted with very considerable dispatch, before Percy, Earl of Northumberland, was aware of their movements. The first warning he had of their presence was the sight of smoke from burning villages set on fire by the raiders. He sent his sons, Ralph and Percy, to Newcastle to rally all available support to their side, while he remained in Alnwick, hoping to catch the Scottish force between his two forces. Meanwhile the Scots had ravaged and burned as far as the gates of Durham as planned and now returned, laden with spoils, to the gates of Newcastle.

Outside the gates of the impregnably walled city there was a good deal of skirmishing and a few minor battles between the two sides. During one of these skirmishes Douglas captured Percy's pennon and taunted him by saying that he would mount it on the walls of his castle at Dalkeith. To this Percy replied proudly that he would not carry it outside Northumberland. The Scot then challenged him to come and fetch it from outside his tent that night, but the Scots were left in peace. The English, imagining the Scots were merely part of a much larger army, were loath to leave the safety of their battlements to attack. In spite of Percy's desire to regain his lost pennon they refused to support him in what seemed to them a foolhardy proceeding. Thinking the odds out of all proportion the English merely counselled patience in the face of what was an accepted misfortune of war.

Failing to draw Percy into battle the Scots then continued on their way to Otterburn, some thirty-two miles north-west of Newcastle, pillaging as they went and driving before them all the cattle and sheep they had looted further south. At Otterburn, they spent the day besieging the castle to no avail. Finally they made camp on a slight hill nearby and took counsel among themselves. Most were in favour of rejoining the main army at Carlisle, but Douglas would have none of this and was in favour of continuing the siege of Otterburn Castle, for he was still hoping that Percy would come in search of his pennon.

Then the English received the news that the main Scots army was at Carlisle and that this was no more than an audacious force of some three hundred men-at-arms with two thousand mounted archers. Since they had at hand a force of about six hundred men-at-arms and eight thousand archers they were more inclined this time to heed Percy's

40

promptings that they should at once move into the attack. Indeed the odds were so greatly in their favour that it must have seemed almost a certainty that they would readily revenge the insults they had swallowed earlier and at the same time pay the Scots back with interest for their raid. Accordingly they marched hastily towards the Scots camp at Otterburn. There they surprised them in the middle of the night when they were supping and taking their ease.

Despite this unfavourable start to the battle, the Scots had prepared a plan for just such an eventuality. In the moonlight they skirmished their way skilfully, fighting a rearguard action until they fell back on pre-pared defences. Then they turned the tables with a vengeance and fell on the flank of the English, taking them completely by surprise. Despite the odds the battle ebbed and flowed for a long time. Although 'out-numbering the Scots by nearly three to one the English were weary from their long forced march.

Sheer weight of superior numbers was beginning to have its effect when Douglas stormed his way singlehanded into the mass of the enemy before being struck down with three spears in his body. He was tended, as the ballad informs us, by his nephew Sir Hugh Montgomery and he urged him and his companions to continue to rally the Scots in his name, since in the darkness his fall had escaped notice. Thus a sooth-sayer's forecast, according to some versions of the ballad, or a dream according to others, was fulfilled that 'a dead man should win the field'.

The Sinclairs and Lindsays, with the Earls of Murray,* March and Dunbar, charged forward to the rallying cry of 'Douglas' and the Scots charged forward with them. The English gave way before taking to their heels and amid the general rout Sir Ralph Percy was captured. The Scots pushing forward in pursuit then encountered the Bishop of Durham and fresh English forces coming too late to Percy's support. Although some of the more impetuous Scots were made prisoner, both sides, uncertain what was happening, withdrew. Apart from losing Douglas, who was buried on the battlefield, the Scots claimed to have lost only a hundred killed and two hundred captured. The English losses, however, were reputedly 1,860 killed and 1,040 captured with more than 1,000 wounded. The Battle of Otterburn fought in the moonlight on Wednesday, 19 August, was thus a notable Scottish victory.

The ballad given here is extracted from Sir Walter Scott's *Minstrelsy of the Scottish Border*. Scott claimed to have obtained it 'from the

* The spellings Moray and Murray are interchangeable and usage tends to alter confusingly from one period to another.

recitation of old persons residing at the head of Ettrick Forest'. This would seem to imply that it was one of the ballads he obtained from Mrs Hogg. Although not the oldest in Child's collection, it is the most attractive. He gives three versions. He also gives two versions of what is probably a later English ballad based on the same occurrence known as 'The Hunting of the Cheviot', or more commonly perhaps as 'Chevy Chase'. For the purposes of comparison the version from the Percy MS is included in the appendix.*

* See p. 233.

42

THE BATTLE OF OTTERBURN

1

from *The English & Scottish Popular Ballads — Child*

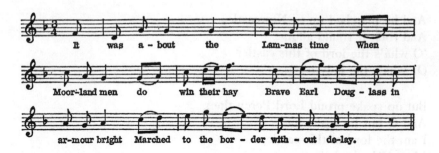

2

from *Minstrelsy of the Scottish Border — Scott*

It fell about the Lammas tide,
When the muir-men win their hay,
The doughty Douglas bound him to ride
Into England, to drive a prey.

He chose the Gordons and the Graemes,
With them the Lindesays, light and gay;
But the Jardines wald not with him ride,
And they rue it to this day.

43

And he has burned the dales of Tyne,
And part of Bambrough shire,
And three good towers on Reidswire fells,
He left them all on fire.

And he marched up to Newcastle,
And rode it round about:
'O wha's the lord of this castle?
Or wha's the lady o't?'

But up spake proud Lord Percy then,
And O but he spake hie!
I am the lord of this castle,
My wife's the lady gay.

'If thou'rt the lord of this castle,
Sae weel it pleases me,
For, ere I cross the Border fells,
The tane of us shall die.'

He took a lang spear in his hand,
Shod with the metal free,
And for to meet the Douglas there
He rode right furiouslie.

But O how pale his lady looked,
Frae aff the castle-wa,
When down before the Scottish spear
She saw proud Percy fa.

'Had we twa been upon the green,
And never an eye to see,
I wad hae had you, flesh and fell;
But your sword sall gae wi me.'

'The Otterbourne's a bonnie burn;
'Tis pleasant there to be;
But there is nought at Otterbourne
To feed my men and me.

'The deer rins wild on hill and dale,
The birds fly wild frae tree to tree;
But there is neither bread nor kale
To fend my men and me.

'Yet I will stay at Otterbourne,
Where you shall welcome be;
And, if ye come not at three dayis end,
A fause lord I'll ca thee.

'Thither will I come,' proud Percy said,
'By the might of Our Ladye;'
'There will I bide thee' said the Douglas,
'My troth I plight to thee.'

They lighted high on Otterbourne,
Upon the bent sae brown;
They lighted high on Otterbourne,
And threw their pallions* down.   *pavilions

And he that had a bonnie boy
Sent out his horse to grass;
And he that had not a bonnie boy
His ain servant he was.

But up then spake a little page,
Before the peep of dawn:
'O waken ye, waken ye, my good lord,
For Percy's hard at hand.'

'Ye lie, ye lie, ye liar loud!
Sae loud I hear ye lie:
For Percy had not men yestreen
To dight my men and me.

'But I have dreamed a dreary dream,
Beyond the Isle of Skye;
I saw a dead man win a fight,
And I think that man was I.'

45

He belted on his guid braid sword,
And to the field he ran,
But he forgot the helmet good,
That should have kept his brain.

When Percy with the Douglas met,
I wat he was fu fain;*   *glad
They swakked their swords, till sair they swat,*   *sweated
And the blood ran down like rain.

But Percy with his good broad sword,
That could so sharply wound,
Has wounded Douglas on the brow,
Till he fell to the ground.

Then he call'd on his little foot-page,
And said, Run speedilie,
And fetch my ain dear sister's son,
Sir Hugh Montgomery.

'My nephew good,' the Douglas said,
'What recks the death of ane!
Last night I dreamed a dreary dream,
And I ken the day's thy ain.

'My wound is deep; I fain would sleep;
Take thou the vanguard of the three,
And hide me by the braken-bush,
That grows on yonder lilye lee.

'O bury me by the braken-bush,
Beneath the blooming brier;
Let never a living mortal ken
That ere a kindly Scot lies here.'

He lifted up that noble lord,
Wi the saut tear in his ee;
He hid him in the braken-bush,
That his merrie men might not see.

The moon was clear, the day drew near,
The spears in flinders flew,
But mony a gallant Englishman
Ere day the Scotsmen slew.

The Gordons good, in English blood
They steepd their hose and shoon;
The Lindsays flew like fire about,
Till all the fray was done.

The Percy and Montgomery met,
That either of other were fain;
They swapped* swords, and they twa swat,   *smote
And aye the blood ran down between.

'Now yield thee, yield thee, Percy,' he said,
'Or else I vow I'll lay thee low!'
'To whom must I yield,' quoth Earl Percy,
'Now that I see it must be so?'

'Thou shalt not yield to lord nor loun,*   *rascal
Nor shalt thou yield to me;
But yield to the braken-bush,
That grows upon yon lilye lee.'

'I will not yield to a braken-bush,
Nor yet will I yield to a brier;
But I would yield to Earl Douglas,
Or Sir Hugh Montgomery, if he were here.'

As soon as he knew it was Montgomery,
He struck his sword's point in the gronde;
The Montgomery was a courteous knight,
And quickly took him by the honde.

This deed was done at the Otterbourne,
About the breaking of the day;
Earl Douglas was buried at the braken-bush,
And the Percy led captive away.

47

Chapter 4

Harlaw

In 1390 Robert II died and was succeeded by his forty-three-year-old son Robert III, a man of little strength of character or purpose, unable to maintain any control over his more powerful subjects. The internecine strife and border warfare continued quite unchecked and almost unheeded, but victory in the latter was not always to the Scots as at Otterburn. In June, 1402, the English defeated a force of border raiders at Nisbet Moor and only three months later, in September, the Scots were given a sharp reminder when an invading army indulging for once in a pitched battle was decisively defeated at Homildon Hill in Northumberland due to ignoring yet again the lethal potential of the English archers. Once again the Scots failed even to come to grips with their foes, but were routed at long range by the murderous accuracy of the long bow.

Robert III died in 1406 shortly after his son James, destined to be James I, had been captured at sea by the English. He was not to return for eighteen years during which time his uncle, the Duke of Albany, became Guardian and to all intents and purposes ruler of the realm. He did little more than his brother or father to check the intrigues among the powerful nobles or to enforce the laws of the land. Near-anarchy prevailed throughout Scotland. There was frequent internecine warfare, and the Battle of Harlaw fought on 24 July, 1411, was an example of this sort of civil strife.

Ostensibly Donald of the Isles raised an army to ensure that his claim to the earldom of Ross was confirmed, if only by physical occupation of the land. He had reason to suspect that Albany was planning to take it from him, as indeed happened afterwards when the Duke passed the title to his son David. In fact he may well have been planning a bid for the throne in the absence of his kinsman James I, or at least for the post of Guardian. It seems likely that at the very least he was attempt-

48

ing to extend his power over a considerable part of Scotland, from Ross as far south as the Tay. Moving southwards with a force of 10,000 men from the Islands and Ross, Donald successfully captured Dingwall and sacked Inverness. He then advanced on Aberdeen, ravaging the countryside on the way.

The country people soon rose in arms against him. Alexander Stewart, Earl of Mar and Ogilvy, the bastard son of the Wolf of Badenoch, and Alexander, Earl of Buchan, gathered men from Mar, Garioch, the Mearns and Angus and these were reinforced by local lairds, the Forbes, Keiths and Leslies, who turned out willingly to defend their homes. The burgesses of Aberdeen under their Provost Robert Davidson also gallantly joined the defence, all inspired no doubt by the knowledge that Donald of the Isles had promised his followers the sacking of Aberdeen as the reward for their success.

The two forces met at Harlaw, slightly north of Inverurie, itself fourteen miles north-west of Aberdeen. This was not simply a battle between Highlander and Lowlander, as has sometimes been represented. There were Highlanders on both sides, although, somewhat naturally, Donald of the Isles had few, if any, Lowlanders in his force. It was basically no more than a bloody battle in a minor civil war, Scot against Scot, with considerable bloodshed on both sides. It was indeed subsequently known as 'Red Harlaw' and the burns were said to have flowed red with the blood of the killed and wounded.

Darkness closed with the battle still in progress and the issue by no means clearly decided. It was not discovered until the following morning that the invading Highland forces had fled the field during the night. Only then were the wounded and weary defenders sure that they had been successful in protecting Aberdeen and the country further south from invasion. Among the casualties were Mar himself, the Provost and many of the burgesses of Aberdeen. It is a measure of the importance attached to the victory that an edict was issued, as was customary after battles of national significance, exempting the heirs of those killed at Harlaw from a number of feudal dues.

Allan Ramsay gives a version of the ballad (in *The Ever Green*), which has the same artificial rhyming as the Raid of the Reidswire, and has been proved to be a translation of Boece's History into verse. The ballad given here is from Child's collection, (1898, Vol. III, part VI) as 'communicated by Charles Elphinstone Dalrymple, Esq., of Kinaldie, Aberdeenshire, in 1888, as obtained from the country people by himself and his brother fifty years before'. It thus dates from the early part of the nineteenth century and not unnaturally after a gap of four hundred years it bears little relation to the facts. It does not even mention the death of Mar. Yet, although the ballad may not be of great age the tune may well be very much older.

THE BATTLE OF HARLAW

1

from *The Scottish Minstrel*

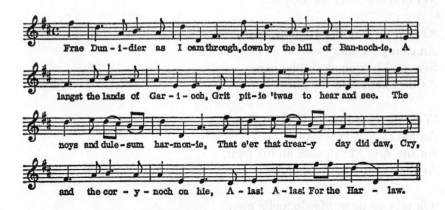

Frae Dun-i-dier as I cam through, down by the hill of Ban-noch-ie, A langst the lands of Gar-i-och, Grit pit-ie 'twas to hear and see. The noys and dule-sum har-mon-ie, That e'er that drear-y day did daw, Cry, and the cor-y-noch on hie, A-las! A-las! For the Har-law.

2

from *The English & Scottish Popular Ballads—Child*

As I cam in by Dunidier,
An doun by Netherha,
There was fifty thousand Hielanmen
A-marching to Harlaw.
Wi a dree dree dradie drumtie dree.

As I cam on, an farther on,
An doun and by Balquhain,
Oh there I met Sir James the Rose,
Wi him Sir John the Gryme.

'O cam ye frae the Hielans, man,
An cam ye a' the wey?
Saw ye Macdonell an his men,
As they cam frae the Skee?'*   *Skye

'Yes, me cam frae ta Hielans, man,
An me cam a' ta wey,
An she saw Macdonnel an his men,
As they cam frae to Skee.'

'Oh was ye near Macdonnel's men?
Did ye their numbers see?
Come, tell to me, John Hielanman,
What micht their numbers be?'

'Yes, me was near, an near eneuch,
An me their numbers saw;
There was fifty thousan Hielanmen
A-marching to Harlaw.'

'Gin that be true,' says James the Rose,
'We'll no come meikle speed;
We'll cry upo our merry men,
And lichtly mount our steed.'

'Oh no, oh no,' says John the Gryme,
'That thing maun never be;
The gallant Grymes were never bate,
We'll try phat we can dee.'

As I cam on, an farther on,
An doun an by Harlaw,
They fell fu close on ilka* side;   *each
Sic fun ye never saw.

52

They fell fu close on ilka side,
Sic fun ye never saw;
For Hielan swords gied clash for clash,
At the battle o' Harlaw.

The Hielanmen, wi their lang swords,
They laid on us fu sair,
An they drave back our merry men
Three acres breadth an mair.

Brave Forbës to his brither did say,
Noo brither, dinna ye see?
They beat us back on ilka side,
An we'se be forced to flee.

'Oh no, oh no, my brither dear,
That thing maun never be;
Tak ye your good sword in your hand,
An come your wa's wi me.'

'Oh no, oh no, my brither dear,
The clans they are ower strang,
An they drive back our merry men,
Wi swords baith sharp an lang.'

Brave Forbës drew his men aside,
Said, Tak your rest a while,
Until I to Drumminnor send,
To fess my coat o' mail.

The servan he did ride,
An his horse it did na fail,
For in twa hours an a quarter
He brocht the coat o' mail.

Then back to back the brithers twa
Gaed in amo the thrang,
An they hewed doun the Hielanmen,
Wi swords baith sharp an lang.

Macdonell, he was young an stout,
Had on his coat o' mail,
An he has gane oot throw them a',
To try his han himself

The first ae straik that Forbës strack,   *made
He garrt* Macdonell reel,
An the neist ae straik that Forbës strack
The great Macdonell fell.

An siccan a lierachie*   *confusion
I'm sure ye never saw
As wis amo the Hielanmen,
When they saw Macdonell fa.

An whan they saw that he was deid,
They turnd an ran awa,
An they buried hin in Leggett's Den,
A large mile frae Harlaw.

They rade, they ran, an some did gang,
They were o' sma record;
But Forbës an his merry men,
They slew them a' the road.

On Monanday, at mornin,
The battle it began,
On Saturday, at gloamin,
Ye'd scarce kent wha had wan.

An sic a weary buryin
I'm sure ye never saw
As wis the Sunday after that,
On the muirs aneath Harlaw.

Gin ony body speer* at you   *inquire
For them ye took awa,
Ye may tell their wives and bairnies
They're sleepin at Harlaw.

Chapter 5

William Dunbar

When at last released by the English in 1424 after his eighteen-year captivity, James I proved himself to be an athlete, a horseman of the first order, a musician and a poet. Aged almost thirty when he finally gained his throne he determined to introduce the rule-of-law throughout his realm. His enactments were aimed at controlling the more powerful of his subjects and proving that the king's rule was paramount. Try as he might, however, he was unable to prevent a considerable degree of internal lawlessness amd strife, more especially in the Borders.

James did not hesitate to employ duplicity, or as some suggested, treachery, to achieve his ends. The Highland chiefs, invited to attend a Parliament in Inverness, found that fifty of their number were promptly arrested and imprisoned. Only three were executed, but the king's power had been demonstrated. Admittedly Alexander, Lord of the Isles, attacked and burned Inverness the following year, but on confronting James's army in Lochaber he was easily defeated, finally making abject submission.

The general spirit of the times was still brutal, savage, treacherous and merciless and James's assassination in 1437 was in keeping. By intrigue and treachery his murderers gained access to the monastery near Perth where he was staying over Christmas. There they butchered the unarmed king without mercy, although he fought them courageously with his bare hands. The rule of the sword remained the principal rule of the realm after all, despite James's efforts to enforce respect for the law. On his death, with the accession of his six-year-old son, James II, intrigue, feud and faction were again the arbiters of existence.

Crichtons, Livingstones and Crawfords fought with each other and with Douglases. The Stewarts and Ruthvens fought at Perth. The Lindsays and Ogilvies fought at Arbroath. Powerful clans, families or factions fought against each other, or allied temporarily against the

English. In 1448 the English were defeated at Gretna on the River Sark. In 1449 they burned Dumfries and Dunbar, whereupon the Scots retaliated by burning Wark and Alnwick.

Even the most powerful in an age which lived by the sword and dagger could die by them. Towards the middle of the fifteenth century the Black Douglases were undoubtedly the most powerful family in Scotland, too powerful by far for their country's good. In 1452 James II, by this time governing his own kingdom, invited William, 8th Earl of Douglas, to Stirling Castle under safe conduct and stabbed him to death. Finally with the aid of the Red Douglas, the Earl of Angus, he attacked the Black Douglases in earnest. By 1455 their power was broken and James had established himself in control of Scotland.

As James gained control of his kingdom relations with England deteriorated. The English once more reiterated their old claim to sovereignty over Scotland. The Scots renewed the 'auld alliance' and began a determined bid to regain Roxburgh and Berwick castles, which were still in English hands. Border warfare continued intermittently, while in England the Wars of the Roses divided the country between Lancaster and York. Then, quite unexpectedly and most unfortunately for Scotland, James was killed in 1460 by the explosion of one of his own cannon at the siege of Roxburgh Castle.* He was only thirty and appeared to be continuing the firm policies of his father. Once again a minor, James III, aged eight, was crowned King of Scotland.

The Queen Mother and Bishop Kennedy of St Andrews guided the young king's policies, but again there was intrigue on all sides and self-interest and civil strife usurped the rule of law. In 1461, seizing his opportunity, as it must have seemed to him, Edward IV negotiated a treaty with John of the Isles, Earl of Ross, whereby he agreed to attack from the north, while the attainted James, 9th Earl of Douglas, the last Black Douglas, was to attack from the south. In 1463 Douglas crossed the border and was defeated by Bishop Kennedy, whereupon a truce was concluded with England in 1464.

In 1466 Kennedy died and the Boyds, with Kerr of Cessford and Hepburn of Hailes, all minor nobles, seized the young king and hence effective control of the country through him. In 1469 Boyd negotiated James's marriage, at about the age of eighteen, to Margaret, daughter of King Christian of Norway, when as part of her dowry the Orkneys and Shetlands came under Scottish rule. Their absence on this task resulted in the overthrow of the Boyds and the rise of their

* A tree in the grounds of Floors Castle, Kelso, marks the spot to this day.

enemies the Hamiltons. Intrigues and factions still dominated affairs of state.

As he grew older, James unfortunately showed none of the strength of character of his father and grandfather. He indulged in favourites and preferred the arts to politics. He was a poor horseman and a worse administrator. His rule was reminiscent of the worst days of Robert II and III. Justice was ignored, punishments and fines were mitigated or dismissed. His entire reign is a confused tangle of internal politics, with faction striving with faction for power.

The poet William Dunbar, who lived from about 1460 to somewhere around 1525, had some bitter comments on the king's rule and its effects. The following extracts from 'The Warldis Instabilitie' speak for themselves:

This waverand warldis* wretchidnes,	*sick world's
The failyeand* and frutles bissiness,	*failed
The mispent tyme, the service vane,	
For to considder is ane pane.	
The sugurit mouthis with myndis thairfra,	
The figurit speiche* with faceis tua,**	*careful speech
	**two faces
The plesand tonungis with hartis unplane,	
For to considder is ane pane.	
The liell* labour lost and liell service,	*loyal
The lang availl on humill wyse,*	*humble ways
And the lytill rewardis agane,	
For to considder is a pane.	
The change of warld fro weill to wo,	
The honourable use is all ago,	
In hall and bour,* in burgh and plane;	*bower
Quhilk to considder is a pane.	
Belief dois leip, traist dois nocht tarie,*	*trust does not wait
Office dois flit, and courtis dois vary,	
Purpos dois change as wynd or rane;	
Quhilk to considder is a pane.	

57

Gude rewle is banist our the Bordour,* *over the border
And rangat ringis* but ony ordour, *rank reigns
With reird* of rebaldis** and of swane;*** *loud noise
                             **revellers ***young men
Quhilk to considder is a pane.

Of one of James's favourites he wrote scathingly:

Ane pykthank* in a prelottis clais, *sycophant
With his wavill* feit and wirrok** tais, *clumsy **lumpy
With hoppir hippis and henches narrow,
And bausy* handis to beir a barrow; *large
With lut* schulderis and luttard** bak, *stooping **bent
Quhilk natur maid to beir a pak;
With gredy mynd and glaschane gane;* *deceptive face
Mell-hedit lyk ane mortar stane,
Fenyeing the feris* off ane lord, *Imitating the authority
And he ane strumbell,* I stand for'd; *by-blow of a strumpet
And ever moir as he dois rys,
Nobles off bluid he dois dispys,
And helpis for to hald thame downe,
That they rys never to his renowne.

As this comparatively mild instance shows, William Dunbar's verse could sometimes degenerate into what amounted to little more than a tirade of abuse, which today is almost incomprehensible in places. Yet it must be appreciated that his work had a considerable and lasting influence on Scottish poetry. Furthermore it must be remembered that what may now seem a mere string of insults was almost certainly by the standards of the day regarded as a vicious satire with considerable effect on public opinion.

In 1482 Edward IV of England acknowledged Albany, James III's brother, as King of Scotland and gave him command of an English army to attack Berwick and cross the border. James summoned his nobles to repel the English, but, led by Archibald 'Bell-the-Cat' Angus,* they seized the King's favourites at Lauder, in particular Cochrane, a stonemason created earl, and hanged them over the bridge outside the town.

* Being told of the mice who put a bell on the cat, Archibald Douglas, Earl of Angus exclaimed that he would 'Bell the Cat', i.e. hang Robert Cochrane, Earl of Mar, and the King's other favourites; ever afterwards nicknamed 'Bell-the-Cat' Angus.

They then forced James to withdraw to Edinburgh. Albany in consequence captured Berwick. In a weak gesture of pacification he was restored to his former rank and honours and made Lieutenant-General, but when he returned to England the following year these honours were promptly forfeited. In 1484 Richard III, having troubles of his own in England, made peace with Scotland.

James next found himself at odds with the Humes, one of the most powerful border families, over the question of the revenues of Coldingham Abbey, which they both claimed. In 1488 the Humes, the Earls of Angus and Argyll, the Hepburns and others in the south seized Prince James, the King's eldest son, and proclaimed him James IV. The Earls of Huntley, Crawford, Errol and Buchan with others in the north remained loyal and following a brief skirmish at Blackness the two sides agreed to an indecisive truce. Soon afterwards they met again at Sauchie burn, close to Bannockburn.

It was perhaps typical of James's entire reign that he buckled on Bruce's sword, but never drew it in action. He also had a powerful charger and, whether he was urged to fly or whether the horse simply ran away with him out of control, when galloping away from the battle he was thrown and stunned. Carried into a nearby dwelling he was quietly assassinated by an unknown figure probably in the service of Lord Gray, one of his oldest enemies. He was thirty-six at his death and his son, James IV, was eighteen, already fit to rule.

Chapter 6

Flodden Field

After the preceding twenty-eight years Scotland required a strong king and with the accession of James IV in 1488 there was a welcome return to a firm rule of law once more. Trade was soon on the increase and there was a fresh spirit of adventure and inquiry in the world of arts and learning. Throughout James IV's reign Scotland steadily increased in prosperity, but unfortunately there was a latent flaw in James's character which was to have dire effects on the nation.

A description of James by the Spanish ambassador, Pedro de Ayala, written in 1498, is to the point. He described the king as 'handsome, of noble complexion and figure'; speaking six languages as well as English and Gaelic; maintaining the law firmly 'without respect to rich or poor'. He was only critical of one aspect of James's character. He noted that James was a poor commander in battle because 'he starts fighting before finishing giving his orders'. It was this fatal flaw as much as any which brought his reign to its cataclysmic conclusion at Flodden.

James accomplished a number of satisfactory reforms during his reign. He began to pacify the Highlands effectively, notably the Lords of the Isles. He also established Edinburgh as the capital of the realm and it was here that he held his Parliaments, rather than moving from place to place. He greatly encouraged the spread of learning and the arts and William Dunbar's poetry reflected the changes. Indeed in almost every way his rule wrought considerable improvements in the country. It was ironic that after twenty-five years his reign should end so fatally for Scotland.

Unfortunately James had all the attributes which go to make up a gallant, if short-lived, platoon commander, but lacked the detached strategic mind of a good army commander. Pedro de Ayala had shrewdly noted this fifteen years earlier and in the interval James's desire for military glory had not diminished. It was due to this as much as any other reason that once committed to war the tragedy of Flodden became almost inevitable.

However, there is no doubt that James was reluctant to go to war in the first place. In 1502 he had agreed to a treaty of 'perpetual peace' with England, prior to marrying Margaret Tudor, Henry VII's eldest daughter, in 1503. Peace was, in fact, preserved until 1513, only a few weeks before Flodden, for, despite considerable provocation from Henry VIII after his accession in 1509, it was obvious that James had little real desire for war with England.

Paradoxically it was the Pope, Julius II, who set the events in train which led to Flodden. Concerned more with uniting Italy under his own temporal rule than with religion, he was engaged in a complex game of power politics balancing each country against the next as it suited his purpose. Having intrigued to get the French into Italy to crush the power of the Venetians, he was then concerned with driving the French out to restore the balance of power in his favour. In 1511 he formed a 'Holy League', an alliance of Spain and Venice against France.

In 1512 the Holy Alliance was joined by Henry VIII eager, like James, for military honour and glory and naturally orientated against France. Combined with Henry's contemptuous attitude towards him this was enough to cause James, not altogether reluctantly, to renew the 'auld alliance'. When the English invaded France in May, 1513, the die was cast. James ignored the advice of his counsellors, and decided to invade England.

The Scots soon assembled 30,000 men, although many of these were far from trained fighting men. The foot soldiers were mostly armed with eighteen-foot-long spears, or pikes, which required discipline, team work and practice to use well. Apart from these they had short swords. The French had also sent a thousand hand culverins and arquebus. Both the pride and the weakness of the Scots army was their extremely unwieldy artillery train, consisting of five large cannon, each requiring thirty-six oxen to move it, and twelve lesser cannon. With the requisite powder and shot the resulting column inevitably slowed down the army's movements very considerably. It was almost certainly because of this that when James crossed the border on 22 August he spent the first fortnight capturing the border castles of Wark, Norham, Ford and Etal, using his cannon to induce them to surrender. Had he instead marched southwards at once, matters might have taken a different turn.

The seventy-year-old Earl of Surrey, deputed by Henry VIII to guard the north against the Scots, had spent the month of August preparing to mobilize his forces and in moving his artillery to Newcastle. Even so it was fortunate for him that James halted to reduce the border strongholds, thus giving him valuable time to complete his preparations and raise his forces. By September he had 20,000 men, well armed with the eight-foot-long axes with curved heads known as bills. These were joined at Alnwick by his son Lord Thomas Howard, Lord High Admiral, with another thousand men from the fleet anchored at sea.

Worried at this stage in case James might retreat over the border, Surrey sent him a challenge to meet him in battle before 9 September at the latest. He had gauged his man well, for James duly agreed to wait for Surrey until the 9th. On his arrival at Wooler on the 8th, however, Surrey found James and the Scottish army awaiting him encamped on Flodden Edge above the Till in a strong strategic position. In numbers they were, if anything, superior to the English. Furthermore, most of Surrey's army had been marching for three days in wet conditions over difficult ground and were short of victuals, with no ale to warm their bellies. From the English viewpoint it was not a promising outlook.

How then was it that the English achieved such a total victory? The crux of the battle was James's failure to prevent the English force under Howard from outflanking his position. In a bold strategic move Surrey sent them forward to outflank the Scots and cross the River Till by the Twizel bridge behind them, thus cutting off their retreat. Meanwhile he followed behind and crossed the Till at Millford. By this move he hoped to draw the Scots off Flodden Edge and while Howard attacked frontally he would take them from the flank, somewhere around Branxton. In the end this was almost exactly what happened.

James only appears to have appreciated what was happening when Howard was already across the Till. In fact this may not have been the colossal blunder it appears on the face of it. There is a likely explanation in the weather conditions. It is acknowledged that the weather was poor with a drizzle falling which made the grass wet and slippery. At that time of year on the east coast in such conditions it is more than probable there was a mist, or haar as it is known locally, which would reduce visibility to near zero. Howard's forces were probably not visible until it was too late. On the other hand a good commander in such circumstances would have had piquets out in various directions keeping in touch with the enemy. For his failure to take this elementary precaution James must stand condemned, but in fact it tends to make the haar theory all the more probable since piquets on one side of the river might well be unable in such conditions to see what was happening on the other bank.

Not only did James apparently fail to post any piquets to report on the enemy movements, he also failed to post any at the fords and bridges over the River Till. With a report on the enemy movements to hand he could readily have sent a small force to deny them the chance of crossing. A light cannon or two, however heavy and ponderous to move, would have been enough to prevent the English from crossing the river and such a setback in their tired state could have been decisive. The probability is that James simply expected the English to act in the manner of ancient chivalry and make a frontal attack on his position. That they might outflank him may never have occurred to him. Such total lack of strategic sense in any army commander may sound impossible today, but was conceivable then. In any age such rigidity of mind bodes ill for the army and this was to prove no exception.

It was not until around midday, or later, that James realized Howard's forces were approaching him from the rear. When he did at last appreciate the English intentions he seems to have panicked quite unnecessarily. He hastily executed a complicated about-face and marched his army about a mile at top speed to Branxton Hill, setting his own camp on Flodden Hill alight for no obvious reason. Since the English army had a more difficult uphill piece of ground to cover the Scots arrived on Branxton Hill before them, but had James been content to stay where he was he would have been perfectly secure. By moving he immediately lost the advantage of a well-fortified position where his army had good fields of fire for their cannon. At Branxton Edge his advantage in ground was by no means so great and his men were thoroughly unsettled. More important still his cannon no longer had suitable fields of fire and could not be depressed sufficiently to affect the issue greatly. On every score he would have been better advised to stay where he was and await the English attack. As it was he did exactly what Surrey had hoped he would do and played into the English hands.

Apart from their undoubted superiority in strategic and tactical command, the English had three other advantages over the Scots, none of which could have been foreseen beforehand. Firstly, the English artillery was greatly superior and better aimed. Whether this was because the Scots were less efficient, or because their guns were no longer suitably sited in their fresh positions and could not be depressed sufficiently to take effect, is not clear. The Scots cannon-fire going overhead merely frightened some of the English raw recuits. The English artillery was noted as being well aimed and effective, ploughing great gaps in the Scots ranks. Secondly, the English bills proved much superior in action to the unwieldy spears of the Scots. Chopped in half by the bills, the Scots had to throw them away and rely on their short swords, or maces, but were unable to get to close quarters with them. Thirdly, the grass was wet and slippery so that charging downhill was no advantage to the Scots. They tended to slide and lose formation, hence the shock effect of the disciplined *schiltrons*, which had won the day at Bannockburn, was dissipated and lost.

The Scots did not arrive at their position on Branxton Hill until between two and three in the afternoon. From there, looking downwards, they were able to see the English army in two solid blocks, with columns like the horns of a bull stretched out towards them on either side of Branxton village. Quite how soon the battle started is not clear, but the Scots do not seem to have been able to withstand the galling English cannon-fire and somewhere between four and five they advanced in the face of heavy fire from the English archers, still one of the most effective and accurate weapons of war. Despite these combined disadvantages they fought on stubbornly and bloodily.

The Scottish left wing under Home successfully defeated the Admiral's right wing, but their subsequent movements are obscure and they seem to have set about plundering the baggage in the rear, taking no further part in the battle. Meanwhile, supported by the timely arrival of Lord Dacre's Borderers from Cumberland under the famed banner of the Red Bull of Dacre, Howard drove the Scots back in front of him and swung round to assist the Earl of Surrey attacking the Scots flank and rear. Lennox and Argyll fell at the head of their Highlanders, who were put to flight. Rothes and Crawford also fell early, but the Scots centre fought strongly, although very soon surrounded.

James then acted entirely as the Spanish ambassador had prophesied. He lost his head completely and charged without further word of command ahead of his men, leading a headlong attack on the English and penetrating, so it is said, within a lance length of Surrey before falling mortally wounded. Many a Scot seems to have gone to his death in a similar way to judge from the description given by an Englishman: 'These fellows were such large, strong men that they would not fall when 4 or 5 bills struck one of them.'

Superior in strategy, tactics, artillery and personal weapons, able to

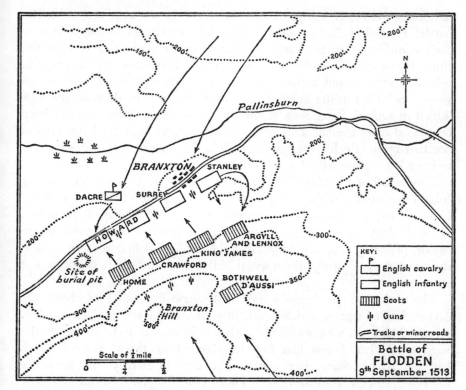

KEY:

⌐	English cavalry
☐	English infantry
▥	Scots
ⱷ	Guns
⇒	Tracks or minor roads

Battle of
FLODDEN
9ᵗʰ September 1513

keep the Scots at arm's length, the English had every advantage once
the battle was joined. Attacked on all sides and hopelessly misled and
outgeneralled, the Scots fought on stubbornly, dying bloodily in the field
rather than yielding. So stubborn indeed was their defence that after
darkness had fallen Surrey berated his commanders for failing to win the
day. On discovering himself in possession of the field the next morning,
however, he knighted them instead.

The Scots losses were estimated at between six and ten thousand
slain, including twelve earls, fourteen lords, one archbishop, three
bishops and sixty-eight knights and gentlemen, apart from James himself. By comparison the English lost merely 1,500 and a few of their
leaders. Yet to the tired and weary English attacking in foul weather
on empty stomachs against a fresh army of superior strength it seemed
like a miracle that they could have won. Small wonder that Surrey had
his doubts when darkness fell on that overcast September day. In the
circumstances it seemed most unlikely that the Scots would be defeated.

Flodden was not merely a defeat. To the Scots it was an unmitigated national disaster. It is significant that there is no Scots ballad on the battle. The only ballads extant are English. The Scots do not even have their own history of the battle written from their point of view at the time. There was no one left alive to write it. The Scots were afterwards reluctant even to put a name to the day. The dead were referred to simply as 'killed in the field', the equivalent of the modern anonymous 'killed in action'. Some idea of the extent of the national disaster may be gained from the fact that there is still a farm near Earlston on the Scottish borders called Sorrowless Field, because it was the only one to have had no one killed at Flodden.

The ballad of Flodden Field is from Deloney's 'Pleasant History of John Winchcomb, in his younger yeares called Jacke of Newberie, etc.,' London, 1633, (9th edition), reprinted by J. O. Halliwell, London, 1859. It may therefore be accepted as a genuine sixteenth-century ballad, probably sung not long after the battle and first printed around the turn of the century. By normal ballad standards it is factually not inaccurate.

The choice of St James's day is historically sound as the Scots declaration of war was dated 26 July, the day after St James's day. Queen Margaret's opposition is also a historical fact, although the suggestion that James had her imprisoned or threatened her with hanging is, of course, hyperbole. The Earl of Surrey, her uncle by marriage, had escorted Margaret Tudor from England for her marriage in 1503, hence the reason for appointing him her chamberlain ten years later.

Although known as Flodden Field in Scotland it was more generally known as the Battle of Brankston in England, here misnamed Bramstone. The ballad also somewhat understandably exaggerates the number of dead, setting them at 12,000. 'Jack with the feather' is a derisory term for James and the reference to 'lapping in leather' in the last verse is merely the first stage in embalming. After the battle James's body was found, sent south and embalmed. This was done by disembowelling, sewing tightly in leather, then enclosing in lead.

66

King Jamie hath made a vow,
Keepe it well if he may!
That he will be at lovely London
Upon Saint James, his day.

'Upon Saint James his day at noone,
At faire London will I be,
And all the lords in merrie Scotland,
They shall dine there with me.'

Then bespake good Queene Margaret,
The teares fell from her eye:
'Leave off these warres, most noble king,
Keepe your fidelitie.

'The water runnes swift and wondrous deepe,
From bottome unto the brimme;
My brother Henry hath men good enough;
England is hard to winne.'

'Away,' quoth he, 'with this silly foole!
In prison fast let her lie:
For she is come of the English bloud,
And for these words she shall dye.'

With that bespake Lord Thomas Howard,
The queenes chamberlaine that day:
'If that you put Queene Margaret to death,
Scotland shall rue it alway.'

Then in a rage King Jamie did say,
'Away with this foolish mome!*   *dolt
He shall be hanged, and the other be burned,
So soone as I come home.'

At Flodden Field the Scots came in,
Which made our English men faine;*   *glad
At Bramstone Greene this battaile was seene,
There was King Jamie slaine.

Then presently the Scots did flie,
Their cannons they left behind;
Their ensignes gay were won all away,
Our souldiers did beate them blinde.

To tell you plaine, twelve thousand were slaine
That to the fight did stand,
And many prisoners tooke that day,
The best in all Scotland.

That day made many a fatherlesse child,
And many a widow poore,
And many a Scottish gay lady
Sate weeping in her bower.

Jack with a feather was lapt all in leather,
His boastings were all in vaine;
He had such a chance, with a new morrice-dance,
He never went home againe.

THE FLOWERS OF THE FOREST

The Flowers of the Forest is the recognized Scots lament for Flodden and for many years in the late eighteenth century was accepted as a genuine song of the period. It was published anonymously and aroused considerable interest and speculation, being widely accepted as an old song rediscovered. James Hogg was convinced that it was not a genuine sixteenth-century piece, but it was Sir Walter Scott who finally discovered the authoress. It was in fact written in the mid-eighteenth century by Miss Jane Elliot, daughter of Sir Gilbert Elliot of Minto, Lord Chief Justice Clerk of Scotland.

Miss Jane Elliot was born in 1727 and died at Mount Teviot in Roxburgh in 1805. The story goes that her father made a wager with her that she could not write any verses on the theme of Flodden. Although her lament is based in part on an even earlier song entitled 'The Flowers of the Forest', written by Mrs Patrick Cockburn of Ormiston, born at Farnielee in Selkirk, Miss Elliot's verses are a far finer piece of poetry. As a lament they are inspired and the song is a masterpiece of sorrow. Played on the pipes it wrenches the heartstrings. It has stood the test of time and deserves its place in any Scots collection.

THE FLOWERS OF THE FOREST

from *Songs of Scotland*

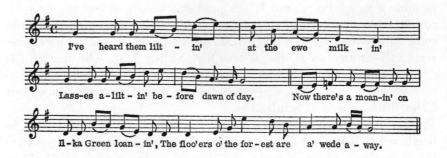

I've heard them lilt-in' at the ewe milk-in'
Lass-es a-lilt-in' be-fore dawn of day. Now there's a moan-in' on
Il-ka Green loan-in', The floo'ers o' the for-est are a' wede a-way.

I've heard the liltin' at our ewe-milkin',
Lasses a-liltin' before dawn o' day;
Now there's a moanin' on ilka green loanin',*   *milking park
The flowers of the forest are a' wede away.

At buchts* in the mornin', nae blythe lads are scornin',   *sheep-pen
Lasses are lanely, and dowie,* and wae;   *sad
Nae daffin',* nae gabbin', but sighin' and sabbin',   *dallying
Ilk ane lifts her leglin and hies her away.

In har'st at the shearin', nae youths now are jeerin',
The bandsters* are runkled, and lyart,** and gray;   *binders of sheaves
At fair or at preachin', nae wooin', nae fleechin',*   **grey streaked
The flowers of the forest are a' wede away.   *flatter

At e'en, in the gloamin', nae swankies* are roamin'   *gallants
'Bout stacks, 'mang the lassies at bogle* to play;   *hide and seek
But each ane sits dreary, lamentin' her dearie,
The flowers of the forest are a' wede away.

70

Dool* and wae for the order sent our lads to the border,   *grief
The English for ance by guile wan the day;
The flowers of the forest, that fought aye the foremost,
The prime o' our land now lie cauld in the clay.

We'll hear nae mair liltin' at our ewe-milkin',
Women and bairns are dowie and wae;
Sighin' and moanin' on ilka green loanin',
The flowers of the forest are a' wede away.

Chapter 7

Johnnie Armstrong

Flodden left Scotland with few leaders. It also left the country with yet another minor on the throne for James V was only a year and a half old on his father's death. Inevitably the first half of the sixteenth century saw continual power struggles among the nobility, in particular between those who favoured England as an ally and those who favoured France. Soon there were to be included the complications of those who favoured the old religion and those who favoured the new.

With the advent of the Duke of Albany as Guardian in 1515, first cousin to James IV, though a Frenchman in all but name, the French party was in the ascendant. On his return to France, however, the Douglas party was triumphant and the English supporters to the fore. Finally James V succeeded in 1528 in becoming his own master at the age of 17 and his first course of action was to effect the banishment of Douglas to England.

James was intent on restoring order in his kingdom and set about it in what was fast becoming a typical Stuart fashion. In 1530 he levied an army of around 12,000 men with which he intended to pacify the borders. Lindsay of Pitscottie described the details as follows:

'The king . . . made a convention at Edinburgh with all the lords and barons, to consult how he might best stanch theiff and riever within his realm. To this effect he gave charge to all earls, lords barons, free-holders and gentlemen to compeir at Edinburgh with a month's victual, to pass with the king to daunton the thieves of Teviotdale and Annandale with all other parts of the kingdom; also the king desired all gentlemen that had dogs that were good to bring them to hunt in the said bounds, which the most part of the noblemen of the Highlands did, such as the earls of Huntly, Argyle and Athol, who brought their deerhounds with them and hunted with his majesty. These lords with many other lords and gentlemen, to the number of twelve thousand men, assembled at Edinburgh and therefrom went with the King's grace to Meggatland in which bounds were slain at that time eighteen score deer. After this hunting the king hanged John Armstrong, laird of Kilnockie, which many a Scotsman heavily lamented, for he was a doubtit man and as good a chieftain as ever was upon the borders either of Scotland or England. And albeit he was a loose-living man, and sustained the number of twenty-four well-horsed able gentlemen with him, yet he never molested no Scotsman. But it is said from the Scots border to Newcastle of England there was not one of whatsoever estate but paid this John Armstrong a tribute, to be free of his cumber, he was so doubtit . . .'

There seems to be little doubt that the favourite Stuart method of offering a safe conduct was successful in enticing Johnnie Armstrong into the king's presence. After that there was no trial, or even the pretence of one. There was merely a summary hanging of Johnnie and his men in the trees of Carlanrig churchyard.* According to the various historical reports the following ballad sums up the affair reasonably accurately. Most of the other ballads have Johnnie Armstrong and his men showing fight when they realize their fate, but the chances are that they were seized and pinioned before they could do so. It does, however, seem likely that Johnnie did indeed give tongue to some proud and typically Border retort on the lines of:

'I haif asked grace at a graceless face.'

Such a retort would have been totally in keeping with the Border mentality, even faced with death. There are at least three versions of the ballad still extant, which indicates the strength of the popular feeling at the time. By all accounts the execution seems to have been regarded as an unwise move, which weakened instead of strengthened the Scots sway in the Border. This version of the ballad comes from Allan Ramsay's *The Ever Green*, Vol II, page 190, which is 'copied from a gentleman's mouth of the name of Armstrang, who is the 6th generation from this John'. This certainly dates it prior to 1724 and it may well be the original sixteenth-century version.

* There is a legend in the Borders that the trees withered and died and that the same has happened to any trees planted there since.

from *The English and Scottish Popular Ballads*

Sum speikis of lords sum speikis of lairds And sic-like men of hie de-gree Of a gen-tle-man I sing a sang Sum tyme called laird of Gil-nock-ie. The King he writes a lov-ing let-ter With his ain hand sae ten-der-ly And he hath sent it tae John-nie Arm-strong to come and speik with him speed-i-ly.

Sum speiks of lords, sum speiks of lairds,
And siclyke men of hie degrie;
Of a gentleman I sing a sang,
Sumtyme calld Laird of Gilnockie.

The king he wrytes a luving letter,
With his ain hand sae tenderly:

And he hath sent it to Johnnie Armstrang,
To cum and speik with him speidily.

The Eliots and Armstrangs did convene,
They were a gallant company:
'We'ill ryde and meit our lawful king,
And bring him safe to Gilnockie!'

'Make kinnen* and capon ready, then,   *oxen
And venison in great plenty;
We'ill welcome hame our royal king;
I hope he'ill dyne at Gilnockie!'

They ran their horse on the Langum howm,*   *low flat ground
And brake their speirs with mekle main;   by river
The ladys lukit frae their loft-windows,
'God bring our men weil back again!'

When Johnnie came before the king,
With all his men sae brave to see,
The king he movit his bonnet to him;
He weind he was a king as well as he.

'May I find grace, my sovereign liege,
Grace for my loyal men and me?
For my name it is Johnnie Armstrang,
And subject of yours, my liege,' said he.

'Away, away, thou traytor, strang!
Out of my sicht thou mayst sune be!
I grantit nevir a traytors lyfe,
And now I'll not begin with thee.'

'Grant me my lyfe, my liege, my king,
And a bony gift I will give to thee:
Full four-and-twenty milk-whyt steids,
Were a' foald in a yeir to me.

'I'll gie thee all these milk-whyt steids,
That prance and nicher at a speir,

With as mekle gude Inglis gilt
As four of their braid backs dow beir.'

'Away, away, thou traytor strang!
Out o' my sicht thou mayst sune be!
I grantit nevir a traytors lyfe,
And now I'll not begin with thee.'

'Grant me my lyfe, my liege, my king,
And a bony gift I'll gie to thee;
Gude four-and-twenty ganging mills,
That gang throw a' the yeir to me.

'These four-and-twenty mills complete
Sall gang for thee throw all the yeir,
And as mekle of gude reid wheit
As all their happers dow to bear.'

'Away, away, thou traytor, strang!
Out of my sicht thou mayst sune be!
I grantit nevir a traytors lyfe,
And now I'll not begin with thee.'

'Grant me my lyfe, my liege, my king,
And a great gift I'll gie to thee;
Bauld four-and-twenty sisters sons,
Sall for the fecht, tho all sould flee.'

'Away, away, thou traytor, strang!
Out of my sicht thou mayst sune be!
I grantit nevir a traytors lyfe,
And now I'll not begin with thee.'

'Grant me my lyfe, my liege, my king,
And a brave gift I'll gie to thee;
All betwene heir and Newcastle town
Sall pay thair yeirly rent to thee.'

Away, away, thou traytor, strang!
Out of my sicht thou mayst sune be!

76

I grantit nevir a traytors lyfe,
And now I'll not begin with thee.'

'Ye lied, ye lied, now, king,' he says,
'Althocht a king and prince ye be,
For I luid naithing in all my lyfe,
I dare well say it, but honesty;

'But a fat horse, and a fair woman,
Twa bony dogs to kill a deir:
But Ingland suld haif found me meil and malt,
Gif I had livd this hundred yeir!

'Scho suld haif found me meil and malt,
And beif and mutton in all plentie;
But neir a Scots wyfe could haif said
That eir I skaithd her a pure flie.*   *I did her a fly's
                                                            worth of harm
'To seik het water beneth cauld yce,
Surely it is a great folie;
I haif asked grace at a graceless face,
But there is nane for my men and me.

'But had I kend, or I came frae hame,
How thou unkynd wadst bene to me,
I wad haif kept the border-syde,
In spyte of all they force and thee.

'Wist Englands king that I was tane,
O gin a blyth man wald he be!
For anes I slew his sisters son,
And on his breist-bane brak a tree.'

John wore a girdle about his midle,
Imbroidered owre with burning gold,
Bespangled with the same mettle,
Maist beautifull was to behold.

Ther hang nine targats at Johnnies hat,
And ilk an worth three hundred pound:

'What wants that knave that a king suld haif,
But the sword of honour and the crown!

'O whair gat thou these targats, Johnnie,
That blink sae brawly abune thy brie?'
'I gat them in the field fechting,
Wher, cruel king, thou durst not be.

'Had I my horse, and my harness gude,
And ryding as I wont to be,
It sould haif bene tald this hundred yeir
The meiting of my king and me.

'God be withee, Kirsty, my brither,
Lang live thou Laird of Mangertoun!
Lang mayst thou live on the border-syde
Or thou se thy brither ryde up and doun.

'And God be withee, Kirsty, my son,
Whair thou sits on thy nurses knee!
But and thou live this hundred yeir,
Thy fathers better thoult never be.

'Farweil, my bonny Gilnock-Hall,
Whair on Esk-syde thou standest stout!
Gif I had lived but seven yeirs mair,
I wad haff gilt thee round about.'

John murdred was at Carlinrigg,
And all his galant companie:
But Scotlands heart was never sae wae,
To see sae mony brave men die.

Because they savd their country deir
Frae Englishmen; nane were sae bauld,
Whyle Johnnie livd on the border-syde,
Nane of them durst cum neir his hald.

Chapter 8

Elliot of Larriston:
Musselburgh Field

The first half of the sixteenth century saw a number of English invasions of Scotland. In 1523, after offering his daughter Mary in marriage to the young James V and being rejected, Henry VIII sent the Duke of Norfolk (Thomas Howard of Flodden) to invade Scotland. He laid waste and burned both Jedburgh and Kelso. In 1542, angered at James V's adherence to the old religion, Henry VIII sent the Duke of Norfolk once again to burn Jedburgh and Kelso. In retaliation James led a counter-invasion, the first time the Scots had crossed the border in force since Flodden, and was decisively defeated at Solway Moss in November. In the following month Mary of Guise, James's French queen, gave birth to a daughter, Mary, and seven days later James died.

Henry VIII, ever hopeful, promptly tried to secure the marriage of the infant Mary to his son Edward, who was to become Edward VI. Although this was at first agreed by a treaty of 1543, it was immediately annulled by the Scots. Thereupon Henry decided on his notorious policy of 'rough wooing' and sent the Earl of Hertford to invade Scotland both in 1544 and again in 1545, during which occasions he burned Edinburgh, Holyrood and Leith, as well as Dryburgh, Melrose and Kelso, succeeding merely in turning the Scots even more strongly against the proposed marriage.

Accustomed to border warfare since the days of Edward I, the Borderers had acquired their own rough philosophy on the subject. Their survival techniques had become finely adjusted over the centuries, for only the hardiest and most alert remained alive. Accustomed to raids from infancy they had acquired a facility for foretelling danger well in advance and avoiding it. The 'early warning system' of bale fires on the hill tops and mounted messengers was very effective in time of trouble. Then the ordinary Borderer would either scatter to the hills, or seek safety in the nearest castle or peel tower, those tall castellated strongholds of defence with which the border was freely sprinkled on both sides. With the doors bolted and barred and the defenders on the alert these were impregnable defences against the ordinary raids, though naturally not able to hold out against an army with siege cannon. From these fastnesses the ordinary Borderers had long grown used to seeing their wooden houses burning and their cattle driven off over the border, comforting themselves with the thought that it would be their turn next. Just now and again a full-scale battle took place and these could be fierce affairs.

Such an occasion is conjured up in James Hogg's famous ballad, 'Lock the door, Larriston'. Written in 1797, it is perhaps one of the finest modern ballads and perfectly captures the spirit of the border raids. Inspired no doubt by the constant repetitions of ballads he had heard in his youth, Hogg produced a border epic eminently suited to the country-side and its history. How well the scene is set with the opening verse, 'The Armstrongs are flying, The widows are crying'. After the roll-call of the English comes that magnificent line 'Why does the joy-candle gleam in thine eyes?' Finally comes the roll-call of the Scots and then the wild climax 'Elliot for aye'. This, one feels, is surely what border war-fare was really like. Here it is epitomized in ballad form.

LOCK THE DOOR, LARRISTON

from *The Lyric gems of Scotland*

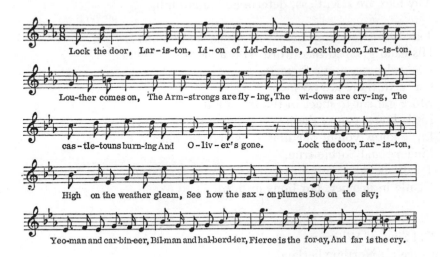

Lock the door, Lar-is-ton, Li-on of Lid-des-dale, Lock the door, Lar-is-ton, Lou-ther comes on, The Arm-strongs are fly-ing, The wi-dows are cry-ing, The cas-tle-touns burn-ing And O-liv-er's gone. Lock the door, Lar-is-ton, High on the weather gleam, See how the sax-on plumes Bob on the sky; Yeo-man and car-bin-eer, Bil-man and hal-berd-ier, Fierce is the for-ay, And far is the cry.

Lock the door, Larriston, Lion of Liddesdale;
Lock the door, Larriston, Lowther comes on;
The Armstrongs are flying,
The widows are crying,
The Castleton's burning, and Oliver's gone.
Lock the door, Larriston; high in the weather gleam
See how the Saxon plumes bob in the sky—
Yeoman and carbineer,
Billman and halberdier,
Fierce is the foray, and far is the cry.

Bewcastle brandishes high his proud scimitar,
Ridley is riding his fleet-footed grey;
Hedley and Howard there,

81

Wandale and Windermere,
Lock the door, Larriston, hold them at bay.
Why dost thou smile, noble Elliot of Larriston?
Why does the joy-candle gleam in thine eye?
Thou bold border-ranger
Beware of thy danger,
Thy foes are relentless, determined, and nigh.

Jock Elliot raised up his steel bonnet and lookit,
His hand grasped the sword with a nervous embrace;
Oh, welcome, brave foemen,
On earth there are no men
More gallant to meet in the fray or the chase.
Little know you of the hearts I have hidden here;
Little know you of our moss troopers' might;
Linhope and Sorbie true,
Tundhope and Milburn too,
Gentle in manner, but lions in fight.

I have Mangerton, Ogilvie, Raeburn, and Netherbie,
Old Sim, of Whitram, and all his array.
Come all Northumberland,
Teesdale and Cumberland,
Here at the Breeker Tower end shall the fray.
Scowled the broad sun o'er the links of green Liddesdale,
Red as the beacon-light tipped he the wold;
Many a bold martial eye
Mirror'd that morning sky
Never more oped on his orbit of gold.

Shrill was the bugle's note, dreadful the warrior shout,
Lances and halberts in splinters were torn;
Helmet and haubert then
Brav'd the claymore in vain,
Buckler and armlet in shivers were shorn.
See how they wane, the proud files of the Windermere,
Howard ah! woe to the hopes of the day;
Hear the wild welkin rend,
While the Scots shouts ascend,
Elliot of Larriston! Elliot for aye!

MUSSELBURGH FIELD

On Henry VIII's death in 1547 the same policy of 'rough wooing' was continued by the Protector, Somerset. In that year he invaded Scotland yet again in an effort to overcome opposition to the marriage of Mary Stuart to Edward VI. His army of 18,000 men was supported by a considerable fleet. On the Scots side the Earls of Angus, Arran and Huntly each commanded 10,000, making an army of 30,000 men. Furthermore they were firmly entrenched in what seemed a completely impregnable position above Musselburgh on Falside Hill. So confident were the Scots of their inevitable victory that they spent the night before the battle dicing with each other for the pick of the noble prisoners and captains they expected to secure. According to the fragment of ballad which survives they considered the English redcoats worth two groats and the white coats sixpence.

Unfortunately for the Scots, they were overconfident and careless. They abandoned their impregnable position and came down to the Plain of Pinkie, or Musselburgh Fields, a flat area just to the south of the town of Musselburgh. They failed to appreciate that numbers were not everything, and that divided command is not likely to win battles.

The English had a considerable advantage in cavalry and artillery, also in strategy and general tactics. Outgeneralled, outmanoeuvred and outgunned the Scots despite their greater numbers stood no chance. After successfully repelling a cavalry charge they were subjected to a sustained and accurate cannonade and were soon in full flight for the marshy low ground towards Dalkeith, or along the sands towards Leith, leaving many dead on the field. Although the English casualties were light it was estimated subsequently that over 10,000 Scots were killed. Child gives the ballad as 'Musleborrowe ffield' from the Percy MS. Unfortunately it is only an incomplete fragment, but although the dates are incorrect Huntly was made prisoner as stated. It was the first year of Edward's reign, not the fourth, and 10 September, not December. Despite this it would appear to be authentically sixteenth century in origin.

On the tenth day of December,
And the fourth yeere of King Edward's raigne,
Att Musleboorrowe, as I remember,
Two goodly hosts there mett on a plaine.

All that night they camped there,
Soe did the Scotts, both stout and stubborne:
But 'wellaway,' it was their song,
For wee haue taken them in their owne turne.

Over night they carded for our English mens coates;
They fished before their netts were spunn;
A white for sixpence, a red for two groates;
Now wisdome wold haue stayed till they had been woone.

Wee feared not but that they wold fight,
Yett itt was turned vnto their owne paine;
Thoe against one of vs that they were eight,
Yett with their owne weapons wee did them beat.

One the twelfth day in the morne
The made a face as the wold fight,
But many a proud Scott there was downe borne,
And many a ranke coward was put to flight.

But when they head our great gunnes cracke,
Then was their harts tirned into their hose;
They cast down their weapons, and turned their backes,
They ran soe fast that the fell on their nose.

The Lord Huntly, wee had him there;
With him hee brought ten thousand men,
Yett, God bee thanked, wee made them such a banquett
That none of them returned againe.

Wee chased them to Dalkeith

Chapter 9

Corichie

Following their success at Musselburgh in 1547, the English seized and fortified the town of Haddington, but the result was precisely the opposite of what they had anticipated. Instead of giving way to the English demands, the Scots turned to the French for assistance. In return for military aid it was agreed that Mary should be brought up in France and marry the Dauphin. The Scots were saved from bondage to the English at the price of bondage to the French. Whereas the supporters of France and the old religion had previously been able to rally national support against the English, now that the French had replaced the English as the threat to national independence, it was the pro-English and Protestant supporters who were able to invoke national support against France.

In 1561 when Mary returned to Edinburgh as Queen of Scots, following the unexpected death of the Dauphin, she was not quite nineteen years old and an acknowledged Roman Catholic in a largely Protestant country. On the whole she managed to avoid being accused of showing undue favour to those of the old religion. Indeed on at least one notable occasion the favour she showed towards a prominent Protestant aroused the jealousy of an eminent Roman Catholic with unfortunate results.

Gordon, Earl of Huntly, head of one of the leading Roman Catholic families in the north-east, as well as chief of a numerous clan, was incensed by the favour he considered Mary was showing towards her half-brother, Lord James Stewart, a Protestant, fat, elderly and choleric, as well as a loyal and powerful supporter of the Crown in the north-east, Huntly expected public recognition of his position, which was not immediately forthcoming. It may well be that he had also learned, or strongly suspected, that Mary had secretly granted the title of Earl of Moray to James Stewart, as was the case, in spite of the fact that Huntly had enjoyed the honours and the income from the title since 1548.

In 1562, whatever the reason, Lord Huntly gathered the Gordons together while the Queen, accompanied by Lord James Stewart and a suitable escort, was making a royal progress in the north-east. With his assembled clan, Huntly stationed himself on the route being taken by the royal party at a place called Corichie, below the Hill of Fair, about eighteen miles west of Aberdeen. There he awaited their arrival, seemingly making little secret of his determination to settle with the new Earl of Moray. However, the royal party obtained due warning since Lord James was able to call on seven or eight hundred of the Forbes's and Leslies to join the royal escort. Although nominally Huntly's vassals, they did not dare to disobey commands given in the Queen's name.

Sensibly enough, Lord James doubted the loyalty of these hastily gathered recruits and sent them into battle first. In the event they made little more than a token advance before retreating in simulated panic pursued by the Gordons. The Queen's escort, however, met them staunchly forming the familiar hedgehog of the *schiltron* with an impenetrable hedge of spears. Huntly and his forces were decisively repulsed. On seeing the way the battle was going, many of Huntly's erstwhile supporters also turned on the Gordons, with the result that considerable numbers were slain.

Among the dead was Huntly himself. It was said that he was thrown from his horse and being old and fat was smothered, but it seems more probable that he died of apoplexy. His sons, John and Adam, were made prisoners and the elder, John, was put to death in Aberdeen the following day, while the estates were forfeited. Shortly afterwards the grant of the Earldom of Moray to Lord James was made public.

The following ballad is included in Child's 1859 collection, Volume VII. It is said to have been composed by one Forbes, a schoolmaster, in Maryculter on Deeside and is almost certainly an eighteenth-century composition. It bears little relation to the facts historically and is openly biased in favour of Huntly, as would of course be the case if the writer's name was Forbes. Needless to say, any suggestion of pressure on the Queen by Lord James, or of any love between Huntly's son and the Queen is nonsense. The ballad is of interest, however, as an example of the north-east dialect in this form and the last verse lapses most unexpectedly into bathos.

86

Murn ye heighlands and murn ye leighlands,
I trow ye hae meikle need;
For thi bonny burn o' Corichie,
His run this day wi' bleid.

Thi hopefu' laird o' Finliter,
Erle Huntly's gallant son,
For thi love hi bare our beauteous quine,
His gar't fair Scotland mone.

Hi his braken his ward in Aberdene,
Thro dreid o' thi fause Murry,
And his gather't the gentle Gordone clan,
An' his father, auld Huntly.

Fain wid he tak our bonny guide quine
An' beare hir awa wi him;
But Murry's slee wyles spoil't a' thi sport,
An reft him o' life and lim.

Murry gar't rayse thi tardy Merns men,
An' Angis, an' mony ane mair.
Erle Morton and the Byres Lord Linsay,
An' campit at the hill o' Fare.

Erle Huntlie came wi' Haddo Gordone,
An' countit ane thousau men;
But Murry had abien twal hunder,
Wi' sax score horsemen and ten.

They soundit thi bougills an' thi trumpits,
An' marchit on in brave array.
Till thi spiers an' thi axis forgatherit,
An' than did begin thi fray.

Thi Gordones sae forcelie did fechtit,
Withouten terrer or dreid,
That mony o' Murry's men lay gaspin,
An' dyit thi grund wi theire bleid.

Then fause Murry feingit to flee them,
An' they pursuit at his backe,
Whan thi haf o' thi Gordones desertit,
An' turnit wi' Murry in a crack.

Wi hether i' thir bonnets they turnit,
The traiter Haddo o' their heid,
An' slaid theire brithers an' their fathers,
An' spoilt an' left them for deid.

Then Murry cried to tak thi auld Gordone,
An' mony ane ran wi' speid;
But Stuart o' hubbriak had him stickit,
An' out gushit thi fat lurdane's bleid.

Then they teuke his twa sonnes quick an' hale,
An' bare them awa' to Aberdene;
But fair did our guide quine lament,
Thi waeful chance that they were tane.

Erle Murry lost mony a gallant stout man;
Thi hopefu' laird o' Thornitune,
Pittera's sons, an' Egli's far fearit laird,
An mair to mi unkend, fell doune.

Erle Huntly mist ten score o' his bra' men,
Sum o' heigh an' sum o' leigh degree;
Skeenis youngest son, thi pryde o' a' the clan,
Was ther fun' deid, he widna flee.

This bloody fecht wis fiercely faught,
Octobris aught an' twenty day.
Chrystis fyfteen hundred thriscore year
An' twa will merk thi deidlie fray.

But now the day maist waefu' came,
That day the quine did grite her fill,
For Huntly's gallant stalwart son,
Wis heidit on thi heidin hill.

88

Fyve noble Gordones wi' him hangit were,
Upon thi samen fatal playne;
Crule Murry gar't thi waefu' quine luke out,
And see hir lover an' liges slayne.

I wis our quine had better frinds,
I wis our country better peice;
I wis our lords wid na discord,
I wis our weirs at hame may ceise.

Chapter 10

Raid of the Reidswire

In 1566 Mary's son, destined to be James VI of Scotland and I of England, was born. In the same year she made her ill-advised journey from Jedburgh to Hermitage Castle. There the Earl of Bothwell, her Warden of the West March, was lying seriously wounded, having been run through the body by a border reiver known as 'Little Jock' Elliot.

'Little Jock' belonged to that powerful border family the Elliots of Liddesdale, amongst whom was the famous 'Lion of Liddesdale' the hero of Elliot of Larriston. 'Little Jock' was a hard-riding reiver of considerable spirit even if short in stature. After his fight with Bothwell his fame spread far and wide in the border country.

Encountering him unexpectedly, Bothwell and his followers had started a chase after 'Little Jock'. Bothwell, in close pursuit of the reiver over Tarras Moor above Newcastleton, fired and wounded him in the hip. A little further on the Earl's horse was bogged down. Thereupon, seeing his pursuer's plight, Jock turned round in spite of his wound and attacked the Warden, running him through with his dagger. Thus, when Bothwell's supporters came up, their first duty was to carry their severely wounded leader to Hermitage Castle rather than continue the chase. 'Little Jock' Elliot himself, in the rhyming manner of the Scot produced two famous verses which ran as follows:

> I vanquished the Queen's Lieutenant,
> And gar'd his fierce troopers flee,
> My name is Little Jock Elliot,
> And wha daur meddle wi' me?
>
> I ride on my fleet-footed grey,
> My sword hanging down by my knee,
> I ne'er was afraid of a foe,
> And wha daur meddle wi' me?

The next two years saw Darnley's murder, the queen's abduction and marriage to Bothwell, her incarceration in Lochleven Castle, her escape and the defeat of her supporters by those of the Regent Morton at the Battle of Langside, finally her flight over the border into England, where after nineteen years of imprisonment she was at last executed. Meanwhile in Scotland the nobility still quarrelled among themselves and the religious schisms grew in intensity as John Knox waxed more militant, foreshadowing the troubles which were to tear the country apart in the ensuing century.

Although the borders remained troublesome with constant raiding on both sides, there were no further major invasions. Gradually the English and Scots were learning to live at peace with each other, due in part to the system evolved over the centuries of regular meetings between the Wardens of the Marches on either side. These posts were filled by prominent families in the West, Middle and East Marches, or divisions. At the regular quarter days they met informally to give judgement on complaints by either side. Where there had been some obvious injustice done on one side or the other the wrong could be redressed by the agreed judgement of both Wardens.

At best this was generally a rough and ready form of justice, but it was an accepted part of the way of life on the borders at this period. There is little doubt that these regular meetings helped to keep the peace on the borders, although sometimes, as at the Reidswire on the Middle March in 1575, they could also be the cause of bloodshed themselves. They could even, as nearly happened on that occasion, prove the cause of a full-scale war.

Although the Wardens normally met in person, they might on occasions appoint deputies to act for them if there was little of importance to discuss or be adjudged, or if they had to be absent on their sovereign's business. In any event the meetings themselves were customarily announced by a regular blast of trumpets, after which it was the accepted practice that the truce should continue until the following sunrise. In the interval no Scot or Englishman could be attacked, or arrested, or the truce broken in any way. In practice, inevitably, there were times when all did not go according to the accepted rules.

The affray of the Reidswire, or the 'Raid of the Reidswire' as the ballad is termed, took place on 5 June, 1575. The Scottish Warden of the Middle March was Sir John Carmichael, who owed his appointment to being a favourite of the Regent, the Earl of Morton. His English

91

opposite number was Sir John Forster, a member of a prominent border family, who probably treated the Scotsman with contempt as a parvenu.

They met at the Reidswire, the generally accepted meeting place on the border between England and Scotland, about ten miles south of Jedburgh on the Carter Bar Hill overlooking the Cheviots. The English were mostly composed of men from Redesdale and Tynedale, the most lawless of the English Borderers, always ready for a fight and notably quarrelsome. The Scots were from Roxburgh, Jedburgh and the surrounding district, and, like Borderers on either side, ever ready for a fight.

In the course of the day's proceedings a complaint by a Scots Borderer against a notorious English freebooter named Farnsten was found proven. Sir John Forster, however, alleged that he had fled justice and was not available for punishment. Since part of the principle of these courts was that each side agreed to produce its malefactors, Sir John Carmichael remonstrated, making some such remark as 'Play Fair!' To this Forster replied with some pointed comments on Carmichael's ancestry and general antecedents, making it plain he did not have any regard for him. Thereupon his followers glad of any pretext for a quarrel let loose a flight of arrows among the Scots.

In a short time a full-scale battle had developed in which Sir John Carmichael was soon taken prisoner. Indeed the English seemed certain of success until the Tynedale men fell to plundering the stalls and sideshows which were always spread out on the hill on such occasions. While they were thus engaged a body of Jedburgh citizens arrived in the nick of time and turned the tables on the English, so that the day ended in complete victory for the Scots.

Among the English prisoners were Sir John Forster, the English Warden, James Ogle, Cuthbert Collingwood, Francis Russell, son of the Earl of Bedford, several of the Fenwick family and other border chieftains. They were sent to Dalkeith where the Earl of Morton was acting as Regent. He detained them there for several days before releasing them with expressions of regard. He also sent Sir John Carmichael to York to satisfy Queen Elizabeth and he too was briefly detained and then honourably dismissed. Thus the danger of a minor skirmish developing into something more serious was averted.

The ballad the 'Raid of the Reidswire' first appeared in print in Allan Ramsay's *Ever Green*, published in 1724. A copy in an early seventeenth-century hand was discovered in 1895 along with an old

MS volume relating to the Carmichael family and this appears to be the earliest known version. Both Allan Ramsay and Sir Walter Scott, who subsequently published a version in his *Minstrelsy of the Scottish Border*, appear to have taken liberties with the text and the spelling. The fact remains, however, that no liberties, however gross, could ever make this ballad either very intelligible or very attractive. Whatever its date, it remains lengthy and prolix. No particular century ever had the monopoly of these vices and the fact that it may in part be genuinely old does not, unfortunately, make it any better.

The first three verses, taken from the *Minstrelsy of the Scottish Border* are included on page 94 to give the reader a clearer picture of the ballad. The full version, for addicts only, is included in the appendix.

The seventh of July, the suith to say,
At the Reidswire the tryst was set:
Our wardens they affixed the day,
And, as they promised, so they met,
Alas! that day I'll ne'er forgett!
Was sure sae feard, and then sae faine —
They came theare justice for to gett,
Will never green to come again.

Carmichael was our warden then,
He caused the country to conveen;
And the Laird's Wat, that worthie man,
Brought in that sirname weil beseen;
The Armestranges that aye hae been
A hardie house, but not a hail,
The Elliots' honours to maintaine,
Brought down the lave o' Liddesdale.

Then Tividale came to wi' speid:
The Sheriffe brought the Douglas down,
Wi' Cranstone, Gladstain, good at need,
Baith Rewle water and Hawick town.
Beanjeddart bauldly made him bound,
Wi' a' the Trumbills, stronge and stout:
The Rutherfoords, with grit renown,
Convoyed the town of Jedburgh out.

Chapter 11

Bonny Earl of Murray: Parcy Reed

Throughout his minority from his coronation in 1567 at a year old, James VI was to be the centre of intrigue, the pawn of noble families, some seeking to restore Mary and the old religion, others striving to support the Kirk and the Protestant religion, yet others simply seeking power. James Earl of Moray, a staunch Protestant and first Regent to be appointed, was murdered in 1570 by the opposing Hamilton faction. Within a year his successor the Earl of Lennox was also killed. The Earl of Mar who followed him died the next year. The Earl of Morton lasted longer, finally being executed in 1581, ostensibly for his part in the murder of Darnley fourteen years earlier. The Duke of Lennox, his supplanter, a Catholic supporter of Mary, was in turn ousted from power by the Earl of Gowrie, who kidnapped the young king in a coup known as the Ruthven Raid. After escaping from his clutches James appointed the Earl of Arran his adviser, ruler in all but name. It was not until 1587, aged twenty-one, when Mary had finally been tried and executed in England, that James could be said to be King in name and deed. Even then he vacillated while the Kirk and the powerful Catholic nobles of the north, the Earls of Huntly, Errol and Angus, clashed with each other. At times near anarchy prevailed virtually unchecked.

The murder of the 'Bonny Earl of Murray' by the Earl of Huntly in 1592 was typical of this laxity of rule. James Stewart, son of Sir James Stewart of Douno, had married Elizabeth the eldest daughter of the first regent, James, Earl of Moray, and on his death in 1570 was created Earl of Moray (or Murray) as his successor. This young Earl of Murray was extremely popular. He was described as 'a comely personage of great stature and strong of body' and was undoubtedly a considerable athlete.

Although the violent enmity between Murray and Huntly was well known, the King weakly and foolishly gave Huntly his royal commission to arrest Murray for suspected treachery. Completely unaware of the charge, Murray was staying with his mother, Lady Stewart of Doune, at her house in Donibristle. Without warning, Huntly besieged the house and demanded that Murray come forth. Getting no satisfaction he set the house on fire, after a short skirmish in which several of the defenders were killed. At last the Earl of Murray was forced to come out, but in the darkness he broke through his enemies and nearly escaped. Unfortunately the tip of his bonnet had caught fire and was still smouldering. This gave away his hiding-place and he was killed.

Despite a considerable public outcry, due to Murray's widespread popularity and the outrageous circumstances surrounding the deed, the King took no action to punish Huntly beyond ordering him to commit himself to ward in Blackness Castle. Huntly, of course, sheltered behind the commission he had been given and took no notice of the King's commands. Eventually popular feeling became so strong that the King was forced to move temporarily to Glasgow until Huntly had obeyed his orders. Even then Huntly was not kept in Blackness long and the crime seems to have gone virtually unpunished.

There are two versions of the ballad 'The Bonny Earl of Murray'. The following, from Ramsay's *Tea-Table Miscellany*, 1750, suggests without any foundation that the Earl was the Queen's lover. The other, from Finlay's Scottish Ballads, suggests, again without foundation, that Huntly's sister was the Countess of Murray. The fact that there are two ballads on the subject, however, indicates the strength of popular feeling and outrage at the time.

The Bonny Earl of Murray

from *Johnson's Musical Museum*

Ye high-lands and ye low-lands, Oh! where have you been? They have slain the Earl of Mur-ray, And they laid him on the green. They have slain the Earl of Mur-ray, And they laid him on the green.

Ye Highlands and ye Lawlands,
Oh where have you been?
They have slain the Earl of Murray
And they layd him on the green.

'Now wae be to thee, Huntly!
And wherefore did you sae?
I bade you bring him wi you,
But forbade you to him slay.'

He was a braw gallant,
And he rid at the ring;
And the bonny Earl of Murray,
Oh he might have been a king!

He was a braw gallant,
And he playd at the ba;
And the bonny Earl of Murray
Was the flower amang them a'.

He was a braw gallant,
And he playd at the glove;
And the bonny Earl of Murray,
Oh he was the Queen's love!

Oh lang will his lady
Look oer the castle Down,
Eer she see the Earl of Murray
Come sounding thro the town!
Eer she see the Earl of Murray
Come sounding thro the town!

While preparing the Armada for the invasion of England in 1588, Philip II of Spain had approached James to join him, but the King rejected his overtures on the grounds that he would be plotting against what could be his own kingdom, hence against his own interests. No such scruples held back Huntly, Errol and Angus, the Catholic Earls in the north, or Maxwell and Hamilton in the south. In 1589 Huntly, Maxwell and Hamilton wrote to Philip suggesting that if he cared to try again his best plan would be to land troops in Scotland prior to invading England. This correspondence was intercepted by Elizabeth, who demanded drastic action against them. It appeared, however, that James had what was delicately termed a 'tendernesse' for Huntly and, although he put him in ward in Edinburgh Castle, the King dined with him, 'kissed him often, and protested he knew he was innocent'. On being freed, Huntly rewarded his clemency by rising against the King, but confronted by James's army at Brig o' Dee he and his companions lost their nerve and surrendered. Once again they were treated with absurd leniency, being merely placed in ward for a few months before being released.

Following such ineffectual punishments it is not surprising that Huntly and the others continued to plot with Spain. In 1592 a conspiracy was revealed to bring 30,000 Spaniards into Scotland. In 1593 Huntly and Errol appeared before the King for their part in this and were told they must renounce popery or leave Scotland. Contemptuously ignoring either alternative they remained in the north and were duly forfeited.

Meanwhile in December, 1593, Maxwell, who had not been involved in this latest plot, was killed in the last large clan battle in the borders between Maxwells and Johnstons at Dryfe Sands, near Lockerbie. The Johnstons, though fewer in number, won the day and so many head wounds were inflicted that they became known as a 'Lockerbie Lick'.

In 1594, when still officially forfeited, Huntly and Errol enforced the release of a known Papal agent arrested in Aberdeen. At this affront to his royal authority James again began to raise an army to march against the northern earls. Before he had gathered enough support, the young Earl of Argyll, with Maclean and his men from the Western Isles and a force estimated at around 6–7,000 men, rashly advanced to attack Huntly and Errol in Strathbolgie, the Huntly stronghold. Only about

1,500 of this force of Highlanders were armed with firelocks. The rest carried claymores and targes. However, they seem to have travelled west with considerable speed as Huntly had very little warning of their approach and did not have time to obtain help from Angus.

Despite his short warning, Huntly raised 1,000 Gordons and a respectable body of horse in the shape of 300 Hays under the Earl of Errol. He also had a decisive advantage in six field pieces under the command of a Captain Ker. The two sides met at Balrinnes in Glenlivet. The Highlanders under Argyll were posted on a steep mountainside, but Errol and Sir Patrick Gordon led the Hays uphill against them. Gunfire from the cannons threw the Highlanders into confusion, but Errol's horse faced with the steep slopes were forced to wheel along the mountainside and received a fusillade of shots. Huntly then made a fierce attack on the centre and captured Argyll's banner. The horse by this time had reached level ground, charged the Highlanders and put them to flight. The clan chief of the Macleans stood firm, but at last he too was driven from the field. Argyll, weeping tears of mortification, left several hundred dead on the field, in particular Campbell of Lochinzell. On Huntly's side only twelve were killed, although amongst these was Huntly's uncle, Sir Patrick Gordon.

The ballad of Glenlivet, or Balrinnes, unfortunately is another of the Hardyknute/Raid of the Reidswire pattern, although since it has its own north-eastern variations, similar to Corichie, or the Hill of Fare, it is worth including two verses here from the copy in Child's 1856 collection, Vol. VII, taken from Dalzell's *Scottish Poems of the Sixteenth Century*. A more readable full version taken from Alexander Gardner's *Border Minstrelsy of Scotland*, 1893, may be found in the appendix:

Macallenmore* cam from the wast   *Argyll
With many a bow and brand;
To wast the Rinnes he thought best,
The Earll of Huntlies land.
He swore that none should him gainstand,
Except that he war fay:
Bot all sould be at his comand
That dwelt be northen Tay

Then Huntli, for to prevent that perrill,
Directit hastilie,
Unto the noble Erll of Erroll,

100

Besought him for supplie.
Quha said 'It is my dietie,
For to give Huntlie support:
For if he lossis Strabolgie
My Slaines will be ill hurt.

The ballad of Glenlivet deals at considerable length with the great victory won by Huntly and Errol, but fails to mention that when faced by their king at the head of an army shortly afterwards, they hastily surrendered. They were duly banished abroad, but within a couple of years were back again and favourably received. Thereafter, however, they appear to have given up their Catholic intrigues. Scotland had plots and conspiracies enough without them.

Yet the Scots did not have the monopoly of murder and intrigue, double-dealing and treachery. It was common to both sides of the border. The murder of Parcy Reed, laird of Troughend, Warden of the Middle March for the English, prominent soldier, popular figure and keen hunter in Redesdale, was a good example. In the course of his duties as Warden, he had offended the Halls, who farmed at Girsonsfield within a couple of miles of his own land at Troughend. They concealed their enmity under pretended friendship and awaited their opportunity to get their revenge. While apprehending various border raiders the Warden had also taken one of a family named Crozier, who openly determined to get their revenge. Unfortunately for Parcy Reed the two families conspired together to lay a trap for him.

The Halls, still pretending friendship, invited him to go hunting. They had a successful day, ending, by a prearranged plan, at a hut in a lonely glen known as Batinghope, one of the sources of the Reedwater, high up in the Cheviots. The Halls then poured water into Parcy Reed's gunpowder and jammed his sword in its sheath. When the Croziers were seen advancing, the Halls pretended alarm and fled, leaving Parcy Reed defenceless. In spite of this he seems to have given a good account of himself before he was killed.

The affair caused considerable indignation in the Borders and the murderous Croziers were driven out of Redesdale where their name was abhorred. The Halls, likewise, were forced to leave their farm and the 'Fause-hearted Ha's' became even more execrated than the Croziers, their name a byword for treachery. For the Borderers, in common with most people of the times, valued loyalty above most virtues and scorned treachery accordingly as the most heinous of crimes.

Child gives two versions of the ballad in his 1898 collection. The following is 'from the late Robert White's papers'. Included in the appendix is the longer but more interesting variation from Richardsons' *Borderer's Table Book*, 1846, 'taken down by James Telfer of Saughtree, Liddesdale, from the chanting of an old woman named Kitty Hall, a native of Northumberland.'

The Liddesdale Crosiers hae ridden a race,
And they had far better staid at hame,
For they have lost a gallant gay,
Young Whinton Crosier it was his name.

For Parcy Reed he has him taen,
And he's delivered him to law,
But auld Crosier has made answer
That he'll gar the house of the Troughend fa.

So as it happened on a day
That Parcy Reed is a hunting gane,
And the three false Halls of Girsonsfield
They all along with him are gane.

They hunted up and they hunted down,
They hunted all Reedwater round,
Till weariness has on him seized;
At the Batinghope's he's fallen asleep.

O some they stole his powder-horn,
And some put water in his lang gun:
'O waken, waken, Parcy Reed!'
For we do doubt thou sleeps too sound.

'O waken, O waken, Parcy Reed!'
For we do doubt thou sleeps too long;
For yonder's the five Crosiers coming,
They're coming by the Hingin Stane.

'If they be five men, we are four,
If ye will all stand true to me;
Now every one of you may take one,
And two of them ye may leave to me.'

'We will not stay, nor we dare not stay,
O Parcy Reed, for to fight with thee;
For thou wilt find, O Parcy Reed,
That they will slay both us and thee.'

'O stay, O stay, O Tommy Hall,
O stay, O man, and fight with me!
If we seek the Troughend again,
My good black mare I will give thee.'

'I will not stay, nor I dare not stay,
O Parcy Reed, to fight for thee;
For thou wilt find, O Parcy Reed,
That they will slay both me and thee.'

'O stay, O stay, O Johnnie Hall,
O stay, O men, and fight for me!
If I see the Troughend again,
Five yoke of oxen I will give thee.'

'I will not stay, nor I dare not stay,
O Parcy Reed, for to fight with thee;
For thou wilt find, O Parcy Reed,
That they will slay both me and thee.'

'O stay, O stay, O Willie Hall,
O stay, O man, and fight for me!
If we see the Troughend again,
The half of my land I will give thee.'

'I will not stay, nor I dare not stay,
O Parcy Reed, for to fight with thee;
For thou wilt find, O Parcy Reed,
That they will slay both me and thee.'

'Now foul fa ye, ye traitors all,
That ever ye should in England won!
You have left me in a fair field standin,
And in my hand an uncharged gun.

'O fare thee well, my wedded wife!
O fare you well, my children five!
And fare thee well, my daughter Jane,
That I love best that's born alive!

'O fare thee well, my brother Tom!
And fare you well his children five!
If you had been with me this day,
I surely had been man alive.

'Farewell all friends! as for my foes,
To distant lands may they be tane,
And the three false Halls of Girsonsfield,
They'll never be trusted nor trowed again.'

Chapter 12

Kinmont Willie: Jock o' the Side

Although the Scots and the English were less likely to find themselves in open warfare, the border scene was still by no means peaceful. Either side was liable to take the law into their own hands on occasions. Murder, rapine, and savagery of all sorts was to be expected. Treachery and intrigue were commonplace. Yet a recognized form of rude justice also existed and loyalty to the death was common enough, by master and man, chieftain and follower. After years of raiding they had freely intermarried and Elliots, Armstrongs and Johnstons were to be found amongst English and Scots on either side of the border.

The ballads of Kinmont Willie, Archie o' Ca'field, and Jock o' the Side, each tell a story typical of the borders. Each has some lines and verses common to the others. Each tells of an epic venture famed throughout the country on either side of the borders in its day. Each is still worth telling.

In many ways Kinmont Willie was a typical Borderer. He was such a notorious reiver that the English were in considerable dread of him and his depredations were famed. Nor was it only in the borders or in the south that he was a byword. In 1586 when the Earl of Angus, accompanied by Home, Buccleuch and others from the borders, had marched to Stirling to remove the Earl of Arran from the King's councils, the Borderers had pillaged the town unmercifully. Particularly notable had been a party of Armstrongs under Kinmont Willie, who not only went off with horses and cattle, but even stole the iron gratings from the windows. When it was subsequently suggested he and his men might be let loose in Edinburgh there was considerable consternation amongst the burghers.

In 1596 the English Warden of the West March for Elizabeth was Lord Scrope, based on Carlisle Castle. His Scots opposite number acting for James VI was Sir Walter Scott of Branxholme, laird of Buccleuch and keeper of Liddisdale. According to the time-honoured custom, as there was little of importance to be decided on, they sent their deputies to keep the day of truce at Dayholm of Kershope, where a small stream marked the border between England and Scotland, separating Liddisdale from Bewcastle. Deputy for the laird of Buccleuch was Robert Scott of Hayning and a Mr Salkeld was deputy for Lord Scrope. The usual trumpet was sounded at the start of the truce indicating that the truce continued until sunrise the following day, by which time all concerned were well away from the scene. The meeting in this instance was friendly and, after a mutual redress of wrongs complained of, the deputy wardens parted in an amicable manner and set off for home.

After the meeting Willie Armstrong of Kinmont, better known by his popular border nickname of Kinmont Willie, was riding home on one side of the Liddel Water, when he was recognized by a party of English, two hundred strong, on the other side. The temptation was too much for them and they crossed the river in breach of the truce agreement. Willie set off at full gallop, but his chance of escape was small. Within three or four miles he was captured and led off to Carlisle Castle.

On hearing the news Buccleuch's first resort was to write a complaint to Mr Salkeld, pointing out the infringement of the truce. Mr Salkeld simply referred the matter to Lord Scrope. On approaching Lord Scrope, Buccleuch found himself referred to Queen Elizabeth. Hoping at this stage to restrict the matter he arranged for an ambassadorial approach through the Scots ambassador to Lord Scrope, but once again received a rebuff. The English argument appeared to be that Kinmont Willie was a well-known offender, that he was in prison and that settled the matter.

Buccleuch, feeling that the matter touched his honour and that of James VI, decided to take matters into his own hands. His first act was to send a female visitor to Kinmont Willie to find out which part of Carlisle Castle he was being imprisoned in and how he was being guarded. At the same time an estimate of the height of the walls was made in order to prepare suitably long scaling ladders. Then Buccleuch assembled two hundred horsemen, who were trysted to meet at Morton Tower, Kinmont Willie's home on the water of Sark in the Debatable Land* ten miles from Carlisle. At one hour before sunset the horsemen duly assembled.

Buccleuch had made his arrangements so that no major incident was

* An area of land about 10 miles by 3½ on the borders and so called because it was frequently 'Debatable' as to which side owned it.

likely to arise which might result in an outbreak of war. He was determined merely to use sufficient force to release a prisoner, who in his view had been taken in breach of the truce. He sent a few scouts on ahead and followed with fifty or sixty horsemen as his fighting party. Behind these again came the main body with ladders, carried two to a horse, and all manner of pickaxes, sledgehammers, crowbars and the like to break down any walls or gates.

They entered England across the Esk about six miles from Carlisle over the ground where the Grahams lived, just as darkness fell. Arriving at the castle in stormy conditions they found that the ladders were too short to reach the top of the battlements, so they set about breaking down the postern gate. As all seemed to be going well Buccleuch withdrew with the main party between the castle and the town to prevent any interference.

The postern gate was soon broken open and the gatekeeper and his assistant tied up. A select few who knew their way about the castle then moved in at speed and broke down the door to Kinmont Willie's prison. At the same time a trumpet was sounded in order to give the impression of a much larger force and a great deal of noise was made. The defenders, including Lord Scrope and Mr Salkeld, promptly locked themselves in and barricaded their doors.

Buccleuch kept a very tight control over his forces and although the castle was virtually theirs to plunder as they wished they merely did what they had come to do and nothing else. No other door than that of Kinmont Willie's prison was broken open and no other prisoner released. The attack had started two hours before dawn and by the time it was over day was breaking. The town and castle were by this time in a state of alarm with bells ringing, drums beating to arms and signal beacons alight. Under cover of this confusion Buccleuch skilfully withdrew his forces.

Arriving at the river where the Grahams were waiting to ambush them in the semi-darkness, he again blew his trumpet and the latter decided that discretion was the better part of valour and allowed him to pass. It may be, however, that as Kinmont Willie was married to a Graham there was an element of collusion. It could well be that the Grahams were to some extent involved and that the same applied to some of the castle defenders, who had turned a blind eye at the right moment. Be that as it may, about two hours after sunrise Kinmont Willie and the Scots forces were back in Scotland once more and the countryside was soon resounding with the news of the feat.

Scrope's account of the affair and his explanation of his failure to prevent it were as follows:

'Yester night, in the dead time thereof, Walter Scott of Harding, the chief of Buccleuch accompanied by 500 horsemen of Buccleuch's and Kinmont's friends, did come armed and appointed with gavlocks and crowes of iron, handpecks, axes, skailing ladders unto an outward corner of the base courts of this castle and to the postern door of the same, which they speedily undermyned and quietly and made themselves possessors of the base courts, broke into the chamber where Will of Kinmont was, carried him away and in their discovery of the watch left for dead two of the watchmen, hurt a servant of mine, one of Kinmont's keepers and were issued again from the postern before they were descried by the watch of the inner ward and ere resistance could be made. The watch, as it would seem, by reason of the stormy night were either on sleep or gotten under some cover to defend themselves from the violence of the weather by means whereof the Scots achieved their enterprise with less difficulty.'

When she received this report Queen Elizbabeth was exceedingly angry and sent a vigorous ambassadorial protest. James replied mildly enough that he felt Scrope was in the wrong, but this did not satisfy Elizabeth. Finally Buccleuch was sent to England. On being taken before Elizabeth, she demanded:

'How dared you undertake such a dangerous and presumptuous venture?'

'What does a man not dare to do?' responded Buccleuch boldly.

Elizabeth was much struck with this reply and said:

'With ten thousand such men our brother of Scotland might shake the firmest throne in Europe.'

After that Buccleuch, rightly named 'the bold', did not have to remain long in England and nothing further was said about his attack on Carlisle Castle.

The ballad version which follows is taken from Scott's *Minstrelsy of the Scottish Border*. Scott wrote: 'This ballad is preserved by tradition in the West borders, but much mangled by reciters, so that some conjectural emendations have been absolutely necessary to render it intelligible.' Child's comment on this, in his 1898 collection, was: 'It is to be suspected that a great deal more emendation was done than the mangling of reciters rendered absolutely necessary.' Child's tart comment is not without reason. He refers in particular to stanzas ten to twelve and there indeed one can detect the hand of the 'Great Romancer

109

of the Borders'. It would, however, be a difficult ballad to spoil and it preserves the spirit of the deed and the times. It is poetic licence which provides the 'fause Sakelds' with rough justice. In fact no English were killed.

O have ye na heard o the fause Sakelde?
O have ye na heard o the keen Lord Scroop?
How they hae taen bauld Kinmont Willie,
On Hairibee to hang him up?

Had Willie had but twenty men,
But twenty men as stout as he,
Fause Sakelde had never the Kinmont taen,
Wi eight score in his companie.

They band his legs beneath the steed,
They tied his hands behind his back;
They guarded him, fivesome on each side,
And they brought him ower the Liddel-rack.

They led him thro the Liddel-rack,
And also thro the Carlisle sands;
They brought him to Carlisle castell,
To be at my Lord Scroop's commands.

'My hands are tied, but my tongue is free,
And wha will dare this deed avow?
Or answer by the border law?
Or answer to the bauld Buccleuch?'

'Now haud thy tongue, thou rank reiver!
There's never a Scot shall set ye free;
Before ye cross my castle-yate,
I trow ye shall take farewell o' me.'

'Fear na ye that, my lord,' quo Willie;
'By the faith o my bodie, Lord Scroop,' he said,
'I never yet lodged in a hostelrie
But I paid my lawing before I gaed.'

Now word is gane to the bauld Keeper,
In Branksome Ha where that he lay,

That Lord Scroop has taen the Kinmont Willie,
Between the hours of night and day.

He has taen the table wi his hand,
He garrd the red wine spring on hie;
'Now Christ's curse on my head,' he said,
'But avenged of Lord Scroop I'll be!

'O is my basnet* a widow's curch?**   *helmet **kerchief
Or my lance a wand of the willow-tree?
Or my arm a ladye's lilye hand?
That an English lord should lightly me.

'And have they taen him Kinmont Willie,
Against the truce of Border tide,
And forgotten that the bauld Buccleuch
Is keeper here on the Scottish side?

'And have they een taen him Kinmont Willie,
Withouten either dread or fear,
And forgotten that the bauld Buccleuch
Can back a steed, or shake a spear?

'O were there war between the lands,
As well I wot that there is none,
I would slight Carlisle castell high,
Tho it were builded of marble-stone.

'I would set that castell in a low,
And sloken it with English blood;
There's nevir a man in Cumberland
Should ken where Carlisle castell stood.

'But since nae war's between the lands,
And there is peace, and peace should be,
I'll neither harm English lad or lass,
And yet the Kinmont freed shall be!,

He has called him forty marchmen bauld,
I trow they were of his ain name,

112

Except Sir Gilbert Elliot, calld
The Laird of Stobs, I mean the same.

He has calld him forty marchmen bauld,
Were kinsmen to the bauld Buccleuch,
With spur on heel, and splent* on spauld,**   *armour **shoulder
And gleuves of green, and feathers blue.

There were five and five before them a',
Wi hunting-horns and bugles bright;
And five and five came wi Buccleuch,
Like Warden's men, arrayed for fight.

And five and five like a mason-gang,
That carried the ladders lang and hie;
And five and five like broken men;
And so they reached the Woodhouslee.

And as we crossed the 'Bateable Land,
When to the English side we held,
The first o' men that we met wi,
Whae sould it be but fause Sakelde!

'Where be ye gaun, ye hunters keen?'
Quo fause Sakelde; 'come tell to me!'
'We go to hunt an English stag,
Has trespassed on the Scots countrie.'

'Where be ye gaun, ye marshal-men?'
Quo fause Sakelde; 'come tell me true!'
'We go to catch a rank reiver,
Has broken faith wi the bauld Buccleuch.'

'Where are ye gaun, ye mason-lads,
Wi a' your ladders lang and hie?'
'We gang to herry a corbie's nest,
That wons not far frae Woodhouselee.'

'Where be ye gaun, ye broken men?'
Quo fause Sakelde; 'come tell to me!'

Now Dickie of Dryhope led that band,
And the nevir a word o lear* had he.   *learning

'Why trespass ye on the English side?
Row-footed outlaws, stand!' quo he;
The near a word had Dickie to say,
Sae he thrust the lance thro his fause bodie.

Then on we held for Carlisle toun,
And at Staneshaw-bank the Eden we crossed;
The water was great, and meikle of spait,*   *much in flood
But the nevir a horse nor man we lost.

And when we reachd the Staneshaw-bank,
The wind was rising loud and hie;
And there the laird garrd leave our steeds,
For fear that they should stamp and nie.

And when we left the Staneshaw-bank,
The wind began full loud to blaw;
But 't was wind and weet, and fire and sleet,
When we came beneath the castel-wa.

We crept on knees, and held our breath,
Till we placed the ladders against the wa;
And sae ready was Buccleuch himse'll
To mount the first before us a'.

He has taen the watchman by the throat,
He flung him down upon the lead:
'Had there not been peace between our lands,
Upon the other side thou hadst gaed.

'Now sound out, trumpets!' quo Buccleuch;
'Let's waken Lord Scroop right merrilie!'
Then loud the Warden's trumpets blew
'O whae dare meddle wi me?'

Then speedilie to wark we gaed,
And raised the slogan ane and a',

114

And cut a hole thro a sheet of lead,
And so we wan to the castel-ha.

They thought King James and a' his men
Had won the house wi bow and speir;
It was but twenty Scots and ten
That put a thousand in sic a stear!*   *commotion

Wi coulters and wi forehammers,
We garrd the bars bang merrilie,
Untill we came to the inner prison,
Where Willie o Kinmont he did lie.

And when we cam to the lower prison,
Where Willie o Kinmont he did lie,
'O sleep ye, wake ye, Kinmont Willie,
Upon the morn that thou's to die?'

'O I sleep saft, and I wake aft,
It's lang since sleeping was fleyd frae me;
Gie my service back to my wyfe and bairns,
And a' gude fellows that speer for me.'

Then Red Rowan has hente him up,
The starkest men in Teviotdale:
'Abide, abide now, Red Rowan,
Till of my Lord Scroop I take Farewell.

'Farewell, farewell, my gude Lord Scroop!
My gude Lord Scroop, farewell!' he cried;
'I'll pay you for my lodging-maill
When first we meet on the border-side.'

Then shoulder high, with shout and cry,
We bore him down the ladder lang;
At every stride Red Rowan made,
I wot the Kinmont's airns* playd clang.   *irons

'O mony a time,' quo Kinmont Willie,
'I have ridden horse baith wild and wood;*   *fierce

115

But a rougher beast than Red Rowan
I ween my legs have naer bestrode.

'And mony a time,' quo Kinmont Willie,
'I've pricked a horse out oure the furs;
But since the day I backed a steed
I nevir wore sic cumbrous spurs.'

We scarce had won the Staneshaw bank,
When a' the Carlisle bells were rung,
And a thousand men, in horse and foot,
Cam wi the keen Lord Scroop along.

Buccleuch has turned to Eden Water,
Even where it flowd frae bank to brim,
And he has plunged in wi a' his band,
And safely swam them thro the stream.

He turned him on the other side,
And at Lord Scroop his glove flung he:
'If ye like na my visit in merry England,
In fair Scotland come visit me!'

All sore astonished stood Lord Scroop,
He stood as still as rock of stane;
He scarcely dared to trew his eyes
When thro the water they had gane.

'He is either himsell a devil frae hell,
Or else his mother a witch maun be;
I wad na have ridden that wan water
For a' the gowd in Christentie.'

JOCK O' THE SIDE

The ballads of Jock o' the Side and Archie o' Cawfield have many verses in common, quite apart from their general resemblance. It could well be that Jock o' the Side relates to an escape from Newcastle prison at a much earlier date, around 1527. The date of Archie o' Cawfield is also uncertain and it is possible that the name of Hall could have been slipped in by someone wishing to glorify their own name. It seems quite likely that it refers to an occasion when the Maxwells had imprisoned one of their arch enemies the Johnstons in the Dumfries Tolbooth and were about to hang him. There is a record of such an escape by a Johnston, again at a much earlier date.

The ballad of Jock o' the Side which follows is from Caw's *Poetical Museum* of 1784. It is also included in Campbell's *Albyn's Anthology*, where it is described as being 'taken down from the recitation of Mr Thomas Shortreed of Jedburgh who learnt it from his father'. The copy of Archie o' Cawfield included in the appendix for comparison is taken from Scott's *Border Minstrelsy*. Child gives six different versions of this ballad in his 1898 collection. It will be appreciated that unlike the Bonny Earl of Murray, where there are two distinct ballads, these are merely variations of the same ballad.

'Now Liddisdale has ridden a raid,
But I wat they had better staid at hame;
For Mitchel o Winfield he is dead,
And my son Johnie is prisner tane.'
With my fa ding diddle, la la dow diddle.

For Mangerton House auld Downie is gane;
Her coats shee has kilted up to her knee,
And down the water wi speed she rins,
While tears in spaits fa fast frae her eie.

Then up and bespake the lord Mangerton:
'What news, what news, sister Downie, to me?'
'Bad news, bad news, my Lord Mangerton;
Mitchel is killd, and tane they hae my son Johnie.'

'Neer fear, sister Downie,' quo Mangerton;
'I hae yokes of oxen four and twentie,
My barns, my byres, and my faulds, a' weel filld,
And I'll part wi them a' ere Johnie shall die.

'Three men I'll take to set him free,
Weel harnessd a' wi best o steel;
The English rogues may hear, and drie
The weight o their braid swords to feel.

'The Laird's Jock and, the Laird's Wat twa,
Oh, Hobie Noble, thou ane maun be;
Thy coat is blue, thou hast been true,
Since England banishd thee, to mee.'

Now Hobie was an English man,
In Bewcastle-dale was bred and born;
But his misdeeds they were sae great,
They banishd him neer to return.

Lord Mangerton them orders gave,
'Your horses the wrang way maun a' be shod;

Like gentlemen ye must not seem,
But look like corn-caugers* gawn ae road.   *hucksters

'Your armour gude ye maunna shaw,
Nor ance appear like men o weir;
As country lads be all arrayd,
Wi branks* and brecham** on ilk mare.'   *halter with wooden
                                                                                head-piece
                                                                        **straw pack-saddle

Sae now a' their horses are shod the wrang way,
And Hobie has mounted his grey sae fine,
Jock his lively bay, Wat's on his white horse behind,
And on they rode for the water o Tyne.

At the Choler-ford they a' light down,
And there, wi the help o the light of the moon,
A tree they cut, wi fifteen naggs* upo ilk side,   *notches
To climb up the wa o Newcastle town.

But when they cam to Newcastle town,
And were alighted at the wa,
They fand their tree three ells oer laigh,
They fand their stick baith short and sma.

Then up and spake the Laird's ain Jock,
'There's naething for't, the gates we maun force';
But when they cam the gates unto,
A proud porter withstood baith men and horse.

His neck in twa I wat they hae wrung,
Wi hand or foot he neer playd paw;*   *never stirred again
His life and his keys at anes they hae tane,
And cast his body ahind the wa.

Now soon they reach Newcastle jail,
And to the prisner thus they call:
'Sleips thou, wakes thou, Jock o the Side?
Or is thou wearied o' thy thrall?'

Jock answers thus, wi' dolefu' tone:
Aft, aft I wake, I seldom sleip;

But wha's this kens my name sae weel,
And thus to hear my waes does seik?

Then up and spake the good Laird's Jock,
'Neer fear ye now, my billie,' quo he;
'For here's the Laird's Jock, the Laird's Wat,
And Hobie Noble, come to set thee free.'

'Oh, had thy tongue, and speak nae mair,
And o thy tawk now let me be!
For if a' Liddisdale were here the night,
The morn's the day that I maun die.

'Full fifteen stane o' Spanish iron
They hae laid a' right sair on me;
Wi locks and keys I am fast bound
Into this dungeon mirk and drearie.'

'Fear ye no that,' quo the Laird's Jock;
'A faint heart neer wan a fair ladie;
Work thou within, we'll work without,
And I'll be bound we set thee free.'

The first strong dore that they came at,
They loosed it without a key;
The next chaind dore that they cam at,
They gard it a' in flinders flee.

The prisner now, upo his back,
The Laird's Jock's gotten up fu hie;
And down the stair him, irons and a',
Wi nae sma speed and joy brings he.

'Now, Jock I wat,' quo Hobie Noble,
'Part o the weight ye may lay on me;'
'I wat weel no,' quo the Laird's Jock,
'I count him lighter than a flee.'

Sae out at the gates they a' are gane.
The prisner's set on horseback hie;

120

And now wi speed they've tane the gate,
While ilk ane jokes fu wantonlie.

'O Jock, sae winsomely's ye ride,
Wi baith your feet upo ae side!
Sae weel's ye're harnessd, and sae trig!
In troth ye sit like ony bride.'

The night, tho wat, they didna mind,
But hied them on fu mirrilie,
Until they cam to Cholerford brae,
Where the water ran like mountains hie.

But when they cam to Cholerford,
There they met with an auld man;
Says, Honest man, will the water ride?
Tell us in haste, if that ye can.

'I wat weel no,' quo the good auld man;
'Here I hae livd this thirty yeirs and three,
And I neer yet saw the Tyne sae big,
Nor rinning ance sae like a sea.'

Then up and spake the Laird's saft Wat,
The greatest coward in the company;
'Now halt, now halt, we needna try't;
The day is comd we a' maun die!'

'Poor faint-hearted thief!' quo the Laird's Jock,
'There'll nae man die but he that's fie;
I'll lead ye a' right safely through;
Lift ye the prisner on ahint me.'

Sae now the water they a' hae tane,
By anes and twas they a' swam through;
'Here are we a' safe,' says the Laird's Jock,
'And, poor faint Wat, what think ye now?'

They scarce the ither side had won,
When twenty men they saw pursue;

Frae Newcastle town they had been sent,
A' English lads, right good and true.

But when the land-sergeant the water saw,
'It winna ride, my lads,' quo he;
Then out he cries, 'Ye the prisner may take,
But leave the irons, I pray, to me.'

'I wat weel no,' cryd the Laird's Jock,
'I'll keep them a', shoon to my mare they'll be:
My good grey mare, for I am sure,
She's bought them a' fu dear frae thee.'

Sae now they're away for Liddisdale,
Een as fast as they coud them hie;
The prisner's brought to his ain fire-side,
And there o's airns they make him free.

'Now, Jock, my billie,' quo a' the three,
'The day was comd thou was to die;
But thou's as weel at thy ain fire-side,
Now sitting, I think, tween thee and me.'

They hae gard fill up ae punch-bowl,
And after it they maun hae anither,
And thus the night they a' hae spent,
Just as they had been brither and brither.

Chapter 13

Bonny John Seton:
The Bonnie House o' Airlie

On Elizabeth's death in 1603 James VI of Scotland became James I of England. The Union of the Crowns effectively prevented any further invasions by either English or Scots. Willy nilly they were united at last and had to learn to live with each other. Though there might be civil war, or internal religious conflict, though armies might invade Scotland from the south, or England from the north, they were never again to be specifically English versus Scots. At last the Scots could learn to live without fear of attack from England and vice versa. Slowly the Borderers on each side could settle down to living in peace. The lawless reivers, living in what James termed his 'Middle Shires', were in danger of being tamed at last.

With the accession of Charles I in 1625 the fatal Stuart lack of judgement soon became apparent. He pursued the unwise policy of trying to impose uniformity of worship in England and Scotland. The result was a riot in Edinburgh at St Giles Cathedral in 1637 and unity amongst Presbyterians of all classes. In a spontaneous and almost unprecedented countrywide upsurge of emotion they subscribed to a National Covenant which, though professing loyalty to the Crown, utterly rejected the innovations that had been introduced into Church affairs.

There is no doubt that the Presbyterian religion, the religion of Calvin, strong, harsh and uncompromising, suited the Scots Lowland temperament particularly well. From the fourteenth to the sixteenth century Scotland possessed the most turbulent, treacherous and self-seeking nobility of any country in Europe. Nor, like England, did it possess a powerful buttress against them in the shape of a wealthy merchant or yeoman middle class. Prior to the Reformation, the church which should have acted as a buttress was too involved with politics and itself far too corrupt to do so.

During the Reformation many of the nobles increased their wealth by the acquisition of church lands and some of them in consequence embraced the new faith readily. The poor, the bulk of the nation, seized on the new religion because it appealed to a people who had lived on the verge of starvation, were accustomed to invasion, insecurity, poverty and wretchedness. They needed a strong, if sometimes harsh, creed with the promise of life hereafter for the true believers. Thus the Lowlanders accepted it wholeheartedly, but in the north, where few proselytizers ever penetrated and where life under the clan system, if still poverty-stricken, was in some ways more secure, the new religion was less successful. By the turn of the sixteenth century, however, even in the north, Presbyterianism was the principal religion. The widespread emotional surge of the National Covenant in 1638 was a proof of the hold the new religion had achieved in Scotland.

In 1638 the General Assembly, justifiably confident in its popular following, refused to accept the authority of the King's Commissioner and, in spite of being prorogued, continued to sit. They then went on to abolish episcopacy and depose the bishops. The so-called Bishops' Wars resulted, during which the Covenanters drew up lists of those who were termed 'enemies of religion'. The Committee of Estates gave the Earl of Argyll a commission to pursue the people so listed with 'fire and sword', until 'brought to their duty, or rooted out and utterly subdued'. The fact that Argyll, chief of the largest and most powerful Highland clan, the clan Campbell, had sided with the Covenant was automatically enough to make most of the other clans take the opposing side. The Campbells were so universally disliked in the Highlands that this was inevitable. The same was to happen in the '15 and the '45 and was at least a contributory cause of the Highland support for the Stuarts.

The following ballad is taken from James Maidment's *North Country Garland*. It describes an action on 18 June, 1639, when Montrose was commanding a Covenanter force attacking the Bridge of Dee, which had been fortified and manned by royalists from Aberdeen. The bridge was bravely defended all that day and part of the next by Lt-Colonel Johnston (not Middleton, as the ballad has it). Lord Aboyne, newly made the King's Lieutenant in the North, was leading a small body of horse which came under Montrose's cannon fire. A gallant gentleman, John Seton of Pitmeddin, was killed and Johnston was badly wounded. Aboyne and his horsemen abandoned the defenders, who also took to flight. The final verses refer to a minor action known as the Raid of Stonehaven, which took place three days before the attack on the Bridge of Dee. Aboyne, with over a thousand Highlanders totally unused to cannon fire, was completely routed after coming under fire from Montrose's cannons.

Upon the eighteenth day of June,
A dreary day to see,
The southern lords did pitch their camp
Just at the Bridge of Dee.

Bonny John Seton of Pitmeddin,
A bold baron was he.
He made his testament ere he went out,
The wiser man was he.

He left his land to his young son,
His lady her dowry,
A thousand crowns to his daughter Jean,
Yet on the nurse's knee.

Then out came his lady fair.
A tear into her ee;
Says, Stay at home, my own good lord,
O stay at home withe me!

He looked over his left shoulder,
Cried, Souldiers, follow me!
O then she looked in his face,
And angry woman was she;
'God send me back my steed again,
But neer let me see thee!'

His name was Major Middleton
That manned the bridge of Dee,
His name was Colonel Henderson
That let the cannons flee.

His name was Major Middleton
That manned the bridge of Dee.
And his name was Colonel Henderson
That dung Pitmeddin in three.

Some rode on the black and grey,
And some rode on the brown,

But the bonny John Seton
Lay gasping on the ground.

Then bye there comes a false Forbes,
Was riding from Driminere;
Says, Here there lies a proud Seton;
This day they ride the rear.

Cragievar said to his men,
'You may play on your shield;
For the proudest Seton in all the lan
This day lies on the field'.

'O spoil him! spoil him!' cried Cragievar,
'Him spoiled let me see:
For on my word,' said Cragievar,
'He had no good will at me.'

They took him from his armour clear,
His sword, likewise his shield;
Yea, they have left him naked there,
Upon the open field.

The Highland men, they're clever men
At handling sword and shield,
But yet they are too naked men
To stay in battle field.

The Highland men are clever men
At handling sword or gun,
But yet they are too naked men
To bear the cannon's rung.

For a cannon's roar in a summer night
Is like thunder in the air;
There's not a man in Highland dress
Can face the cannon's fire.

Among those named as an 'enemy of religion' to be 'brought to their duty, or rooted out and utterly subdued' was the Roman Catholic Earl of Airlie. He did not wait to be rooted out or subdued. Afraid that he might be forced to sign the Covenant, he left his home in the care of his eldest son, Lord Ogilvie, and departed to England. Fortunately for him, Montrose, whose duty it was to execute the commission of the Committee of Estates, was not inclined to do so very thoroughly. He was content to invest Airlie Castle, enforce a surrender, then garrison it and go elsewhere.

Argyll was not content, however, to leave matters thus easily. He caused Airlie to be pillaged, burnt and destroyed. All the 'goods, gear, corn, cattle, horses, holt, sheep' were removed and only the bare ground left. According to at least one writer Lady Ogilvie was heavily pregnant at the time and asked leave to be allowed to remain in Forthar, their other castle, until the child was delivered. Not only was this not permitted, but Forthar was also pillaged and destroyed. Whether Argyll was present, as the ballad suggests, is very doubtful, since he wrote a letter still extant, dated July, 1640, to one Dugald Campbell: 'You need not let them know you have directions from me to fire it'. The ballad which follows is from Smith's *Scottish Minstrel*, vol. II.

The Bonnie House o' Airlie

from *The Lyric gems of Scotland*

1

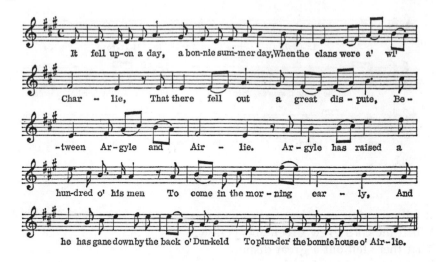

It fell up-on a day, a bon-nie sum-mer day, When the clans were a' wi' Char - lie, That there fell out a great dis-pute, Be- -tween Ar-gyle and Air - lie. Ar-gyle has raised a hun-dred o' his men To come in the mor-ning ear - ly, And he has gane down by the back o' Dun-keld To plun-der the bonnie house o' Air-lie.

from *Songs of Scotland*

2

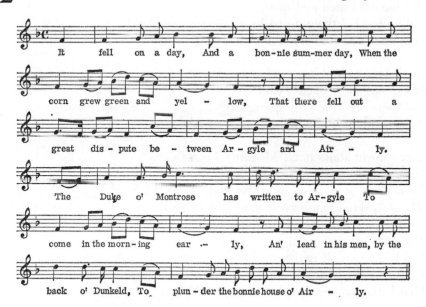

It fell on a day, And a bon-nie sum-mer day, When the corn grew green and yel - low, That there fell out a great dis-pute be - tween Ar-gyle and Air - ly. The Duke o' Montrose has written to Ar-gyle To come in the morn-ing ear - ly, An' lead in his men, by the back o' Dunkeld, To plun - der the bonnie house o' Air - ly.

O' Ar-gyll has writ-ten to Mont-rose To see gin the fields they was fair-ly And to see whether he should stay at hame. Or come to plun-der Air-ly.

It fell on a day, on a bonny summer day,
When the corn grew green and yellow,
That there fell out a great dispute
Between Argyle and Airley.

The great Argyle raised five hundred men,
Five hundred men and many,
And he has led them down by the bonny Dunkeld,
Bade them shoot at the bonny house of Airley.

The lady was looking oer her castle-wa,
And O but she looked weary!
And there she spied the great Argyle,
Come to plunder the bonny house of Airley.

'Come down stairs now, Madam,' he says,
'Now come down and kiss me fairly';
'I'll neither come down nor kiss you,' she says,
'Tho you should na leave a standing stane in Airley.'

'I ask but one favour of you, Argyle,
And I hope you'll grant me fairly
To tak me to some dark dowey glen,
That I may na see the plundering of Airley.'

130

He has taen her by the left shoulder,
And O but she looked weary!
And he has led her down to the top of the town,
Bade her look at the plundering of Airley.

'Fire on, fire on, my merry men all,
And see that ye fire clearly;
For I vow and I swear by the broad sword I wear
That I winna leave a standing stane in Airley.

'You may tell it to your lord,' he says,
'You may tell it to Lord Airley,
That one kiss o his gay lady
Wad hae sav'd all the plundering of Airley.'

'If the great Sir John had been but at hame,
As he is this night wi Prince Charlie,
Neither Argyle nor no Scottish lord
Durst hae plundered the bonny house of Airley.

'Seven, seven sons hae I born unto him,
And the eight neer saw his dady,
And altho I were to have a hundred more,
The should a' draw their sword for Prince Charlie.'

In 1641 it became clear to Montrose that Argyll was planning to take over supreme power in Scotland, supplanting the king in deed if not in name. No match for Argyll as a conspirator, Montrose attempted to expose his intentions, only to find the tables neatly turned. His own actions and statements became the subject of an investigation by the Committee of the Estates, the executive committee of the Scots parliament, containing representatives of the Three Estates, the Lords, the Church and the Commons.

In June, 1641 Montrose was imprisoned, while Argyll intrigued against him and foiled his attempts to obtain a trial at which he might have been able to prove his case. When Charles I himself came north in August agreeing to ban episcopacy and all the other Covenanters' demands, Montrose was unable to obtain an interview with him. On the outbreak of rebellion in Ireland in October the king returned south, after making Argyll a Marquis. The day before he left Scotland Montrose was freed from prison, on a probationary basis. In March of 1642 he was informed that the case against him had been closed at Argyll's discretion. The new Marquis plainly thought that he had nothing further to fear from his discomfited opponent.

By this time Montrose was thoroughly disenchanted with the Covenanters' attitudes and naturally remained steadfastly opposed to Argyll. He retired to his country home in Kincardine while he pondered his future actions. At Argyll's instigation he was offered high military command in the Covenanters' army, for the Campbell chieftain could recognize ability when he saw it and had noted his qualities of leadership during the Bishops' Wars. Montrose temporized, for he and the Covenanters had nearly reached the parting of the ways. It must have been at this time that he wrote the song for which he is famed, the expression of his ardent patriotism.

> My dear and only love, I pray
>   That little world of thee
> Be governed by no other sway
>   Than purest monarchy;
> For if confusion have a part,
>   Which virtuous souls abhor,
> And hold a Synod in thine heart,
>   I'll never love thee more.
>
> As Alexander I will reign,
>   And I will reign alone;

My thoughts did ever more disdain
   A rival on my throne.
He either fears his fate too much,
   Or his deserts are small,
That dares not put it to the touch,
   To win or lose it all.

And in the Empire of thine heart
   Where I should solely be,
If others do pretend a part
   Or dare to vie with me,
Or if Committees thou erect,
   And go on such a score,
I'll laugh and sing at thy neglect,
   And never love thee more.

But if thou wilt prove faithful then,
   And constant of thy word,
I'll make thee glorious by my pen,
   And famous by my sword:
I'll serve thee in such noble ways
   Was never heard before;
I'll crown and deck thee all with bays,
   And love thee more and more.

Chapter 14

Alford

In August, 1643, the General Assembly agreed to a request from the English Parliament to send an army south to assist them against the king. For Montrose this was the last straw. In his view, when the Covenanters obtained the king's agreement to their demands they had in effect made a bargain with him; and this they now proposed to break. He himself moved south to Oxford to offer his services to Charles. Meanwhile the Assembly and the Estates signed the Solemn League and Covenant, which was supposed to supersede the National Covenant. There was, however, a significant difference; signing the National Covenant had been a free expression of belief; those who did not sign the second Covenant were liable to suffer confiscation of their estates and imprisonment.

Throughout the Autumn of 1643 Montrose urged that he be allowed to lead a rising in Scotland, but the king prevaricated endlessly. The fatal Stuart inability to make the correct decision, or indeed any decision based on realities, showed itself to the full. Finally, in February, 1644, he designated Montrose his Lieutenant-General. He was promised troops from Ireland and horse from Newcastle's army to enable him to break his way through the Lowlands to the Highlands. In March he set out from Oxford.

In April he occupied Dumfries without opposition, but no fresh troops flocked to his banner. Too many of the Lowlanders were strong for the Covenant and the Borderers preferred to sit astride the fence. He was soon driven out of Dumfries and forced to return to England. He then marched to Morpeth and, with the aid of six cannons from the Duke of Newcastle's army, he took the town in May. In the same month he was made a Marquis, but he seemed no nearer breaking through to the Highlands and at this stage his task must have seemed well nigh hopeless. His friends urged him to abandon his commission.

In the end, with only two companions, Montrose slipped through the Covenanters' forces in disguise. It must have been a desperate venture for his features were well known and at least one of his erstwhile followers recognized him on the way and wished him luck. After four days travel, mostly by night, they reached comparative safety near Perth, but there was no news of any forces rallying to him.

Fortunately in a few days he received word from Alasdair Macdonald, who with 1,600 followers had come over from Ireland in July in response to Charles's commands. He had attacked the Campbell lands in Ardnamurchan, then, cut off by Argyll, had marched boldly into Lochaber, but had attracted few recruits. He now appealed to the King's Lieutenant for help and orders. Accordingly Montrose instructed him to meet at Blair. Accompanied by Patrick Graham, a well-known local figure, Montrose marched to Blair and arrived just in time to prevent a battle between the Irish forces and the clansmen of Atholl. As the two figures marched between the opposing forces they were recognized by both sides and acclaimed by Irish and Highlander alike. The nucleus of his army was formed on the spot.

It was not a particularly inspiring force, but Alasdair's men, reduced by this time to 1,100, were seasoned campaigners, fighting in three separate regiments and armed with matchlocks, pikes, clubs and claymores. The Highlanders, though poorly armed, were experts with the bow, able to kill a running deer with a single arrow. They were also lean, hardy and able to survive on short rations when required, as well as to move fast in their native mountains. Their cavalry, however, was limited to three horses and their total numbers were only 2,200.

Pitiful as their numbers may have seemed they had several points in their favour which were not at once apparent. They were only opposed at that time by second-rate troops. The main Scottish army under Leven was in the south. It must also be remembered that Montrose was an inspired strategist and leader of men. Furthermore, he was a student of Gustavus Adolphus, who had introduced several revolutionary concepts of warfare. Amongst these innovations was the principle of three files firing together, one kneeling, one stooping and one upright, which Montrose was to use with great effect. Another was the use of shock tactics by cavalry charging home at full gallop instead of as previously merely trotting within gunshot and discharging their weapons.

Towards the end of August Montrose led his forces south from Blair. On their march on 3 August they encountered Lord Kilpont and David Drummond, the Master of Madderty, Montrose's brother-in-law, leading a force of five hundred bowmen to attack Alasdair and his men. On learning who was now leading the Irish they willingly joined Montrose as an unexpected and welcome reinforcement. On the following day, Sunday, 1 September, they encountered 7,000 infantry with 700 cavalry and nine cannon under Lord Elcho, drawn up three miles west of Perth at Tippermuir.

Lord Elcho commanded the right wing, Lord Murray of Gask the centre and Sir James Scott the left, on slightly rising ground. His horse were divided between the two wings equally. Montrose, with only 2,700 men against nearly 8,000 drew up his force three deep in a long line to prevent himself being outflanked by such superior numbers. His Irish regiments under Alasdair he stationed in the centre, Lord Kilpont and his five hundred archers he placed on the left and he himself led the Atholl men on the right.

Montrose sent the Master of Madderty forward to Elcho under flag of truce to inform him that he was acting under the King's Commission and reminding him of his due allegiance. He also advocated a truce to avoid profaning the Sabbath. Elcho's reply was that he had deliberately chosen 'the Lord's day for doing the Lord's will'. Furthermore quite against all civilized custom he sent the Master of Madderty to Perth as a prisoner under escort, apparently with every intention of hanging him after the battle.

Elcho's first move as the two armies advanced was to send a squadron of horse forward against the Highlanders, hoping to provoke a charge from ill-disciplined troops. The Gustavus Adolphus tactics of three lines firing at once, even though the rear rank merely let loose a volley of stones proved enough to send the horse flying and halt Elcho's advance. Close on their heels out of the smoke charged the Highlanders and Irish shouting their war cries as Montrose gave the order to attack. Elcho's centre and right wing gave way and his guns were overrun in a few minutes. The ill-trained Fife levies were soon in full flight and the only real resistance came from Sir James Scott on the rising ground, but he too was soon forced to run.

Estimates of the Covenanters' casualties varied between several hundred and as many as two thousand. It seems to be generally agreed, however, that not many were killed in the actual battle, but most in the rout afterwards. The arms and ammunition which Montrose obtained on the battlefield must have proved extremely welcome, especially the nine captured cannon. It did not take him long to reach Perth, which at once surrendered, and where, with the discipline so characteristic of

136

him, he refused to allow any looting. It soon appeared, however, that his Highlanders had gained sufficient spoil on the battlefield to need to return home to off-load it, as was their custom. By 4 September Montrose was reduced nearly to his original Irish regiments and he decided it was time to move on since no further recruits appeared to be rallying to him.

On his way through Angus to Aberdeen he acquired some seventy-five cavalry under Lord Airlie and Nathaniel Gordon. On 12 September he was outside Aberdeen and found Burleigh awaiting him with 2,000 foot, 500 cavalry and some heavy artillery. Against this Montrose had around 1,500 foot and 75 horse. Furthermore Argyll was approaching from the south with a strong force of Covenanters.

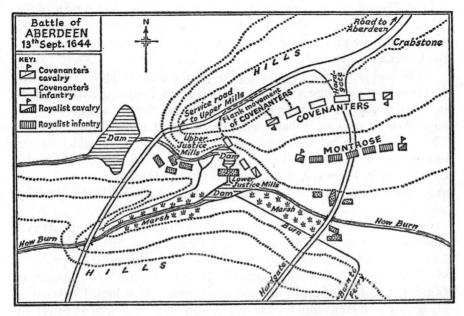

Montrose began by sending an envoy to the burgesses of Aberdeen to demand their surrender. He warned them that if they did not accept no quarter would be given to any remaining in the city and that it would be advisable to send their women and children to safety. A drummer boy with the envoy was treacherously shot as he returned and this aroused Montrose to uncharacteristic wrath. He promised Alasdair and his men permission to sack the city if they won the battle. He then prepared his forces for action.

He kept the Irish in the centre with Nathaniel Gordon, an

experienced but rash commander, on the left and Sir William Rollo on the right. His cavalry he divided equally on each wing, interspersing bowmen and musketeers between them to increase their effectiveness, an old device of the European wars. He began the action with an attack on the Covenanters' front which was protected by some houses. These were soon captured and one or two ineffective cavalry assaults were repulsed.

An attempt by the Covenanters to outflank Montrose's left wing was nearly successful, but was held by Nathaniel Gordon's men until Sir William Rollo brought reinforcements from the right to repel it effectively. A cavalry attack driven home on the weakened right wing was allowed to pass through by the Irish and the horsemen were shot as they passed. The charge was turned into a rout by the prompt return of Sir William Rollo and his men. Montrose, sensing the turn of the battle, which had gone on for some hours, then gave the order to charge and the Covenanters turned and fled in disorder.

As he had promised, Montrose allowed the Irish to plunder the city. Just how much damage was done, or how many people the Irish killed, it is hard to say. The Covenanters were such strenuous and bigoted propagandists in such cases that it was unwise to trust any of their figures. They even managed to invent massacres and martyrs which never existed and in an instance like this might have been expected to make the most of it. However, the number of dead citizens, is only estimated at between 118 and 140 which hardly amounts to wholesale slaughter by any standards.

On 16 September Montrose left Aberdeen and on the 19th Argyll entered the city. The long-suffering citizens were then subjected to further demands and levies. Meanwhile Montrose continued to Speyside, via Tomintoul. In Badenoch he fell ill and did not recover until 4 October. On the 24th, for once, his intelligence failed him. Unaware of his enemy's whereabouts he was nearly cornered by Argyll at Fyvie on the Ythan. After a short skirmish Argyll was content to withdraw, although his forces were much stronger. Heavily outnumbered, Montrose promptly retreated none the worse.

Montrose now experienced trouble with his Lowland supporters, who did not mix well with the Highlanders. The Highlanders did not favour the suggestion of carrying the attack southwards into the Lowlands and the Lowlanders did not relish spending the winter in the Highlands. Promises of safe conducts from Argyll had their effect and considerable numbers of the Lowlanders slipped away.

138

As much to keep his forces occupied as anything else, Montrose next proposed attacking Argyll, who by this time was in Dunkeld. Hearing this news Argyll did not wait for more. He withdrew to Edinburgh and surrendered his commission as General-in-Chief of the Estates Army on the specious grounds that he had been insufficiently supported. William Baillie, a professional general under Leven, was chosen as his successor.

At this stage, while Montrose was still undecided as to his next move, Alasdair appeared at Blair with reinforcements. He brought five hundred Macdonalds from Clanranald, Glengarry, Keppoch and the Isles. He brought also the Macleans of Morvern and Mull, the Farquharsons of Braemar and the Stewarts of Appin, all inspired by a profound hatred of Argyll and the Clan Campbell who had ravaged their lands so often. The Central Highlands were united at last against their mutual enemy and Montrose decided to attack the Campbell headquarters at Inveraray.

On 11 December, with his small army of 3,000 men, Montrose left Blair. His route lay along Loch Tayside, past Crianlarich, through Glenorchy and down past Loch Awe, raiding and burning each clachan and settlement as they went, driving the cattle before them. Intelligence of this reached Argyll in Edinburgh and he moved speedily to Inveraray where all seemed peaceful, despite rumours of disturbances in Lorn. Suddenly like a blast of thunder came the news that Montrose's forces were almost on top of Inveraray itself. Argyll barely had time to board a fishing boat and sail down Loch Fyne to the safety of his castle at Roseneath before the Highlanders were busy plundering the capital of the Campbell territory. Once again by the sheer speed of his movements and the audacity of his attacks Montrose had accomplished the seemingly impossible.

General Baillie was ordered to send sixteen companies of foot to Argyll's assistance. As Argyll himself had been injured in a fall from his horse they were put under the command of Sir Duncan Campbell of Auchinbreck. Once again, however, Montrose was a step ahead of his opponents. By mid January, 1645, he had left Inveraray, marching through the Pass of Brander over Connel and ferrying across Loch Etive. The advance went on by Glencoe and Glen Spean until he reached Kilcumin (subsequently Fort Augustus) at the south end of Loch Ness on 29 January. Although he had been reinforced on the way by 150 Stewarts of Appin, many of the Atholl Highlanders and others had returned home with their plunder. Barely 1,500 of his original 3,000 remained.

Despite his lack of numbers Montrose next proposed attacking Seaforth who had 5,000 levies, referred to as a 'mere rabble', in Inverness, thirty miles to the north. Then he learned that Argyll with 3,000 men was only thirty miles behind him at Inverlochy. He was now sandwiched between two greatly superior forces, both fresh, while his own men were weary. Although the Seaforth force was the larger he was certain of beating it. The Campbells, combined with Baillie's reinforcements, though numerically smaller, represented a much tougher problem. Characteristically and correctly he resolved to tackle them first.

On 31 January, by way of Culachy and Glen Roy and the famous 'Parallel Roads' Montrose performed an epic flanking march, arriving at Roy bridge on the morning of 1 February. Fortunately for him he had excellent guides with intimate local knowledge and he next skirted the lower edges of Ben Nevis, through snow-clad glens. He travelled the final thirteen miles between Roy bridge and Inverlochy without being sighted except by a small scouting party, who were promptly killed. That night Montrose and his men camped overlooking the Campbell army without fires and with no food beyond cold meal washed down with icy water.

On the morning of 2 February, when the pipes sounded their challenge from the hill above Inverlochy, Argyll in his galley on Loch Eil realized that the unbelievable had happened and that Montrose, who two days before had certainly been at Loch Ness, was now upon him. Auchinbreck drew up his army with the Lowlanders on each wing and the Campbells in the centre. Montrose had his Irish on each wing and himself led the Highlanders in the centre.

The battle began with the Irish on each wing charging downhill on the Lowlanders, who, despite their previous battle experience, broke and fled at this new and unnerving spectacle. The Highlanders in the centre drove back the Campbells who fought bravely, despite the sight of their clan chief sailing to safety down the loch. Finally they also broke and were mercilessly slaughtered by their age-old foes. Although the Lowlanders were given quarter, the dead on the Covenanter's side was said to equal the entire strength of Montrose's force, whereas their casualties were put at single figures. The power of the Clan Campbell never recovered from that terrible slaughter. To Montrose it seemed to signal the end of the Covenanter's cause.

After a few days rest in Inverlochy Montrose marched on past the heavily fortified Inverness and so to Elgin. Here he was joined by 300 Grants under their laird. Even more welcome were 200 Gordon horse led by Lord Gordon, who was to become Montrose's closest friend and confidant. Seaforth also came to make peace and was welcomed. All this brought Montrose's forces up to around 2,000 men and 200 horse.

Without a secure base and constantly subject to attack he was forced to keep on the move. He now marched eastwards once more towards Aberdeen, arriving nearby on 9 March. His advance continued through Angus, harried by General Sir John Hurry with 600 horse. Numerous Covenanter pockets of resistance were burned, including Brechin, but near Coupar Angus Montrose encountered General William Baillie with an army of 3,000 of Leven's best regulars. Despite a challenge to attack, Baillie was not to be drawn. He remained where he was, blocking the way south.

Montrose then moved west to Dunkeld, intent on entering the Lowlands by a different route. Here, however, his Highlanders started slipping away, as his Lowlanders had done earlier, for they had no desire to leave the security of the mountains. He soon realized that to attack the Lowlands with his greatly reduced strength was no longer feasible. Convinced that Hurry and Baillie had moved down to Fife to guard the fords over the Forth he decided instead to move against Dundee. A Covenanter stronghold only twenty-four miles away, it seemed a tempting prize.

He sent half his force on to Brechin to await him and with 600 foot and 150 horse attacked Dundee. It seems to have proved a simple matter to breach the walls and take it by storm, since the burghers refused to surrender at once. His men were busy looting and drinking themselves insensible when he received the alarming news that Hurry and Baillie were not, as he had thought, over the Tay in Fife, but were approaching with 3,000 foot and 800 horse within a mile of Dundee. The situation appeared desperate and he was urged to fly, which he refused to do. Instead he set about beating some sense into his men.

Somehow or other he separated them from their booty and sobered them sufficiently to send 400 ahead and hold back 150 horse and 200 of his best musketeers in reserve as a rearguard. They withdrew to the east as Baillie's forces entered Dundee from the west. By this time it was dark, but in the clear light of a northern April night Hurry followed with his horse close on the Highlanders' heels as they marched along the sea coast. A brief skirmish and some sharpshooting made him withdraw and Baillie, deciding that Montrose was making for Brechin to join up with his other force, attempted to cut him off by taking the more direct inland route. This was exactly what Montrose had hoped for and close

141

on midnight he turned sharp left and slipped round Baillie's army towards the hills.

By dawn Montrose was on the south Esk only three miles from the hills and had received news of the escape of his other force from Brechin. Here he allowed his men to rest. After marching something like sixty miles in thirty-six hours and fighting several engagements, quite apart from storming and sacking Dundee and their drunken pillaging thereafter, no doubt they slept like dead men. Even had Baillie been upon them it is unlikely if they would have been able to resist at that stage.

It was not long before Baillie discovered that he had been tricked and sent Hurry and his horse after them. With great difficulty Montrose managed to arouse sufficient marksmen to make Hurry withdraw and give the remainder of his force time to cover the last three miles to the safety of the hills. Unexpectedly faced with vastly superior forces of disciplined soldiers, caught in the middle of sacking a town, forced to march through the night and harried by enemy cavalry, even so Montrose, consummate strategist and leader that he was, had succeeded in saving his men to fight again another day. This may not have been a victory, but it deserves as much praise as any action in which Montrose took part.

The Convenanters' forces were now divided. Baillie, with 2,000 men and 500 horse remained near Perth. Hurry with 1,200 foot and 150 horse moved north. Their idea was to crush Montrose between them, but this plan did not take into account his force's remarkable mobility and his outstanding genius as a commander. With only 500 foot and 50 horse he confronted Baillie's vastly superior army on 17 April and decided that discretion was the better part of valour. He removed himself to Doune in the Trossachs by the 20th and there found some reinforcements. He was on Deeside by the end of April and here he collected Lord Gordon with 1,000 foot and 200 horse, thus bringing his forces up to 2,000 foot and 250 horse.

Meanwhile, further north, Hurry had raised something like 4,000 foot and 400 horse with the aid of the Covenanters of Moray and Elgin and of Seaforth who had changed sides again. As he appeared to be threatening the Gordon country in Strathbogie, Montrose felt bound to move to defend his allies. Astutely Hurry withdrew in front of him, apparently falling back on Inverness, hoping that Montrose would follow him out of the friendly Gordon country. He withdrew from Elgin to Forres and from thence to Nairn, hoping not only to lead Montrose into hostile country, but also to gain fresh reinforcements from Seaforth.

Learning that Montrose had followed him and despairing of Seaforth's aid, Hurry at last turned to the attack about midnight on 8 May. Montrose was encamped at Auldearn, a small village about two miles east of Nairn. It was a wet and moonless night and Hurry justifiably did not expect the royalist pickets to be far from their camp. While still five miles or so from Auldearn, Hurry accordingly ordered his army to clear their guns of their wet powder with a volley. The Irish guards heard the fusillade and reported the news to Montrose. Aware of what it almost certainly portended he took up defensive positions at dawn.

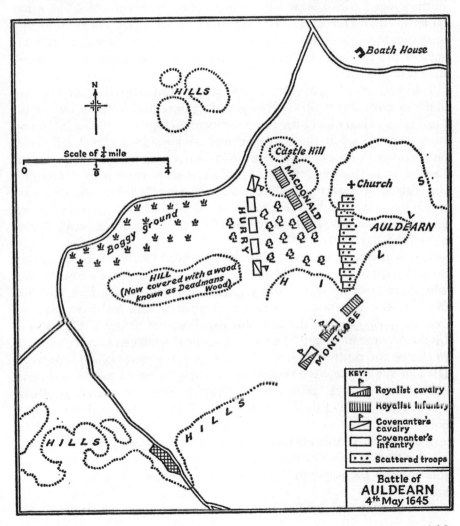

The focal point of the village and obvious defensive position was the Castle Hill. Here Montrose posted Macdonald and part of the Irish force in front of his standard in the hope that Hurry would launch his main attack against them across ground which was boggy and difficult going for his horse. He also posted a few scattered musketeers in the village in the hollow with instructions to keep up a rapid fire to give an impression of strength. His main body of foot and his cavalry under Lord Gordon he kept on the left flank concealed behind a ridge of rising ground. His forces were thus deployed in a horseshoe formation suited to the ground with a weak right wing and a strong concealed left wing on an even weaker hinge. The plan was to decoy the enemy into the unfavourable ground between the bog and the castle. It was a brilliant spur of the moment strategic plan and it met with even more success than it deserved.

Hurry advanced on Macdonald's severely outnumbered force. The five hundred Irish found themselves pitted against nearly three thousand. Fortunately Hurry had little room for manœuvre, as Montrose had foreseen. Constrained by the boggy ground on one side and the Castle Hill on the other he could only advance with one regiment, the Campbells of Lawers, in the lead and the other three in reserve close behind. Despite the Irish Macdonalds' magnificent feats of arms they were driven backwards by sheer weight of numbers. Macdonald and his men, however, fought like heroes until Hurry and his four main regiments were committed beyond recall.

It was at this stage that Montrose sent Lord Gordon forward at the head of the horse in a full-blooded cavalry charge. Hurry's own horse, which had been having difficulty advancing, was sent reeling into his foot soldiers. Montrose then followed up hard with his main force of foot in a charge on the unprotected flank of Hurry's regiments. Inspired by the moment, Macdonald somehow managed to rally his men to charge the centre yet again. The effect was catastrophic for Hurry. His four regiments were slaughtered and the reserves turned and fled.

The Covenanters' casualties at Auldearn were estimated at about 2,000. Hurry, one of the last to leave the field, escaped with about 100 horse. Apart from a number of Macdonald's men the royalist army had few casualties. It was another brilliant strategic victory for Montrose, but this time in defence rather than attack and against a general who had shown much the same ability to mount a surprise attack as Montrose himself.

During May and June of 1645 Montrose recouped his strength and

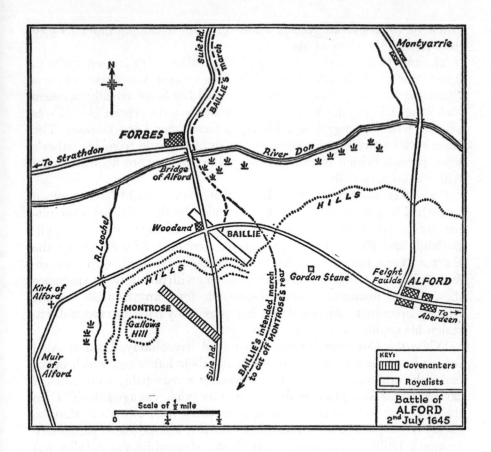

Battle of
ALFORD
2nd July 1645

tried to draw Baillie into battle. At Keith towards the end of June
Baillie refused a challenge from Montrose to move from a strong position and meet him on level terms in the open. Quite understandably he
replied that he was not accustomed to moving at his enemy's con-
venience. However, as Montrose had hoped, he followed the royalist
force when they withdrew and on 2 July the two armies met above the
Don at Alford.

Montrose had taken the direct route south over the Don, then a river
with wide boggy banks. He had crossed at the ford by the village of
Forbes and had then taken up a strong position on the Gallows Hill, a
gradual eminence to the south-west. His forces were drawn up mostly on
the reverse slope so that to Baillie they would appear negligible in
numbers and easily outflanked by marching over the ford and to the
east, rather than attacking by direct assault. His idea was to draw

Baillie on to dangerous ground where a retreat would put him in boggy ground with the river at his back.

The two forces were about equal in numbers with around 1,500 to 2,000 foot on each side, but Baillie had around 500 horse whereas Montrose had only 250. Montrose divided his horse equally between each wing. His Badenoch Highlanders composed the centre, his left was a small Irish contingent and his right was under Lord Gordon. The latter was particularly incensed at the sight of cattle from his father's lands penned behind the Covenanters' lines and swore he would deal with Baillie personally.

Once over the ford it is probable that Baillie would have declined battle had he not been thoroughly overruled by the Advisory Committee travelling with him, which included amongst others Argyll, Burleigh and Elcho. These peripatetic committees appointed by the Estates were a hazard to which the Covenanter Generals were increasingly subjected. Often composed of ministers with no military experience these absurd institutions were responsible for many Scottish defeats. Already in conflict with his, Baillie had previously tried unsuccessfully to resign his command. It was now too late.

While the Covenanter force was halted irresolutely, Lord Gordon led his horse in a violent charge against their left wing, which broke under the onslaught. For a while thereafter a reasonably well matched cavalry mêlée took place as the Covenanter horse engaged them. Then the foot came to Lord Gordon's support, using their swords to stab the enemy horses, which were soon in full retreat, leaving the royalists free to attack Baillie's unprotected left flank. Meanwhile the royalist left wing had also charged and there was a general advance. In a few minutes Baillie's forces were completely swamped and utterly overcome.

Argyll only narrowly escaped being cut down on his third horse, as he made for safety. Lord Gordon was actually reaching forward to grasp Baillie by the belt when he was struck down by a bullet which was said to have come from behind and the Covenanter general was thus also able to make his escape by the narrowest of margins. Although Montrose had won the day it was at bitter personal cost. Lord Gordon was an inspired leader and his closest personal friend.

By his victory at Alford on 2 July, Montrose was triumphant in the Highlands. Both Hurry's and Baillie's armies had been destroyed in two successive battles within two months of each other. Unfortunately all was nullified by Cromwell's victory at Naseby on 4 June. The royalist cause was already lost.

The following is a fragmentary series of verses taken from *The Thistle of Scotland:* A Selection of Ancient Ballads (with notes) by Alexander Laing, Aberdeen, 1823. The verses are reasonably accurate factually. Montrose had spent the previous night at the Castle of Asloun and Baillie had been encamped at Leslie, halting during his advance south at a farm called Mill Hill, before crossing the river. Lord George Gordon, however, commanded the right wing, not the left, but the verses do him justice, indicating that he was widely appreciated, even by his enemies.

The Grahames and Gordons of Aboyne
Camp'd at Drumminor bog;
At the castle there they lay all night,
And left them scarce a hog.

The black Baillie, that auld dog,
Appeared on our right,
We quickly raise up frae the bog,
To Alford march'd that night.

We lay at Lesly all night,
They camped at Asloun;
And up we raise afore daylight,
To ding the beggars doun.

Before we was in battle rank,
We was anent Mill Hill;
I wat full weel they gar'd us rue,
We gat fighting our fill.

They hunted us and dunted us,
They drave us here and there,
Untill three hundred of our men,
Lay gasping in their lair.

The Earl of Mar the right wing guarded,
The colours stood him by;
Lord George Gordon the left wing guarded,
Who well the sword could ply.

There came a ball shot frae the west,
That shot him through the back;
Although he was our enemy,
We grieved for his wreck.

We cannot say 'twas his own men,
But yet it came that way;
In Scotland there was not a match,
To that man where he lay.

Chapter 15

Kilsyth: Philiphaugh

After Alford Montrose waited some time for reinforcements to arrive. It was not until the end of July that they finally assembled at Dunkeld, amounting to around 4,500 foot and 500 horse. Meanwhile Baillie was also collecting fresh forces, hampered as always by the Advisory Committee, which made it virtually impossible to exercise proper discipline or control. (Regardless of his record Argyll was still a prominent member.) Despite these difficulties this Covenanter force finally amounted to 6,000 foot and 800 horse. At last the rival armies met on the Campsie Fells near Kilsyth on 15 August.

Montrose had encamped in a strong position above Kilsyth and on 14 August, although further reinforcements under Lanark were only twelve miles away, Baillie was urged by his Advisory Committee to attack. At dawn on the 15th the Covenanters began their advance. Even within sight of the enemy the Advisory Committee overruled their general's proposed strategy and insisted on an outflanking march, which led to the Covenanters' own flank being exposed.

Near the head of the glen between the two armies were several small cottages which promised to make a strongpoint and Montrose prudently seized them and occupied them in advance. As the Covenanters moved forward on their flank march some of their force, against orders, attacked these cottages and were repelled. The Highlanders were not content with merely throwing their attackers back. Seeing their enemy's flank unexpectedly exposed they charged it too, which had the unexpected and entirely undeserved effect of cutting the Covenanters' army in half.

The advance force of the Covenanters was now met by the Gordons, who seemed to make little headway. Aboyne, with the Gordon horse, went to their rescue, but with little effect. Finally Lord Airlie and the Ogilvies went into the fray and the tide began to turn in Montrose's favour. As Nathaniel Gordon and the rest of the royalist horse joined the battle the Covenanters broke and fled. Their forces were scattered. Argyll, Baillie and the other leaders, better horsed, managed to save their own skins, but there were few survivors from the 6,000 foot who had started the day. This was the decisive battle. Montrose had now cleared the Covenanters' forces out of Scotland.

Throughout Scotland Montrose was acclaimed. One after another the noble houses rallied to his standard. Edinburgh surrendered and presented its humble submission. The prisons were emptied of the royalists

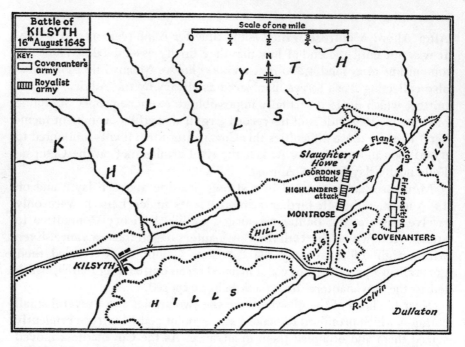

who had been incarcerated. Everywhere Montrose was triumphant and hailed as the victor. The King's commission appointing him viceroy of Scotland was sent to him and amongst his first acts he knighted Alasdair for his gallant campaigning. He sent word back that he hoped to travel south with 20,000 men.

Montrose had forgotten how hopeless it was to rely on Highland troops in the south. As he lay encamped at Bothwell, in August and early September, his Highlanders faded away to their mountain homes. Even Alasdair departed for Argyll with half his Irish following, bent on a campaign of revenge against Argyll. Although he promised to return

150

he did not do so and four months later after an ineffectual and blundering campaign he returned to Ireland.

On 4 September Montrose broke camp and marched south. He was left with only 1,200 foot, including some 500 Irish, and a little over 1,000 horse, mostly Scottish gentry. By 12 September his small force was encamped in a field called Philiphaugh, a low lying plain beyond the town of Selkirk and the Ettrick Water. Montrose and his horse were mostly in the town, his foot were on the plain, divided from each other by the river, an oversight which was to prove fatal. This was Covenanter country, hostile to the Highlanders and Montrose. Here he lacked the good intelligence he could rely on in the Highlands and he spent the night of 12 September unaware that Leslie's army was close at hand.

General Sir David Leslie with 4,000 cavalry and 2,000 foot had advanced north along the coast, via Berwick and Tranent. He had a Committee of Advice with him, but they were not to affect the issue as they subsequently did at the fatal field of Dunbar. From Tranent Leslie struck suddenly and unexpectedly inland to the south. On the night of 12 September he had successfully approached within five miles of Selkirk and encamped there, without warning reaching Montrose.

On the morning of 13 September, aided by local guides opposed to the royalists and under cover of a thick mist, he made a surprise attack on Montrose's camp. Leslie had divided his forces in two and 2,000 horse abruptly swept down out of the mist on the royalists as they were mustering in the morning. Although the 500 Irish fought desperately in shallow trenches they had dug the night before, they scarcely had a chance. The first Montrose heard of the attack was the sound of shots being fired. Hastily mounting his horse and leading 150 men into action he twice charged the vastly superior force across the river with little effect. He was finally persuaded to give up the hopeless struggle and save himself. By that time it was painfully clear that the royalist force was completely overwhelmed.

The Covenanters might subsequently invent massacres and martyrs as evidence of how they were victimized, but nothing they could ever invent could equal their own appalling behaviour after Philiphaugh. Three hundred women and children, the Irish camp followers, were butchered on the spot. Some two hundred cooks and horseboys were also killed without mercy. Although the remaining Irish fighting men had surrendered on terms of safe conduct they were cut down or shot as they stood. One of the bloodthirsty ministers who watched this with satisfaction and even took part in it, was heard to say exultantly, 'The wark

151

goes merrily on'. Those of Montrose's supporters and leaders who were captured were also promptly executed, among them Sir William Rollo, brother-in-law to Argyll, who had been one of Montrose's closest aides since his first taking the commission as the King's Lieutenant-General.

The brilliant year of success was over. Yet what a year of victories it had been. No other campaign in Scotland could ever equal it. As leader, tactician, strategist and warrior Montrose stood head and shoulders above his contemporaries.

The following Whiggish ballad is taken from Scott's *Minstrelsy of the Scottish Border*. It credits Leslie with half as many men as he had and Montrose with nine times as many. The 'aged father' apparently fought at Solway Moss in 1542, 103 years previously, also at Dunbar, when Leslie was defeated by Cromwell five years after Philiphaugh in 1650. This would seem to date the ballad at least twenty years after the event.

On Philiphaugh a fray began,
At Hairheadwood it ended;
The Scots outoer the Graemes they ran,
Sae merrily they bended.

Sir David frae the Border came,
Wi heart an hand came he;
Wi him three thousand bonny Scots,
To bear him company.

Wi him three thousand valiant men,
A noble sight to see!
A cloud o mist them weel conceald,
As close as eer might be.

When they came to the Shaw burn,
Said he, 'Sae weel we frame,
I think it is convenient
That we should sing a psalm.'

When they came to the Lingly burn,
As daylight did appear,
They spy'd an aged father,
And he did draw them near.

'Come hither, aged father,'
Sir David he did cry,
'And tell me where Montrose lies,
With all his great army.'

'But first you must come tell to me,
If friends or foes you be;
I fear you are Montrose's men,
Come frae the north country.'

153

'No, we are nane o Montrose's men,
Nor eer intend to be;
I am Sir David Lesly,
That's speaking unto thee.'

'If you're Sir David Lesly,
As I think weel ye be,
I am sorry ye hae brought sae few
Into your company.

'There's fifteen thousand armed men
Encamped on yon lee;
Ye'll never be a bite to them,
For aught that I can see.

'But halve your men in equal parts,
Your purpose to fulfill;
Let ae half keep the water-side,
The rest gae round the hill.

'Your nether party fire must,
Then beat a flying drum;
And then they'll think the day's their ain,
And frae the trench they'll come.

'Then, those that are behind them maun
Gie shot, baith grit and sma;
And so, between your armies twa,
Ye may make them to fa.'

'O were ye ever a soldier?'
Sir David Lesly said;
'O yes; I was at Solway Flow,
Where we were all betrayd.

'Again I was at curst Dunbar,
And was a prisoner taen,
And many weary night and day
In prison I hae lien.'

154

'If ye will lead these men aright,
Rewarded shall ye be;
But, if that ye a traitor prove,
I'll hang thee on a tree.'

'Sir, I will not a traitor prove;
Montrose has plunderd me;
I'll do my best to banish him
Away frae this country.'

He halvd his men in equal parts,
His purpose to fulfill;
The one part kept the water-side,
The other gaed round the hill.

The nether party fired brisk,
Then turnd and seemd to rin;
And then they a' came frae the trench,
And cry'd, The day's our ain!

The rest then ran into the trench,
And loosd their cannons a':
And thus, between his armies twa,
He made them fast to fa.

Now let us a' for Lesly pray,
And his brave company,
For they hae vanquishd great Montrose,
Our cruel enemy.

Chapter 16

Montrose

After the disastrous annihilation of his force at Philiphaugh, Montrose spent the rest of 1645 and the first six months of 1646 in the Highlands in largely abortive attempts to raise another effective army. Then, in May, Charles placed himself in the hands of the Scots and wrote to Montrose commanding him to give up his fight against the Covenanters. Only after Charles had repeated his command in July could Montrose bring himself to accept the inevitable and negotiate his followers' surrender. The terms he was offered and accepted were better than might have been expected. With the exception of himself, the Earl of Crawford and Sir John Hurry, who had changed sides after Kilsyth and was still with him, all Montrose's followers were granted free pardon. Montrose, Crawford and Hurry were to go into exile before 1 September. For the moment, loyal to his king's commands, Montrose left the scene.

In February, 1647, the Covenanters surrendered Charles at Cromwell's demand, despite the fact that he and his 'Independents' still refused to acknowledge the Solemn League and Covenant. Immediately the country was deeply divided between the militant faction of bigoted Covenanters headed by Argyll and those in sympathy with the King led by the Duke of Hamilton. Towards the end of 1647, under a secret agreement, Charles engaged to accept the Solemn League and Covenant and in return Hamilton's followers engaged to support him against the English Parliament. The supporters of this 'Engagement', known as 'Engagers', proved to have a majority in the Scots Parliament and for once broke away from the tyranny of the kirk bigots, but the country was bitterly divided.

The bitterness of feeling and depth of division within the country can be gauged by subsequent events. Despite denunciations from the pulpits, in August, 1648, Hamilton led a hastily levied and inadequately trained army south into England to support Charles. Attacked by Cromwell's seasoned Ironsides at Preston in Lancashire, this inexperienced force proved no match for them and was soundly defeated. Most of the foot were made prisoner and Hamilton himself was executed. In Scotland the extremists hailed this defeat with delight and, led by Argyll, welcomed Cromwell to Edinburgh. The 'Engagers' were forced to forfeit civil and military office, thus dividing the county even more deeply.

The bitterness of feeling and depth of division can be gauged by subsequent events. When Charles I was executed on 30 January, 1649, there was an abrupt revulsion of feeling throughout Scotland, even among the strongest sectarians. For a brief period the country was even more deeply split as intrigue vied with intrigue. Charles II was proclaimed King conditionally on signing the two Covenants and the English Parliament was accused of breach of the Solemn League and Covenant. Naively the Scots still regarded this as binding on the Parliamentarians.

In April, 1650, Montrose was sent from the Continent on an ill-considered and ill-fated expedition to the north. Landing from Orkney in Caithness, in an area he barely knew, with untried supporters, the result was almost a foregone conclusion. Relying on defective intelligence he was surprised by a superior force of horse at the Battle of Carbisdale on the Oykel in Ross and Cromarty in May. His own horse was overwhelmed and his foot scattered and slain. Forced to take to the hills he was betrayed by the dastardly Neil Macleod of Assynt, whose name became a byword for treachery throughout the Highlands. Montrose was taken south to Edinburgh, badgered and pestered by militant preachers at every halt. With the prospect of Charles II arriving the Covenanters hastened to dispose of their old enemy. On the grounds that his attainder of 1644 had never been revoked, he was condemned to be hung. The night before his execution, while in a crowded smoke-filled cell, he penned the following:

> Let them bestow on every airth a limb,
> Then open all my veins, that I may swim
> To Thee, my Maker, in that crimson lake;
> Then place my parboiled head upon a stake,
> Scatter my ashes, strew them to the air —
> Lord! Since Thou knowest where all these atoms are,
> I'm hopeful Thou'lt recover once my dust,
> And confident Thou'lt raise me with the just.

There may have been better verse, but in the circumstances these few lines are past praise. The spirit that could produce them transcends all the sectarian differences and petty quarrels which reft the country. Small wonder that next day all the witnesses, both friend and foe, testified that his noble appearance awed the crowds and that his march to the scaffold came near to being a triumphant procession.

One observer wrote: 'He stept along the streets with so great state, and there appeared in his countenance so much beauty, majesty and gravity as amazed the beholder, and many of his enemies did acknowledge him to be the bravest subject in the world, and in him a gallantry that braced all the crowd.' Even a Cromwellian agent was moved to note: 'I never saw a more sweeter carriage in a man in all my life.' Thus, for the last time, Montrose triumphed unexpectedly, setting an unassailable example even in the manner of his dying.

The following verses by Ian Lom, translated by Sheriff Nicolson, are from the *Beauties of Gaelic Poetry*, Mackenzie, 1841. With their magnificent Celtic allegory they go far to explaining the Highlander's feeling for 'The Great Montrose'. The final verse relates to the oft-told tale that McNeil of Assynt was paid in meal which was sour.

158

I'll not go to Dunedin
Since the Graham's blood was shed,
The manly, mighty lion
Tortured on the gallows.

That was the true gentleman,
Who came of line not humble,
Good was the flushing of his cheek
When drawing up to combat.

His chalk-white teeth well closing,
His slender brow not gloomy!—
Though oft my love awakes me,
This night I will not bear it.

Neil's son of woeful Assynt,
If I in net could take thee,
My sentence would condemn thee,
Nor would I spare the gibbet.

If you and I encountered
On the marshes of Ben Etive,
The black waters and the clods
Would there be mixed together.

If thou and thy wife's father,
The houscholder of Leime
Were hanged both together,
'Twould not atone my loss.

Stript tree of the false apples,
Without esteem, or fame, or grace,
Ever murdering each other
'Mid dregs of wounds and knives!

Death-wrapping to thee, base one
Ill didst thou sell the righteous,
For the meal of Leith,
And two-thirds of it sour!

Chapter 17

Dunbar: Rullion Green

Montrose had only been hung and quartered a few weeks when Charles II took ship to Aberdeen. No doubt he saw one of Montrose's limbs publicly displayed there on his arrival. Certainly he must have seen his head on a spike on the Edinburgh Tolbooth. The death of such a loyal supporter cannot have endeared the Covenanters to him, or filled him with any trust in their loyalty. On the other hand, with their pathetic belief in the binding value of the Covenants, they insisted he should subscribe to them both. Convinced that thereafter he was bound to them, they then turned to face Cromwell.

In June of 1650 the Scots army consisted of only 2,500 horse and 3,000 foot. Furthermore the Covenanters had dismissed many of their old commanders as 'Engagers'. A fresh army had to be hastily raised and trained, officered at least in part by clerks and others unused to fighting. Even though their numbers eventually reached 22,000, it is not surprising that General Sir David Leslie avoided combat with Cromwell's seasoned troops, relying on the familiar and well tried Scots scorched earth and harrying tactics of many previous campaigns.

When he invaded Scotland on 22 July Cromwell had 16,354 battle-hardened soldiers, the equal of any in Europe. He had planned, however, to obtain his supplies by sea and the weather conspired to defeat him. It was wet and cold and contrary winds kept his ships harbour-bound in the south. Soaked to the skin and without tents until well into August even his experienced Ironsides began to fall sick. Towards the end of August he was reduced to around 11,000 men, composed of 3,500 horse and 7,500 foot. Even so he no doubt felt a match for the Scots had he been able to bring them to battle.

His initial plan had been to march to Leith and await supplies there, but, failing to engage the Scots or obtain sufficient from the countryside, he was forced to fall back on Musselburgh in late August. On 30 August he decided to withdraw to Dunbar, which he intended to fortify as a convenient base for his sick to recover in and for reinforcements from Berwick to land at. It is possible he was even considering withdrawing his forces by sea, but he was still hoping principally to get to grips with the Scots forces. On 31 August, as he retreated through Haddington, his forces were severely harried by the Scots. On the morning of 1 September he waited in vain for four hours on the west of Haddington but still failed to bring the Scots to battle. Leslie merely followed him to Dunbar and took up a strong position on the Brunt and Doon hills above the port, commanding the possible line of withdrawal to the south.

At this stage Leslie merely had to stay in his strong position on Doon Hill and there was virtually nothing the English could do. If Cromwell tried to march to Berwick Leslie was perfectly placed to intercept him. If he tried to embark by sea he would be bound to lose a good portion of his wagon train, apart from his horses and rearguard. If he stayed he might find himself besieged.

Unfortunately for Leslie, he not only had to contend with Cromwell, he also had to contend with the customary Advisory Committee of bloodthirsty ministers, full of fire and invective but tactical and strategic half-wits. Seeing Cromwell's army drawn up between Doon Hill and Dunbar beneath them, they immediately announced with conviction:

'The Laird has delivered them into our hands!'

Convinced that this was the opportunity to beat the English at last, despite all Leslie's arguments, they insisted he must take his forces down from their secure position on Doon Hill and attack. Had they known their history they would have remembered that they were making the identical mistake an earlier Scots army had made against the English under Edward I in 1296.

Seeing the Scots army coming down the hill on to level terms, the English generals could be forgiven for saying in their turn:

'The Lord has delivered them into our hands.'

It was significant that the Covenanters' army used as their field word 'The Covenant' while the English used 'The Lord of Hosts'. Each was confident the Almighty was on their side, but Cromwell had the advantage of being his own master and unhampered by amateur tacticians. As the Scots took up their positions at the foot of the Doon Hill, along the line of the Brox Burn and effectively blocking his route to Berwick, he was able to formulate a sound strategical plan.

The Scots, by any standards, were slow in making their move. From mid-morning on the 2nd for the rest of the day they seem to have been busy taking up their positions. All the time their movements were being attentively studied by Cromwell and his principal staff officers from the safety of Broxmouth House on the Dunbar side of the Brox Burn. Cromwell and Lambert, his Major-General, soon saw the weakness of Leslie's new position. Cramped between the slopes of Doon Hill and the steep-sided upper reaches of the Brox Burn the Scots left flank had no room for manœuvre.

Near the sea the Brox Burn was much less of an obstacle, being little more than a foot deep. It was here that the Scots had grouped much of their horse, obviously with the intention of taking advantage of this easy crossing when they attacked. However, they did not get into position in time to attack on the 2nd and during the wet and windy night Cromwell busied his troops in preparing to get their blow in first at dawn. The noise of his troop movements was lost in the storm and with the approach of dawn he was ready for his counter-stroke.

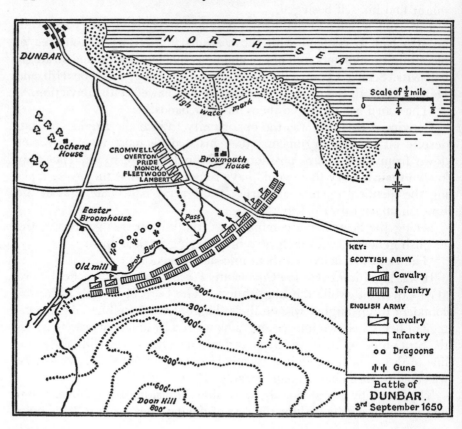

The English horse had been brought into position to attack the Scots right wing and outflank their army from the sea. At 4 am, as dawn broke, Cromwell gave the signal to attack, although his troops had only just got into position. The Scots were taken by surprise in a position intended for attack not defence, but at first they put up a resolute fight and there was some fierce action. Then Cromwell completed his out-flanking movement from the sea and swept down on the unprotected Scottish flank.

The Scots on the right were the Highlanders under Campbell of Lawers, the same who had been defeated by Montrose at Auldearn. They now fought bravely, but were overwhelmed by superior numbers. Under successive cavalry charges the right wing of the Scots army was shattered. Some stood firm and were for the most part killed, but the rest were soon pushed in upon the left and began to break. The left flank followed suit without even taking part in the battle.

As Cromwell had foreseen, the successful flank attack had driven the Scots regiments back on each other without room for recovery or manœuvre. Between 4 am and sunrise the Scots army was completely overwhelmed. Driven before the English horse like cattle, they them-selves ironically nicknamed the battle 'Dunbar Drove'. Their casualties were estimated at about 3,000 killed principally by the Ironsides as they fled. About 10,000 were captured. Of these an unknown number died of hunger in Durham Cathedral, where they were confined, and the rest were sold into slavery in the Colonies.

The effect of the battle of Dunbar was twofold. Firstly, to a very great extent it ended the tyranny of the kirk and the rule of the perfervid bigots. There was now a split between those who saw and approved the necessity to enlist the royalists in their support, the 'Resolutioners', and those who disapproved, the more fanatical 'Remonstrants'. The kirk was never again to be such an absolute master of the country. Secondly, the battle gave Cromwell command of the south of Scotland and enabled him to go on to take Edinburgh, but even this did not as yet give him complete control of the country.

General Lambert defeated a Royalist force at Inverkeithing on 20 July, 1651, but this still was not the last blow. Accompanied by Charles II, Leslie marched south to Worcester. There, on 3 September, Cromwell decisively defeated the largely Scots army under Leslie. Charles fought bravely and by a series of hairsbreadths succeeded in making good his escape. A year to the day after Dunbar, Cromwell was master of Scotland as well as England. Had he faced Montrose

163

instead of Leslie on either occasion it might have been a very different story.

Thereafter Cromwell continued much the same disguised totalitarian government in Scotland that he exercised in England. The more bigoted Presbyterians were disgusted to discover the degree of religious tolerance he insisted on allowing to such Protestant sects as Quakers and Baptists. Inevitably the Scots discovered that government by martial rule was not so very different from government by kirk rule and a few years of each was sufficient to make the Restoration seem doubly welcome when it came in 1660.

One result of the Restoration was the trial and execution of the Marquis of Argyll. Letters he had written to General Monk advising him of royalist movements at the time of the Battle of Worcester were produced as evidence of his treachery. By an interesting twist of fate his head appeared on a spike on the Edinburgh Tolbooth just as Montrose's was removed. At Charles II's command, the latter's limbs and head were reverently gathered together and given a state funeral.

With the Restoration there came also a return to Episcopacy. In 1662 the formal restoration of Bishops was announced. Furthermore those ministers who had been admitted since the rights of lay patrons to appoint clergymen had been abolished in 1649 were ordered to gain the approval of bishop and patron. Some 270 indignantly refused to do so and when, as a consequence, they were banned from their pulpits, they held open air meetings, or conventicles, in the fields. In the west and south-west of Scotland the feeling aroused was particularly strong and here the deprived ministers outnumbered the others by two to one.

Had Charles and his counsellors merely tried to impose a moderate form of 'Jacobean episcopacy', such as had existed under James I, all might have been well. Then moderate opinion might have triumphed and could well have forced a general acceptance of some such compromise. Persecution merely brought the worst and most bigoted elements to the fore. A further act of 1663 imposing fines on all who refused to attend the approved church and banning deprived ministers from living within twenty miles of their old kirk roused even deeper resistance. The seeds of violence and bloodshed were being sown once more.

In 1666 there was a spontaneous uprising, which began in Dumfriesshire. Sir James Turner, a soldier of fortune who had been deputed to collect the arbitrary fines for not attending the episcopal church, was seized with his men and disarmed. Then the ill-organized rabble, for it

164

was little more, started to march to Edinburgh, gathering sympathizers in Ayrshire and Lanarkshire on the way, in particular Colonel Wallace and Major Learmonth, both well-known Covenanters. In the capital they confidently expected to be joined by more supporters, for in Lanarkshire their numbers were estimated as close to the 3,000. In fact the reverse happened. The weather broke and the rain poured down, making the road a quagmire and soaking them to the skin. Far from being joined by others their own numbers steadily decreased as they marched. By the time they were close to Edinburgh they had lost half their own forces and gained no fresh recruits.

They had already started to turn back when they learned that General Tam Dalziel of the Binns had been sent out from Edinburgh to deal with them. Thereupon they halted at Rullion Green in the Pentland Hills and took up their position on a knoll, determined to give a good account of themselves under the leadership of Colonel Wallace. Meanwhile General Dalziel had marched to Calder to intercept them on the Lanark road, only to discover that they had already passed through Colinton to the other side of the Pentlands. He then led his horsemen over the hills and finally found the Covenanters waiting for him at Rullion Green.

In spite of their almost total lack of arms and military training they withstood two charges. The third charge, however, made them break and run, utterly routed. Despite his reputation among the Covenanters for devilish cunning and cruelty, General Dalziel did not pursue them. In part, admittedly, this may have been because his horse were mostly local gentlemen with some degree of sympathy for the misguided west country labourers who formed the main part of the uprising. Only about fifty Covenanters were killed and about the same number made prisoner.

The following ballad is from Scott's *Minstrelsy of the Scottish Border*, Vol. II, p. 246. He in turn obtained it from a Mr Livingston of Airds, who had taken it down verbatim from the recitation of an old woman on his estate. It is notably inaccurate regarding numbers, but though derisory in tone treats the wretched Whigs quite tolerantly.

The gallant Grahams cam from the west,
Wi' their horses black as ony craw;
The Lothian lads they marched fast,
To be at the Rhyns o' Gallowa.

Betwixt Dumfries town and Argyle,
The lads they marched mony a mile;
Souters and taylors unto them drew,
Their covenants for to renew.

The Whigs, they, wi' their merry cracks,
Gar'd the poor pedlars lay down their packs;
But aye sinsyne they do repent
The renewing o' their Covenant.

At the Mauchline muir, where they were reviewed,
Ten thousand men in armour showed;
But, ere they cam to the Brockie's burn,
The half o' them did back return.

General Dalyell, as I hear tell,
Was our lieutenant-general;
And Captain Welsh, wi' his wit and skill,
Was to guide them on to the Pentland Hill.

General Dalyell held to the hill,
Asking at them what was their will;
And who gave them this protestation,
To rise in arms against the nation?

'Although we all in armour be,
It's not against his majesty;
Nor yet to spill our neighbour's bluid,
But wi' the country we'll conclude.'

'Lay down your arms, in the King's name,
And ye shall a' gae safely hame';
But they a' cried out, wi' ae consent,
'We'll fight for a broken Covenant.'

'O well,' says he, 'since it is so,
A wilfu' man never wanted woe';
He then gave a sign unto his lads,
And they drew up in their brigades.

The trumpets blew, and the colours flew,
And every man to his armour drew;
The Whigs were never so much aghast,
As to see their saddles toom* sae fast.   *empty

The cleverest men stood in the van,
The Whigs they took their heels and ran;
But such a raking was never seen,
As the raking o' the Rullion Green.

Chapter 18

Loudon Hill: Bothwell Bridge

Although easily enough suppressed, the ineffectual rising which terminated in the so-called Battle of Rullion Green resulted in an attempt at conciliation on the part of the authorities. In the nature of things this did not last long. Events had already gone too far. As bitterness moved them to excess the very name Covenanter began to take on a subtly different connotation, implying an extremist rather than merely one who had signed the Covenant. As repression increased in the west, for instance in 1678 when landlords were made answerable for their tenants, so, increasingly, armed men began to attend the conventicles. The government, taking alarm, sent 6,000 armed Highlanders into Ayrshire for a month to enforce the law, but the 'Highland Host', as they were nicknamed, merely increased the general bitter discontent and ill-feeling in the west.

On 3 May, 1679, Archbishop Sharp of St Andrews was waylaid by a party of vengeful Covenanters led by Hackston of Rathillet and John Balfour of Kinloch, the latter a notorious ruffian. The archbishop, a strong supporter of the government's measures, was travelling across Magus Muir, about two miles outside St Andrews, in a coach with his daughter. The coach was halted and the archbishop dragged out to be shot and stabbed. Despite the fact that they loudly proclaimed that God had delivered him into their hands they made a singularly untidy job of finishing him off. It was only because Balfour, known as Burly, overheard the archbishop's daughter call to the servants for assistance that he realized that the archbishop was not yet dead. He rode back and split his skull with his sword. The small band then rode off congratulating themselves on having accomplished 'the Lord's work'.

While proclaiming Presbyterianism in its narrowest form, these Covenanters were strangely superstitious, accepting many odd beliefs completely at variance with any form of Christianity. For instance many

168

of them believed in the need to use silver bullets on their more prominent enemies, whom they genuinely imagined to be in league with the devil. They firmly believed many other manifestly absurd statements, such as that wine turned to blood in the goblets of some of their enemies while they were drinking. Apart from their facility for blackening the name and character of anyone opposed to them, they were remarkable for their ability to rationalize their own actions, including cold-blooded murder, as in the case of Archbishop Sharp. They invented totally false massacres and martyrs, building a formidable but mostly mythical history of persecution around some undoubtedly harsh treatment. Since they themselves believed implicitly in their own propaganda it was all the more effective.

In June, 1679, after the murder of Sharp, there followed the Covenanter victory at the Battle of Drumclog, or Loudon Hill. John Graham of Claverhouse, later Earl of Dundee, had captured three Covenanters and an outlawed minister on 31 May. On 1 June a conventicle was held at Loudon Hill on the borders of Ayrshire and Lanark. Although Claverhouse was known to be in the neighbourhood there was an attendance of 250 armed men, who moved to Drumclog, a farm in swampy ground about two miles east of Loudon Hill. The commander was Robert Hamilton with 'Burly' and others concerned in killing the archbishop also in attendance.

Claverhouse wrote a frank account of the battle that ensued as follows:

'I thought that we might make a little tour, to see if we could fall upon a conventicle; which we did, little to our advantage. For, when we came in sight of them, we found them drawn up in battle upon a most advantageous ground, to which there was no coming but through mosses and lakes. They were not preaching and had got away all their women and children. They consisted of four battalions of foot, and all well armed with fusils and pitchforks, and three squadrons of horse. We sent, both, parties to skirmish, they of foot and we of dragoons; they run for it and sent down a battalion of foot against them (the dragoons). We sent three score of dragoons who made them run again shamefully. But in the end (perceiving that we had the better of them in skirmish) they resolved a general engagement and immediately advanced with their foot, the horse following. They came through the loch and the greatest body of all made up against my troop. We kept our fire until they were within ten paces of us. They received our fire and advanced to shock. The first they gave us brought down the cornet, Mr Crafford and Captain Bleith. Besides that with a pitchfork they made such an opening in my sorrel horse's belly that his guts hung out half an ell, and yet he carried me off a mile; which so discouraged our men that they sustained not the shock but fell into disorder. Their horse took the occasion of this and pursued us so hotly that we got no time to rally. I saved the standards but lost on the place about eight or ten men, besides wounded. But the dragoons lost many more. They are not come easily off on the other side, for I saw several of them fall before we came to the shock. I made the best retreat the confusion of our people would suffer.'

From Claverhouse's account it is plain that the Covenanters easily had the best of the day at Loudon Hill, or Drumclog, as the battle came to be known. Although no relation of Claverhouse the cornet he mentioned being killed was named Graham. The Covenanters finding the name embroidered on his shirt took him for Claverhouse and hacked the body about obscenely, cutting off the nose and spearing out the eyes. With characters of Balfour of Kinloch's kidney present such behaviour is quite understandable. However, the victory for the extremists inspired numbers of more moderate Covenanters to join them.

The ballad which follows is taken from Scott's *Minstrelsy of the Scottish Border*. The description of 'Burly' as 'noble' indicates the pronounced Whig bias. Although admittedly powerful and determined, as well as being lauded throughout the ballad and in Covenanter mythology, he was a thoroughly unpleasant, squat and cross-eyed ruffian. No mention is made, needless to say, of the treatment the unfortunate cornet's corpse received. Compared with the previous ballad, however, the intensity of feeling becomes plain.

The Battle of Loudon Hill

from *The Scottish Minstrel*

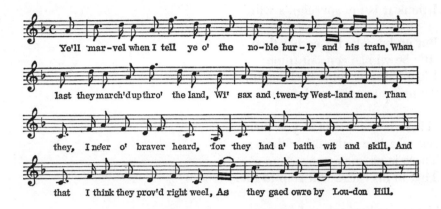

Ye'll 'mar-vel when I tell ye o' the no-ble bur-ly and his train, Whan
last they march'd up thro' the land, Wi' sax and twen-ty West-land men. Than
they, I ne'er o' braver heard, for they had a' baith wit and skill, And
that I think they prov'd right weel, As they gaed owre by Lou-don Hill.

Loudon Hill, or Drumclog

You'l marvel when I tell ye o
Our noble Burly and his train,
When last he marchd up through the land,
Wi sax-and twenty westland men.

Than they I neer o braver heard,
For they had a' baith wit and skill;
They proved right well, as I heard tell,
As they cam up oer Loudon Hill.

Weel prosper a' the gospel-lads
That are into the west countrie
Ay wicked Claverse to demean,
And ay an ill dead may he die!

For he's drawn up i battle rank,
An that baith soon an hastilie;

171

But they wha live till simmer come,
Some bludie days for this will see.

But up spak cruel Claverse then,
Wi hastie wit an wicked skill,
'Gae fire on yon westlan men;
I think it is my sovreign's will.'

But up bespake his cornet then,
'It's be wi nae consent o me;
I ken I'll neer come back again,
An mony mae as weel as me.

'There is not ane of a' yon men
But wha is worthy other three;
There is na ane amang them a'
That in his cause will stap to die.

'An as for Burly, him I knaw;
He's a man of honour, birth, an fame;
Gie him a sword into his hand,
He'll fight thysel an other ten.'

But up spake wicked Claverse then—
I wat his heart it raise fu hie—
And he has cry'd, that a' might hear,
'Man, ye hae sair deceived me.

'I never kend the like afore,
Na, never since I came frae hame,
That you sae cowardly here suld prove,
An yet come of a noble Graeme.'

But up bespake his cornet then,
'Since that it is your honour's will,
Mysel shall be the foremost man
That shall gie fire on Loudoun Hill.

'At your command I'll lead them on,
But yet wi nae consent o me;

For weel I ken I'll never return,
And mony mae as weel as me.'

Then up he drew in battle rank—
I wat he had a bonny train—
But the first time that bullets flew
Ay he lost twenty o his men.

Then back he came the way he gaed,
I wat right soon as suddenly;
He gave command amang his men,
And sent them back, and bade them flee.

Then up came Burly, bauld an stout,
Wi's little train o westland men,
Wha mair then either aince or twice
In Edinburgh confind had been.

They hae been up to Loudon sent,
An yet they're a' come safely down;
Sax troop o horsemen they hae beat,
And chased them into Glasgow town.

In open rebellion at last, the victors of Drumclog found supporters flocking to their standard. The steadily swelling army of Covenanters eventually camped at Hamilton beside the Clyde in early June. They were still there on the 19th, on the south side of the river, unable to decide on their future course of action, when news was brought of a royalist army approaching under the Duke of Monmouth. The narrow bridge, known as Bothwell Bridge, was commanded by cannons of the Covenanter's forces manned by resolute men. However, by 22 June the Duke of Monmouth's army was encamped on the north side of the river within a quarter of a mile of the bridge and the Covenanters still had not decided on any plan of action.

The Duke marched his army to a slight rise overlooking the Covenanter's position and a deputation from their camp was sent to parley with him. They explained their demands, which were principally against Popery, but which they had still not clearly formulated amongst themselves. Monmouth listened to them courteously and replied that they must lay down their arms before any further action could be taken. He gave them one hour to comply with his instructions.

The deputation returned and were still arguing when the hour was up. Then the royalist army bombarded the bridge until the defenders ran out of powder with which to reply. While the Covenanters were still preparing for battle, Monmouth's forces crossed the bridge and advanced on them. At their first fire the Covenanter horse wheeled about and threw the foot into disorder. The entire force panicked and fell into confusion. Almost at once 1,200 men surrendered and the rest fled.

The ballad which follows is taken from Scott's *Minstrelsy of the Scottish Border*. Once again the pronounced Whig bias is extremely plain. The strange first four verses concern an incident which happened after the battle. Some dragoons were chasing some Covenanters when they encountered William Gordon of Earlston, a strong Covenanter, on his way to join the force at Hamilton, unaware that it was already all over. He stoutly resisted their attempt to take him prisoner and was killed. His son, Alexander, was of more moderate persuasion and though present at Bothwell Bridge managed to escape. It is hardly necessary to point out that Claverhouse, then merely Captain John Graham, was not guilty of insubordination and an attempt to revenge his cornet's death, nor, in some strange manner, of arranging Monmouth's execution six years before his time.

174

'O billie, billie, bonny billie,
Will ye go to the wood wi me?
We'll ca our horse hame masterless.
An gear them trow slain men are we.'

'O no, O no!' says Earlstoun,
'For that's the thing that mauna be;
For I am sworn to Bothwell Hill,
Where I maun either gae or die.'

So Earlstoun rose in the morning,
An mounted by the break o day,
An he has joind our Scottish lads,
As they were marching out the way.

'Now, farewell, father! and farewell, mother!
An fare ye weel, my sisters three!
An fare ye well, my Earlstoun!
For thee again I'll never see.'

So they're awa to Bothwell Hill,
An waly, they rode bonnily!
When the Duke o Monmouth saw them comin,
He went to view their company.

'Ye're welcome, lads,' then Monmouth said,
'Ye're welcome, brave Scots lads, to me;
And sae are you, brave Earlstoun,
The foremost o your company.

'But yield your weapons ane an a',
O yield your weapons, lads, to me;
For, gin ye'll yield your weapons up,
Ye'se a' gae hame to your country.'

Out then spak a Lennox lad,
And waly, but he spoke bonnily!
'I winna yield my weapons up,
To you, nor nae man that I see.'

Then he set up the flag o red,
A' set about wi bonny blue:
'Since ye'll no cease, and be at peace,
See that ye stand by ither true.'

They stelld their cannons on the height,
And showrd their shot down in the how,
An beat our Scots lads even down;
Thick they lay slain on every know.

As eer you saw the rain down fa,
Or yet the arrow frae the bow,
Sae our Scottish lads fell even down,
An they lay slain on every know.

'O hold your hand,' then Monmouth cry'd,
'Gie quarters to yon men for me;'
But wicked Claverhouse swore an oath
His cornet's death revengd sud be.

'O hold your hand,' then Monmouth cry'd,
'If ony thing you'll do for me;
Hold up your hand, you cursed Graeme,
Else a rebel to our king ye'll be.'

Then wicked Claverhouse turnd about —
I wot an angry man was he —
And he has lifted up his hat,
And cry'd, God bless his Majesty!

Than he's awa to London town,
Ay een as fast as he can dree;
Fause witnesses he has wi him taen,
An taen Monmouth's head frae his body.

Alang the brae, beyond the brig,
Mony brave man lies cauld and still;
But lang we'll mind, and sair we'll rue,
The bloody battle of Bothwell Hill.

Chapter 19

Killicrankie: Haughs o' Cromdale

Despite this crushing defeat at Bothwell Bridge, the following year in 1680 the more extreme Covenanters signed what became known as the 'Sanquhar Declaration' so called because it was defiantly affixed to the town cross in Sanquhar. In effect it was a straightforward statement of rebellion since it disowned Charles II as king because it claimed he had broken the Covenant. Amongst the principal signatories were two ministers, Donald Cargill and Richard Cameron. The latter's followers called themselves Cameronians and in due course became a byword for extremism.

A month after signing the declaration Cameron and some of his company were surprised by a party of dragoons on Airds Moss, not far from Drumclog. In the short and desperate action which followed Cameron was killed. The following year Cargill was captured and executed. Yet despite continued persecution the extreme Covenanters persevered in their meetings and the practice of their faith. Although there were no further pitched battles on the scale of Bothwell Bridge, the remainder of Charles's reign was termed by the Covenanters the 'Killing Time' as more or less open warfare existed between the Covenanters and Claverhouse's dragoons.

Until 1685 there is no doubt that the Covenanters were much persecuted. It was principally the die-hard Cameronians in the west who continued to resist, sniping at dragoons and ambushing occasional patrols. On Charles's death in 1685 James II and VII came to the throne. In 1687, by two Declarations of Indulgence, he gave complete toleration to all his subjects, including Romanists, Covenanters and Quakers. The persecution was over.

Civil war, however, was far from over. James's reign lasted only until 1688, by which time he had alienated the greater part of his subjects by his obvious leaning towards Roman Catholicism. Those who had

177

welcomed the Restoration were in most cases as willing to welcome the Revolution and the advent of James's son-in-law, Prince William of Orange, and his daughter Mary, as King and Queen.

In December, 1688, John Graham of Claverhouse, who had recently been made Viscount Dundee, was with James in the south. He is reputed to have spoken as follows:

'The question, sire, is, whether you shall remain in Britain or fly to France? Whether you shall trust the returning zeal of your native subjects or rely on a foreign power? Here, I say, you ought to stand. Keep possession of a part, let it be ever so small, and the whole will return to you by degrees. Resume the spirit of a king and summon your subjects to their allegiance. Your army, though dispersed is not disheartened. Give me but your commission and I will carry your standard through England at its head and drive before you these Dutch and their prince.'

Unfortunately the natural Stuart ability to make the wrong choice prevailed and James duly left for Europe, never to return to England again. The Stuart legacy of civil disorder and bloodshed, however, was yet to cause the country much disturbance and grief. It was not until the middle of the eighteenth century that the failure of the '45 brought peace at last.

The famous song 'Bonnie Dundee' celebrated an unavailing attempt by Claverhouse to sway the Convention called by William III in Edinburgh to ratify his succession. Despairing of carrying the vote and afraid of an attempt on his person he rode off at the head of his mounted followers, causing consternation among the faint-hearted citizens. His departure had the effect of causing many who favoured his views to withdraw also and those who favoured William were left without opposition. Meanwhile Dundee withdrew to the Highlands and set about raising an army. This is well summed up in the song.

BONNIE DUNDEE

To the Lords of Convention, 'twas Claverhouse spoke,
Ere the King's crown go down there are crowns to be broke.
Then each cavalier that loves honour and me,
Let him follow the bonnets of Bonnie Dundee.
Come fill up my cup, come fill up my can,
Come saddle my horses, and call out my men;
Unhook the west port, and let us gae free,
For it's up wi' the bonnets of Bonnie Dundee.

Dundee he is mounted, he rides up the street,
The bells they ring backward, the drums they are beat,
But the provost (douce man) said, 'Just e'en let it be,
For the toun is weel rid o' that de'il o' Dundee.'
Come fill up my cup, etc.

There are hills beyond Pentland, and lands beyond Forth,
If there's lords in the south, there are chiefs in the north;
There are brave Duinnewassals three thousand times three,
Will cry 'Hey for the bonnets of Bonnie Dundee.'
Come fill up my cup, etc.

Then awa' to the hills, to the lea, to the rocks,
Ere I own a usurper I'll crouch with the fox;
And tremble false whigs in the midst o' your glee,
Ye hae no seen the last o' my bonnets and me.
Come fill up my cup, etc.

In the Highlands Claverhouse soon raised some 1,500 men including some raw, half-naked Irish auxiliaries sent by James. When the news reached the south he was declared a fugitive outlaw and General Mackay, a Highlander and ardent Presbyterian, who had spent many years in Holland, was sent by William III with four regiments of foot and one of dragoons to hunt him down. Although Mackay's strategy was indifferent his courage was never in question. He would have made a good Colonel of a regiment but he was never intended for a general.

He and Claverhouse conducted a series of pointless marches and counter-marches without doing battle, which served Mackay no purpose. As had been the case with Montrose, the speed with which Claverhouse and his Highlanders moved completely baffled his opponent. Claverhouse, however, had little of Montrose's genius for strategy. He failed to accomplish anything in his series of feints and marches until in late July he heard that sympathizers in Atholl had seized Blair Castle. Claverhouse hastened to their aid and decided that this was the opportunity he had been awaiting.

With the reinforcements he now acquired Claverhouse had close on 3,000 men. He turned on the slower-moving Mackay and sent him word to prepare for battle. Mackay had only just come through the narrow Pass of Killiecrankie and his baggage train was miles behind. Taken by surprise, many of his troops lacked ammunition, but he could not face the disgrace of turning round and retreating from the man he was supposedly pursuing. Instead he drew up his troops in preparation for battle on the flat ground between the river Garry and the hills just beyond the Pass to the north. It was 27 July, 1689.

Claverhouse on the high ground prepared for his attack. He sent some Atholl men to guard the pass for stragglers, assuring them that he would win the day. His men he led in the flying column form, which had always been favoured by Montrose, by which each clan by itself charged in narrow columns, 'upon the raw', or in a row. The Macleans under their chief formed the right. The Macdonalds of Skye formed the left. The Camerons led by Lochiel, the Macdonells of Glengarry, the followers of Clanranald and the Irish auxiliaries formed the centre under command of Claverhouse himself. Behind was a troop of horse under Sir William Wallace. Beneath them on the plain Mackay's eight battalions of some 4,500 men and two troops of horse were deployed on the plain.

For some hours the two armies stood looking at each other without taking any action. Finally, at five in the afternoon, there was some skirmishing, but it was not until eight in the evening that Claverhouse led the charge in person. The Highlanders poured down the hillside in close columns with their tartans streaming, swords and targes held high, pipes skirling their challenge and the roar of battle in their throats. Within a few yards of the enemy they fired their muskets and hurled them in the faces of those still standing.

The left wing of Mackay's army was pierced almost at once and did not stand the shock above seven minutes. They were driven off by the Macleans with great slaughter and chased across the River Garry or into the pass, though most were slain in the river. The Macdonalds on the left of the Highland line, reinforced by the doubtful Irish auxiliaries, were not at first so successful. When the Chief of the Macleans and Cameron of Lochiel with his men took the Dutch and Colonel Hastings's regiment in the flank, however, they soon gave way. Colonel Hastings's regiment then withdrew in good order, covering the retreat of the remainder.

Few of Mackay's army who fled through the pass made good their escape for the Atholl men were waiting for them above. Those running away were attacked, driven into the Garry and drowned or shot. Although the right wing of Mackay's army was never dispersed and broken as the left had been, they had a difficult fighting retreat over the moors to the upper Tummel. In the morning Mackay found that he had lost half his army.

While directing the last attack, however, Claverhouse himself had been mortally wounded. He survived the battle and was carried into the nearby house of Orrat just above the plain, where he wrote an account of the victory to James in his own hand. By the morning he was dead. His body was taken to Blair Atholl and he was buried in the vault there. His attempt to emulate Montrose was over and James's hopes were buried with him.

A rather macabre aftermath of the battle was recorded in Orrat house. The men had all been at the battle and the lady of the house and all the other females had fled to the safety of the hills. They did not return for several days and found the walls and beds bloodstained as if many had died there. About a week after their return they were troubled by an unpleasant smell and at last found a dead Whig soldier lying in a dark cupboard where he must have concealed himself and died of his wounds. It is still known as the Soldier's Hole.

In James Hogg's *Jacobite Relics* there are two ballads on the battle in Scots and one in Latin. The version included here has a catchy tune and one has to admire the sheer audacity of the man who could rhyme

181

'Killicrankie, O' with 'auntie, O'. The sentiments expressed are pure exuberance and contempt for Whigs rather than Jacobite fervour. Even as early as this, however, 'King Willie' was not popular in the Highlands. The other ballad,* though by no means accurate, contains greater detail.

* See Appendix.

The Braes o' Killicrankie

from *The Lyric Gems of Scotland*

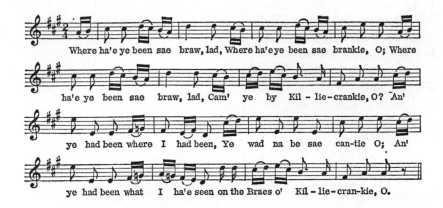

Where ha'e ye been sae braw, lad, Where ha'e ye been sae brankie, O; Where ha'e ye been sae braw, lad, Cam' ye by Kil-lie-crankie, O? An' ye had been where I had been, Ye wad na be sae can-tie O; An' ye had been what I ha'e seen on the Braes o' Kil-lie-cran-kie, O.

Killicrankie (Song XIX) Hogg:

Whare hae ye been sae braw, lad?
Whare hae ye been sae brankie, O?
Whare hae ye been sae braw, lad?
Came ye by Killicrankie, O?
An ye had been where I hae been,
Ye wad-na been sae cantie,* O;
An ye had seen what I hae seen,
I' the braes o' Killicrankie, O.

I faught at land, I faught at sea,
At hame I faught my auntie, O;
But I met the devil and Dundee
On the braes o' Killicrankie, O.
An ye had been, etc.

The bauld Pitcur fell in a furr,
And Clavers got a clankie, O,
Or I had fed an Athol gled

*cheerful

183

On the braes o' Killicrankie, O.
An ye had been, etc.

O fie, Mackay, what gart ye lie
I' the bush ayont the brankie, O?
Ye'd better kiss'd King Willie's loof,*   *hand
Than come to Killicrankie, O.
It's nae shame, it's nae shame,
It's nae shame to shank* ye, O;   *send off
There's sour slaes* on Athol braes,   *sloes
And deils at Killicrankie, O.

When Claverhouse fell the command was taken by Colonel Alexander Cannon of Galloway, who had been sent over by James with the Irish troops. Instead of pursuing Mackay, Cannon allowed him to withdraw safely to Stirling. The clan chiefs then wished to appoint the Earl of Dunfermline as their leader but, on referring the matter to James, inevitably he made the wrong choice and Cannon was confirmed in the post.

Determined to show his mettle, Cannon detached his horse, 500 strong, to take Perth and the rich stores there, but, meeting Mackay instead, they were effectively annihilated. Meanwhile Cannon attacked Dunkeld, where he had learned there was a small force of 900 Cameronians under their celebrated leader, the poet Colonel William Cleland. Unfortunately Cannon led his men so badly and the Cameronians fought so desperately despite the death of their Colonel that his much larger force was soundly beaten in a running battle lasting for several hours. The Highlanders drew off disgusted with his leadership.

After this disastrous battle the Highlanders told Cannon to his face that he was a fool and unfit for command. They then broke open his strongbox and helped themselves to the contents, leaving him to return to Ireland while they appointed Lochiel in his place. However, James, with his ability to compound an error several times over, sent Cannon back in the spring to take command over the Highlanders once more. Few things could more clearly have demonstrated their loyalty to the Stuarts than the fact that they accepted Cannon again as their commander.

With 1,500 picked men Cannon marched into Strathspey and encamped on the Haughs of Cromdale, his men lodging in hamlets all over the valley, except for a hundred posted near the church. The laird of Grant finding his lands harried, promptly sent for help to Sir Thomas Livingstone, who arrived on 28 April, 1690, with seventeen troops of dragoons and three regiments of foot, to which the laird of Grant added some 800 of his clan. On 30 April this force marched through the night guided by the Grants and attacked the Jacobite army while it was still asleep just before dawn. Cannon was captured in his nightshirt and despite sporadic attempts at resistance the bulk of the army was forced to take flight. Four hundred of the clans were killed, but the remainder escaped in the mist which had concealed their attackers and their resistance had been such that Livingstone's men were content to let them go. For the moment at least the fighting was at an end.

The ballad of 'The Haughs of Cromdale' is taken from Hogg's *Jacobite Relics*. It was originally produced to describe this battle and as it has a catchy tune was soon being sung all over the Highlands. This seems to have been too much for some unknown bard and, in an effort to redeem the description of this defeat of the clans in 1690, he added on a somewhat highflown description of Montrose's victory at Auldearn over the Covenanter army in 1645. Thus the two battles, forty-five years and a considerable number of miles apart, were unceremoniously joined together. The gallant Montrose, who had been dead for over forty years, was brought to life in verse to win another battle. The result is a horribly muddled ballad, but one which has been immensely popular. To the strains of the pipes playing this tune the Highlanders have charged and won battles all round the world.

The Haws o' Cromdale

from *The Scottish Minstrel*

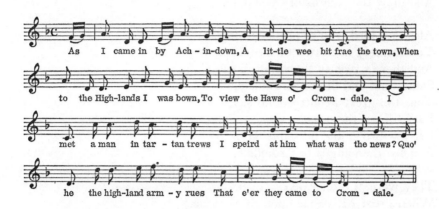

As I came in by Ach-in-down, A lit-tle wee bit frae the town, When to the High-lands I was bown, To view the Haws o' Crom-dale. I met a man in tar-tan trews I speird at him what was the news? Quo' he the high-land arm-y rues That e'er they came to Crom-dale.

As I came in by Auchindoun,
A little wee bit frae the toon,
When to the Highlands I was bound,
To view the haughs of Cromdale,
I met a man in tartan trews,
I speer'd at him what was the news;
Quo' he the Highland army rues,
That e'er we came to Cromdale.

We were in bed, sir, every man,
When the English host upon us came,
A bloody battle then began
Upon the haughs of Cromdale.
The English horse they were so rude,
They bath'd their hoofs in Highland blood,
But our brave clans, they boldly stood
Upon the haughs of Cromdale.

But, alas! we could no longer stay,
For o'er the hills we came away,

187

And sore we do lament the day,
That e'er we came to Cromdale.
Thus the great Montrose did say,
Can you direct the nearest way?
For I will o'er the hills this day,
And view the haughs of Cromdale.

Alas, my lord, you're not so strong,
You scarcely have two thousand men,
And there's twenty thousand on the plain,
Stand rank and file on Cromdale.
Thus the great Montrose did say,
I say, direct the nearest way,
For I will o'er the hills this day,
And see the haughs of Cromdale.

They were at dinner, every man,
When great Montrose upon them came,
A second battle then began,
Upon the haughs of Cromdale.
The Grant, Mackenzie and M'ky,
Soon as Montrose they did espy,
O then, they fought most valiantly!
Upon the haughs of Cromdale.

The M'Donalds they return'd again,
The Camerons did their standard join,
M'Intosh play'd a bloody game,
Upon the haughs of Cromdale.
The M'Gregors fought like lions bold,
M'Phersons, none could them controul,
M'Lauchlins fought, like loyal souls,
Upon the haughs of Cromdale.

M'Leans, M'Dougals, and M'Neils,
So boldly as they took the field,
And make their enemies to yield,
Upon the haughs of Cromdale.
The Gordons boldly did advance,
The Frasers fought with sword and lance,

The Grahams they made the heads to dance,
Upon the haughs of Cromdale.

The loyal Stewarts with Montrose,
So boldly set upon their foes,
And brought them down with Highland blows,
Upon the haughs of Cromdale.
Of twenty thousand Cromwell's men,
Five hundred fled to Aberdeen
The rest of them lie on the plain,
Upon the haughs of Cromdale.

Chapter 20

Sheriffmuir

At the time of the Civil War, when the Highlanders under Montrose were opposed to the Lowlanders and the Clan Campbell under Argyll, the pattern of the future was set. The Lowlanders, defeated in battle, conceived an irrational fear of the Highlanders. Speaking different languages, living utterly different lives, they completely failed to understand each other. The Clan Campbell on the other hand, had suffered a blow to their military pride and were out for revenge. Still secure in their mountain retreats the Highlanders could not be expected to appreciate that the clan system, a way of life unchanged since the days of the Romans, would have to adapt to a changing world or perish. Clashing head-on with the developing civilization of the eighteenth century it was inevitable that they would be crushed.

With the battle of Cromdale, all resistance to William and Mary was overcome. Free pardons were granted to all who took an oath of submission before 1 January, 1692. MacIan, chief of the Macdonalds of Glencoe, was six days overdue owing to heavy snowfalls. The Lowland authorities inspired by the Master of Stair, the Lord Advocate, who loathed all Highlanders, and the Earl of Breadalbane, a neighbour of the Macdonalds of Glencoe, who disliked their constant depredations on his cattle and land, persuaded William III to sign an order for their extirpation. In his letters Stair made his intentions plain:

'Glencoe hath not taken the oath, at which I rejoice . . . it will be a proper vindication of the public justice to extirpate that sept of thieves . . . It were a great advantage to the nation that thieving tribes were rooted out and cut off. It must be quietly done, otherwise they will make shift for both men and their cattle . . . Let it be secret and sudden.'

The planned massacre of the Macdonalds of Glencoe was an extraordinarily cold-blooded bureaucratic muddle. On 3 February a hundred and twenty Campbell soldiers led by Campbell of Glenorchy, a relation by marriage to MacIan, were billeted on the Macdonalds. Their orders were to wait ten days until the 13th at a chosen hour at night when soldiers were to arrive from Ballachulish and from Breadalbane to block both ends of the Pass. Then they were to put all the Macdonalds to the sword. All this seems unnecessary preparation for a force of some fifty fighting men and a total population of about one hundred and fifty!

Inevitably the Campbell soldiers disliked their task. After ten days as guests of the clan, playing and eating with them, it could scarcely be otherwise. They may have been hereditary enemies, but they were not devoid of humanity. When the appointed day came several of the soldiers gave their hosts indirect warnings of what was to come, which were sufficient to set them on the alert. Others appear to have taken care to make enough noise approaching the houses to allow the inhabitants time to escape.

A blizzard that night prevented the troops arriving to block the Pass as intended and in the end there were only thirty-eight men, women and children assassinated, among them MacIan, although probably as many again died on the hills from exposure. The remainder escaped, due to some extent to the connivance of the Campbells, and spread the tale of infamy throughout the land. The breach of trust and the deliberate planning of the attempted massacre roused the indignation of the entire country, but particularly in the Highlands. It also created a deep dis-trust of the authorities in Edinburgh and London. William III, whose signature was on the order for the deed, became the most hated man in the Highlands. Yet apart from general indignation and moral censure nothing seems to have been done. In 1695 after a rather perfunctory inquiry the Master of Stair was removed as Lord Advocate and sub-sequently made Earl of Stair. The massacre remained an unforgiven wrong, passing into legend in the Highlands.

Between 1698 and 1700 the Scots' hopes of founding a colony on the Isthmus of Darien, now Panama, foundered, largely due to the open hostility of the English towards the plan. The two Parliaments and the rival commercial interests of the two countries clashed violently. The Darien scheme cost large sums of money as well as lives and investors throughout Scotland lost heavily. There was bitter anti-English feeling as a result and the Union of the Crowns seemed endangered. After Anne's accession in 1702, however, the move towards complete Union was at last successful and in 1707 the Union of the Parliaments was finally achieved. The two countries were united under the title of Great Britain and the Hanoverian succession was assured.

In 1708 the French sent James, the Old Pretender, and a fleet with 6,000 troops to the Firth of Forth, hoping to exploit Scottish discontent with the Union in the middle of Marlborough's wars. Although they reached their destination they were prevented from disembarking by the timely arrival of the navy. The fleet was then chased back to France ignominiously with the loss of a warship and several transports. This was the most the French ever attempted in the Jacobite cause. In the opinion of many at the time if James had landed alone he would have carried the country with him, despite the Kirk's long standing distrust of his faith, so widespread was the discontent.

The death of Queen Anne in 1714 found the Jacobites quite unready and lacking in leadership and George I of Hanover was duly proclaimed King without opposition. It was through no effort on his part that James found himself belatedly proclaimed King in 1715. His supporter was the Earl of Mar, a vainglorious and ambitious Tory, who had felt himself slighted since his prominent part in promoting the Union. After sounding out the Highland chiefs under the guise of holding a hunting party in August, Mar raised the Royal Standard at Braemar on 6 September, proclaiming James III and VIII as King. Unfortunate as ever, James by then lacked backing in France following the death of his royal patron, Louis XIV, a few days before the rising began.

On 16 September the Earl of Mar moved to Perth with some 6,000 men. At this stage the only force of any strength opposing him in Scotland was the Earl of Argyll with some 2,500 men in Stirling Castle. Had Mar forced his way south at that point Argyll would have been powerless to stop him and something might have been achieved, but he merely stayed in Perth. Admittedly he was accumulating more troops meanwhile, for the Highlanders of Lochaber were flocking to his banner until eventually he had an estimated 12,000, but time was not on his side.

Largely on his own initiative Mackintosh of Borlum led a thousand men across the Forth in small boats in an attempt on Edinburgh. Faced by 500 horse from Stirling he moved by night to link up with a small force of Lowland and northern England Jacobites. The augmented force then continued south to Lancashire hoping for more recruits, but failed to find them. At Preston on 13 November, the same day as Sheriffmuir, they encountered a government army under General Wills. After fierce fighting in the streets and heavy casualties on both sides the remaining 1,500 Jacobites surrendered.

Meanwhile Mar had already advanced hesitantly on Stirling and then retired to Perth. On 12 November he advanced again as far as Kinbuck. The government army under Argyll camped some two miles further south at Dunblane. Although Argyll's force was little more than 3,000 and Mar must have had at least twice the numbers no decisive victory for either side resulted at Sheriffmuir on 13 November when the two armies met. Argyll's right wing sent Mar's left wing reeling backwards across the Allan Water, but Mar's right wing decisively routed Argyll's left wing and sent them back to Stirling at the run. Hence by the time darkness fell neither side could claim a victory and neither was sure which had won, but since Argyll remained in Stirling blocking the route south he at least maintained his advantage in that respect. Indeed from that moment, to all intents and purposes, the rising was finished. Thereafter it slowly fizzled out.

The following ballad is taken from Child's 1848 collection, but is to be found in many other collections, including notably, Hogg's *Jacobite Relics*. It reads rather like a *Who's Who* of the battle, with reference to almost every person of note present and some who can no longer be traced. The mention of Rob Roy is not without interest. He took no part in the battle, as the ballad indicates, because he did not wish to take up arms against his patron Argyll and it would have been against his conscience to fight against James. The chorus emphasizes the uncertainty and inconclusiveness of the whole battle. Another more modern ballad, by Burns, is included in the appendix. There are several others. It seems to have been a very popular subject. None is inspired.

There's some say that we wan, and some that they wan,
And some say that nane wan at a' man!
But one thing I'm sure, that at Sherra-muir,
A battle there was that I saw, man.
And we ran and they ran, and they ran, and we ran,
But Florence ran fastest of a' man.

Argyle and Belhaven, not frightened like Leven,
Which Rothes and Haddington saw, man:
For they all, with Wightman, advanc'd on the right, man,
While others took flight, being raw, man:
And we ran, etc.

Lord Roxburgh was there, in order to share,
With Douglas, who stood not in awe, man:
Volunteerly to ramble with Lord Loudon Campbell,
Brave they did not suffer for a', man:
And we ran, etc.

Sir John Schaw, that great knight, with broad sword most bright,
On horseback he briskly did charge, man:
A hero that's bold, none could him withhold,
He stoutly encountered the targemen.
And we ran, etc.

For the cowardly Whittam, for fear they should cut him,
Seeing glittering broadswords with a pa', man:
And that in such thrang, made Blair edicang,
And from the brave clans ran awa, man.
And we ran, etc.

The great Colonel Dow, gade foremost, I trow,
When Whittam's dragoons ran awa', man:
Except Sandy Baird, and Naughton the laird,
Their horse shaw'd their heels to them a', man.
And we ran, etc.

Brave Mar and Panmure were firm, I'm sure,
The latter was kidnapt awa' man:

With brisk men about, brave Harry retook
His brother and laugh'd at them a' man.
And we ran, etc.

Brave Marshall and Lithgow and Glengary's pith too,
Assisted by brave Loggia, man,
And Gordons the bright, so boldly did fight,
That the redcoats took flight and awa', man.
And we ran, etc.

Strathmore and Clanronald cried still, 'Advance Donald',
Till both of those heroes did fa', man:
For there was such hashing and broad swords a-clashing,
Brave Forfar himself got a claw, man.
And we ran, etc.

Lord Perth stood the storm, Seaforth but lukewarm,
Kilsyth and Strathallan not slaw, man:
And Hamilton pled, the men were not bred,
For he had no fancy to fa', man:
And we ran, etc.

Brave gen'rous Southesk, Tullibardin was brisk,
Whose father indeed would not draw, man,
Into the same yoke, which serv'd for a cloak,
To keep the estate 'twixt them twa, man.
And we ran, etc.

Lord Rollo not fear'd, Kintore and his beard,
Pitsligo and Ogilvie, a' man:
And brothers Balfours, they stood the first show'rs,
Clackmannan and Burleigh did claw, man.
And we ran, etc.

But Cleppan fought pretty, and Strowan the witty,
A poet that pleases us a', man:
For mine is but rhyme, in respect of whats fine,
Or what he able to draw, man.
And we ran, etc.

For Huntly and Sinclair, they both play'd the tinkler,
With consciences black as a craw, man:
Some Angus and Fife men, they ran for their life, man,
And ne'er a Lot's wife there at a', man:
And we ran, etc.

Then Laurie, the traitor, who betray'd his master,
His king and his country an' a' man,
Pretending Mar might give orders to fight,
To the right of the army awa', man.
And we ran, etc.

Then Laurie, for fear of what he might hear,
Took Drummond's best horse and awa, man;
'Stead of going to Perth, he crossed the Firth,
Alongst Stirling Bridge and awa, man:
And we ran, etc.

To London he pressed and there he profess'd,
That he behav'd best o' them a', man:
And so, without strife, got settled for life,
A hundred a-year to his fa, man.
And we ran, etc.

In Borrowstouness he resides with disgrace,
Till his neck stand in need of a thraw' man;
And then in a tether, he'll swing from a ladder,
And go off the stage with a pa', man.
And we ran, etc.

Rob Roy there stood watch on a hill for to catch,
The booty, for aught I saw, man:
For he ne'er advanc'd from the place he was stanc'd,
Till no more was to do there at a', man.
And we ran, etc.

So we all took the flight and Moubray the wright,
And Letham the smith was a braw, man,
For he took a fit of gout, which was wit,

196

By judging it time to withdraw, man:
And we ran, etc.

And trumpet Maclean, whose breeks were not clean,
Through misfortune he happen'd to fa' man:
By saving his neck, his trumpet did break,
And came off without music at a', man.
And we ran, etc.

So there such a race was as ne'er in that place was,
And as little chace was at a', man:
From each other they run, without toak of drum,
They did not make use of a paw, man.
And they ran, etc.

Whether we ran or they ran, or we wan or they wan,
Or if there was winning at a', man,
There no man can tell, save our brave genarell,
Who first began running of a', man.
And we ran, etc.

With the Earl of Seaforth and the Cock of the North·
But Florence ran fastest of a', man,
Save the laird o' Phinavon, who sware to be even
Wi' any general or peer o' them a', man.
And we ran, etc.

Despite James's belated arrival at Peterhead on 22 December, nothing could revive the jaded spirits of his forces. Towards the end of January Argyll received considerable reinforcements and began to advance. On 31 January the Jacobite forces evacuated Perth and moved to Dundee and thence to Montrose. It was from there that James sailed once more for France. The rising of '15 was over. It seemed as if the Old Pretender's hopes were at an end, yet it was to be only three years before the next attempt was made.

After intriguing for help from both Sweden and Spain the Jacobites received aid from Spain as a means of revenging the defeat of their fleet off Cape Passaro. Two forces, one of 5,000 Spaniards under the Duke of Ormonde and one of 300 under the Earl Marischal, George Keith, sailed from Spain in March, 1719. The larger was caught in a storm and blown back to port. The smaller, consisting of only two frigates, landed in the Western Isles. There Keith learned that Lord Tullibardine had been appointed Commander-in-Chief of the Jacobite forces, a post he had confidently expected to be his. Thereafter, relations between the two leaders deteriorated daily until they were no longer on speaking terms.

On 25 April the small force anchored in Loch Alsh off the mainland. They disembarked the troops, stores and guns and sent the ships home. It was there that they learned that the other force had been storm-bound and returned to Spain. Then three English warships sailed into the loch and bombarded Eilean Donan Castle, which the Jacobites were utilizing as a magazine. A small party of 45 Spaniards acting as garrison surrendered to a landing party. The main force, some way inland, was unable to assist them. Small wonder that they began to lose heart, or that the commanders quarrelled so strongly with each other that they camped three miles apart.

A heartening but incorrect rumour that Ormonde and his forces were arriving after all brought about a thousand recruits from the Highland clans. Then came the news of the approach of General Wightman with about 1,100 men up Glenshiel. Tullibardine and Keith agreed to hold a strong position on each side of the River Shiel, but there was little co-operation between them even in the face of the enemy. The two forces met on the evening of 10 June and General Wightman was able to attack systematically with four small mortars, thus dealing with any resistance at a distance. By dark the Highlanders were in full flight. In the morning the Spanish troops surrendered. The Battle of Glen Shiel was over.

The 1720s saw the arrival of General Wade in the Highlands and between 1726 and 1733 he built the famous roads linking Inverness with Perth and the Great Glen to facilitate troop movements. He also built Fort George at Inverness and Fort Augustus at the south end of Loch Ness as companions to Fort William, already built at the head of Loch Linnhe, thus completing a protective chain of fortresses to control the Highlands. He enrolled the first Independent Companies of Highland Volunteers to keep watch on the clans and because of their dark tartan they soon became known as the 'Black Watch', the forerunners of the famous regiment.

The Scots and the English were still in uneasy harness. The imposition of taxes, especially the hated malt tax, which affected the distilling of whisky and brewing of ale and was widely regarded as a breach of the articles of the Union, was the cause of protest riots. In 1725 during such a riot in Glasgow a party of soldiers under a Captain Bushell fired on a mob and killed several people. Bushell, though tried and convicted, was pardoned to the indignation of the citizens. In 1736 what subsequently became known as the Porteous riots arose in somewhat similar circumstances. At the hanging of a smuggler, who had become a popular hero through helping his companion to escape at the expense of his own freedom, Captain Porteous, in charge of the guard, nervously ordered them to fire on the crowd, which he feared was becoming unruly. He was tried and convicted, but subsequently granted a respite, the prelude to a reprieve. The mob thereupon broke into the prison and took Porteous to the Grassmarket where they hanged him before dispersing in an orderly manner. Even though Scotland was outwardly reasonably law abiding by the 1740s, there were still powerful emotions just beneath the surface.

Chapter 21

Prestonpans

In 1739 Britain was at war with France once more, but by now Prince Charles Edward Stuart, son of the Old Pretender, was a well built young man of nineteen, filled with a burning desire to regain what he regarded as his throne. The Jacobite cause, only faintly glowing, was ready enough to burst into flame if given sufficient encouragement. In 1744 the French, never loathe to use the Scots to further their own ends, planned an attack through the Highlands with 3,000 French troops, who were to be supported by the Clans. At the same time a larger force of 12,000 was to be put ashore near London under the leadership of Prince Charles himself.

By February, 1744, the transports filled with troops and the escorting warships were ready to move when a British fleet appeared offshore. This, combined with a violent storm which wrecked many of the French ships, put an end to the plans for an invasion. Thereafter the French abandoned the whole idea, possibly with a certain feeling of relief.

Despite the failure of this expedition the young Prince announced his intention of coming over to Scotland in the summer of 1745. His supporters were aghast at the idea and sent word to dissuade him, but with typical Jacobite inefficiency their message never reached him. In July the Prince set off on board a French privateer escorted by a French warship of 60 guns. The warship was involved in a naval action with an English ship, H.M.S. *Lion*, and the privateer continued alone. Thus against all odds the Young Pretender, landed at Eriskay, an island in the outer Hebrides, on 23 July, 1745, accompanied by some nine others, of whom only three were Scots. By any standards it seemed an unlikely start to a successful attempt on a throne.

The first Highlander to whom the Prince spoke was reportedly MacDonald of Boisdale, who proved completely and outspokenly against his clan taking part in any such venture. Despite this unfavourable beginning the Prince continued to try to raise supporters. When Donald Cameron of Lochiel, chief of the powerful Clan Cameron, agreed to give his support other waverers followed. Within three weeks Charles Edward felt confident enough to make a public announcement of his intentions.

On 19 August the Jacobite standard was raised at Glenfinnan at the head of Loch Shiel. King James III and VIII was formally proclaimed king and his son, Prince Charles Edward Stuart, his regent. Already several prisoners had been taken in small actions by gathering clansmen against government troops they had encountered on their way to Glenfinnan. Some of these were subsequently to pass on greatly inflated estimates of the number of Highland supporters. At this stage they were not much above 1,300, but they were put as high as 3,000 in reports reaching Sir John Cope, the general commanding the government forces in Scotland.

From that moment at Glenfinnan when the standard is raised the scene unfolds with all the terrible inevitability of a Greek tragedy. Ranged against the young Prince and his Highlanders are the Campbells and other loyal clans, the Lowlanders and the English. The entire power of a prosperous state is ready to be mounted against him but its leaders, in the north at least, are elderly and slow to act. On his side he has youth, impetuosity, the courage and toughness of the Highlanders and some sound advisers, though some bad ones as well. He lacks finance and is cursed with the fatal Stuart ability to listen to the wrong man at the wrong time. At first, however, all appears to go well.

Sir John Cope, by no means the poltroon he is portrayed in verse, was cursed with contrary news of the Prince's whereabouts and forces. It was not until 8 August that he had definite confirmation of the Prince's arrival in the Highlands. He was then positively commanded by the Lords' Justices to move to the Highlands with as large a force as he could muster to nip the rising 'in the bud'. He only managed to raise some 1,400 raw recruits who had never been in battle. His principal cavalry officer, Colonel Gardiner, was sick and totally unfit for action, while his dragoons were unreliable to say the least and their horses, just in from grass, too soft for any lengthy marching. Although he was able to raise some cannon he had no regular gunners to man them. Yet obedient to his orders he moved north from Stirling on 20 August. For lack of fodder his horse were left at Stirling.

By the 25th Cope's army had reached Dalnacardoch and there he received first hand, if exaggerated, eye-witness accounts of the strength and intentions of the Prince's forces. He was warned that it was their intention to block the Corryarrack Pass against him and since he was well aware that it was easily held by a small force against a larger one he decided not to attempt it. His alternatives were to turn back to Stirling, in which case he might have been overtaken, or bypassed by the Highlanders, or move on to Inverness, where he might hope to raise some of the well-affected clans. He rightly chose the latter course, which left the road to Perth open to Prince Charles. It was not Cope's fault that he found no volunteers on his arrival in Inverness. By 4 September, realizing that it was essential he returned south to protect the Lowlands, Cope was demanding shipping urgently from his subordinates in Edinburgh. On the same day Charles Edward was entering Perth. The race to Edinburgh was on.

Prince Charles advanced southwards from Perth on 11 September and Gardiner's dragoons retreated before him without offering any resistance. By the 15th the dragoons had withdrawn to the outskirts of Edinburgh and on the same day continued their retreat to Preston, finally halting at Colonel Gardiner's small estate at Bankton near Prestonpans. There they demonstrated their complete unfitness for action by panicking at a false alarm and breaking up during the night into two separate parties, one ending up in North Berwick, the other in Dunbar.

On the 16th Edinburgh was taken by the Jacobite army in a quiet surprise attack during the night with little or no bloodshed. Cope and his forces, having marched to Aberdeen by the 11th and taken ship from there, arrived just too late to prevent this happening. Instead he was forced to disembark at Dunbar on the 17th. By the evening of the 19th he had assembled his forces and marched them to Haddington, preparatory to advancing on Edinburgh. On the 20th he marched them via the open, winding coast road rather than the direct but enclosed upper route, which was open to ambush. Outside Tranent they encountered the advance guard of the Jacobite army and it was at this point, on the open ground outside Preston, that Cope rightly decided to fight. The flat ground provided him with room to manœuvre his horse.

Prince Charles, learning of the arrival of Cope's army at Dunbar, had set about requisitioning arms and ammunition for his men. On the 19th they marched from Duddingston with a force of around 2,300, very similar in size to Cope's army. They had just crossed the River Esk and were on the site of the old battle of Pinkie when the advance guard reported the government army near Preston. Lord George Murray, one of the Prince's chief military advisers, led his men on to take Falside

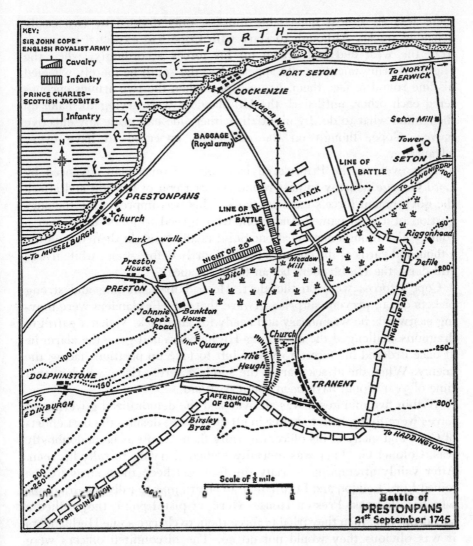

KEY:
SIR JOHN COPE –
ENGLISH ROYALIST ARMY
▨ Cavalry
▥ Infantry
PRINCE CHARLES –
SCOTTISH JACOBITES
▢ Infantry

FORTH

PORT SETON

To NORTH
BERWICK

COCKENZIE

Wagon Way

Seton Mill

BAGGAGE
(Royal army)

Tower

LINE OF
BATTLE

SETON

To LONGNIDDRY

PRESTONPANS

ATTACK

LINE OF
BATTLE

Riggonhead

Church

150'

Park walls

NIGHT OF 20th

Defile

200'

Preston
House

Meadow
Mill

To MUSSELBURGH

Ditch

PRESTON

NIGHT OF 20th

250'

Johnnie
Cope's
Road

Bankton
House

Church

300'

Quarry

The
Heugh

TRANENT

DOLPHINSTONE

150'

AFTERNOON
OF 20th

To
EDINBURGH

100'

300'

Birsley
Brae

To HADDINGTON

200'
250'

From EDINBURGH

Scale of ¼ mile

0   ¼   ½

Battle of
PRESTONPANS
21st September 1745

Hill, south of the village of Walliford and west of Tranent, the highest
ground in the vicinity, where the Scots forces had encamped before
Pinkie in 1547. On breasting the hill they came in full view of Cope's
forces in the plain below and each army raised a defiant cheer at the sight
of the other.

When the Prince's generals came to examine Cope's position they
began to appreciate that although they had the high ground they could
could not use it to advantage. Between them and the government army

there was an almost impassable morass, only divided by two easily defended tracks. Although to start with Cope had expected an attack from the west and had drawn up his forces accordingly, when the Highland army unexpectedly appeared to the south he merely wheeled his line round to face them. From 2 pm, when the two armies encountered each other, until dark the Highlanders were trying to make up their mind what to do. By nightfall neither side had made any effective moves. Cope, though on the defensive, appeared to have every advantage.

That evening the Prince's advisers agreed on a plan advanced by Lord George Murray to pass round the east end of the bog and attack the government force's exposed flank. This was improved by the suggestion of a local named Anderson, who agreed to guide them over a route which though narrow at one point finally brought them out within a thousand yards of the enemy's flank. Shortly before 4 am, while it was still dark, the Highlanders began their advance.

Cope's forces were on the alert. He had fires burning and strong pickets out to prevent surprise. Aware that the Highlanders were moving eastwards he was uneasy and ready for an attack. When a patrol of dragoons challenged the advancing Highlanders and gave the alarm he at once ordered his forces to wheel left to take up positions facing the enemy. When the attack started the sun had barely risen, which at that time of year would have been about 6.30 am.

Within five minutes it was all over and the demoralized government forces were flying helter skelter in all directions, despite the best efforts of Cope and many of his officers to rally them. Unfit as he undoubtedly was, Colonel Gardiner was mortally wounded trying to rally his men. After vainly attempting to rally the foot and keep them steady Cope joined Lord Loudon and Lord Hume in an attempt to rally the dragoons who had fled past Preston House. Here, at pistol point, they rallied a squadron, but when they tried to force them to charge some Highlanders it was obvious they would not do so. The discomfited officers were forced to trot up Birsley Brae to Tranent by a track still known as 'Johnnie Cope's Road'. Subsequently Cope was faced with the humiliation of reporting the defeat of his own force to the garrison commander at Berwick.

How was it that the Highlanders achieved such an instant victory? Apart from the advantage of local advice on the ground, which proved invaluable and brought them within striking distance of the enemy on their flank, they also had the cover of mist. At that time of year, especially on the east coast, a thick mist clinging a few feet above the ground is a very common phenomenon in the early morning, especially over boggy ground or newly cut stubble. Several accounts of the battle mention mist, but since it swiftly vanished with the onset of the sun, it is probable that everyone was too pre-occupied to make a note of it afterwards. If the Highlanders stalked as close as possible under cover of it on their knees, as seems likely, then the débâcle becomes more readily understandable. Even without the mist a description of their tactics at this period provided by General Stewart of Garth makes the picture of what happened much clearer:

'They advanced with the utmost rapidity towards the enemy, gave fire when within a musket length of the object, and threw down their pieces, then drawing their swords and holding their dirk in their left hand along with their target, darted with fury on the enemy through the smoke of their fire. When within reach of the bayonets of their opponents, bending their left knee they contrived to receive the thrust of the weapon on their targets, then raising the target arm and with it the enemy's point, they rushed in upon the defenceless soldier, killed him at a blow and were in a moment within the lines, pushing right and left with sword and dagger, often bringing down two men at once. The battle was thus decided in an almost incredibly short time and all that followed was mere carnage.'*

It must have been extremely demoralizing for the raw Hanoverian forces. One moment they were freshly wheeled into position and standing facing writhing tendrils of mist when suddenly they saw the Highland hordes rising up only a few yards away, as if from nowhere. Then to receive a volley of shots at close range and an immediate whirlwind assault while the smoke from the muzzle loaders was still choking and blinding them would have been enough to make hardened troops break and run. All this accompanied by wild Highland war cries and the blood-curdling skirl of the pipes made it small wonder that Cope found it impossible to keep his troops steady, or that it was over so soon. Cope was perfectly correct at his subsequent court martial, prior to his acquittal, when he said simply that his troops had been seized by 'a sudden Panick'. Considering the circumstances their casualties were not so great, being only some 3–400 killed and around 500 wounded, although nearly 1,500 were made prisoner. On the Jacobite side they lost only six officers killed.

* From *Sketches of the Character, Manners and Present State of the Highlanders of Scotland.*

The popular song, *Hey Johnnie Cope*, composed by an East Lothian farmer of rhyming propensity, a phenomenon still to be found in the county, is an example of how far from the truth and how misleading a ballad can be, even when written at the time of the events it sets out to describe. It appears that a Mr Skirving went down to the beach in the afternoon when the battle was long over and was held up by some Highlanders who relieved him of the contents of his pockets and scared him nearly out of his wits, as he himself was honest enough to admit. He described the scene as a frightful one, with heads, limbs and bodies lying about, demonstrating the effects of the Highland claymore strokes.

It is a gross libel on the wretched Cope to suggest, as the ballad does, that he was asleep, or that he was cowardly about his retreat. Nor, of course, did Cope have a horse ready with a view to flight. He was mounted simply because every Commanding Officer was mounted at the time. The 'coals' mentioned in the chorus is simply a reference to the local coal pits, one of which was very close to the battlefield. Tranent was then entirely a mining town.

Mr Skirving's other, more elaborate, but lesser known ballad on the same subject, entitled the 'Battle of Tranent Muir, or Prestonpans' is dealt with in the appendix.

JOHNNIE COPE

from *Scottish Songs* Balmoral Edition

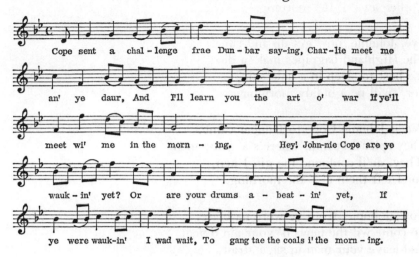

Cope sent a chal-lenge frae Dun-bar say-ing, Char-lie meet me an' ye daur, And I'll learn you the art o' war If ye'll meet wi' me in the morn-ing. Hey! John-nie Cope are ye wauk-in' yet? Or are your drums a-beat-in' yet, If ye were wauk-in' I wad wait, To gang tae the coals i' the morn-ing.

Cope sent a letter frae Dunbar,
'Charlie, meet me an' ye daur,
And I'll learn you the art of war,
If you'll meet me in the morning.'
Chorus
Hey! Johnnie Cope, are ye wauking yet,
Or are your drums a-beating yet;
If ye were wauking I would wait,
To gang to the coals i' the morning.

When Charlie look'd the letter upon,
He drew his sword the scabbard from;
'Come, follow me, my merry, merry men,
And we'll meet Johnnie Cope i' the morning.'

Now Johnnie, be as guid's your word,
Come let us try baith fire and sword;
And dinna rin awa' like a frighted bird,
That's chased frae its nest i' the morning.'

When Johnnie Cope he heard o' this,
He thought it wad na be amiss
To hae a horse in readiness,
To flee awa' i' the morning.

Fye, Johnnie, now get up and rin,
The Highland bagpipes mak' a din;
It's best to sleep in a hale skin,
For 'twill be a bluidy morning.

When Johnnie Cope to Dunbar came,
They spier'd at him, where's a' your men?
'They, de'il confound me gin I ken,
For I left them a' i' the morning.'

Now, Johnnie, troth ye were na blate,
To come wi' the news o' your ain defeat,
And leave your men in sic a strait,
Sae early i' the morning.

'I' faith,' quo' Johnnie, 'I got a fleg,
Wi' their lang claymores and philabegs;
If I face them again, de'ill break my legs,
Sae I wish ye a good morning.'

Chapter 22

Falkirk: Culloden

His victory at Prestonpans was undoubtedly the peak of Charles's campaign in the '45. At that moment Scotland seemed to be his, apart from the castles of Stirling and Edinburgh and the various Highland forts. Yet recruits were strangely slow in coming in and the loyal clans, the Campbells in the west, the Munros, Mackays and Sutherlands in the north, remained against the rising, while Macleod and Macdonald of Skye also came out in favour of Hanover. Even the Grants, Mackenzies, Mackintoshes and Gordons remained divided, though Lady Mackintosh whose husband was loyal to Hanover, herself a cousin of Lord George Murray, raised 500 of the Clan Mackintosh for the Prince. One way and another within six weeks the Prince had mustered 5,000 foot and 500 horse, plus a variety of cannon from two French ships and the promise of further French support. Against this, however, the government had great numbers of troops returning from Holland, along with 6,000 Dutch troops and considerable numbers of loyal militia volunteers in most English counties.

On 3 November Prince Charles set off for England, firmly convinced that many would flock to his standard. On the 15th, Carlisle surrendered without a shot being fired, but it was no longer fortified or suitable for defence and was badly undermanned. The elderly and by this time somewhat ineffective Field-Marshal Wade sent a relieving party through heavy snow, but it arrived too late. On learning that the castle had already fallen it returned to Newcastle.

The capture of Carlisle was the only success of the march south. By 3 December they were in Derby, the furthest south they were to go. Here it became obvious, even to Prince Charles, that no fresh recruits were joining his standard. With a mere 5,000 men he was against three armies amounting to around 30,000 men. At least two of these rival armies were approaching him from different directions. The retreat began on 6 December.

The Jacobite army was nearly cornered in Wigan by the approach of the Duke of Cumberland's army from the south and Wade's army from Newcastle in the east. Fortunately for them, they slipped through the net. There was one minor action outside Penrith, but the Jacobites managed to withdraw to Carlisle without serious fighting. There the Prince insisted, against his advisers' counsels, on leaving a garrison which was doomed to certain surrender as soon as his main force withdrew to Scotland.

On Christmas Day the Highlanders entered Glasgow, the Whig capital of Scotland, which had raised a militia regiment for Hanover. It was accordingly only poetic justice when Charles requisitioned clothes for his ragged army from the City. Meanwhile the Jacobites in Perth had raised a force of nearly 4,000, almost as many as he had taken south with him. Further good news was the withdrawal of the youthful and energetic Duke of Cumberland to command the troops in the south standing by to defend the country against the threat of invasion from France. The elderly Wade was replaced in the north by the blustering General Henry Hawley, who had fought at Sheriffmuir. He had accordingly a poor view of the capabilities of the Highlanders as fighters and on 12 January issued the following directive to his troops:

'The manner of the Highlanders way of fighting which there is nothing so easy to resist If Officers & men are not prepossess'd with the Lyes & Accounts which are told of them. They Commonly form their Front rank of what they call their best men, or True Highlanders, the number of which being allways but few, when they form in Battallions they commonly form four deep & these Highlanders form the front of the four, the rest being Lowlanders & arrant scum.

'When these Battallions come within a large Musket shot, or three score yards, this front Rank gives their fire & Immediately thro' down their firelocks & Come doen in a Cluster with their Swords & Targets making a Noise & Endeavouring to pearce the Body, or Battallions before them becoming 12 or 14 deep by the time they come up to the people they attack.

'The sure way to demolish them is at 3 deep to fire by ranks diagonaly to the Centre where they come, the rear rank first, and even that rank not to fire till they are within 10 or 12 paces but If the fire is given at a distance you probably will be broke for you never get time to load a second Cartridge, & If you give way you may give your foot for dead, for they being without a firelock or any load, no man with his arms, accoutrements &c. can escape them, and they give no Quarters, but if you will but observe the above directions, they are the most despicable Enimy that are.'

On 16 January Hawley reached Falkirk with an army of around 8,500, including horse and artillery. The Jacobites with about 8,000 decided to attack him at Falkirk, advancing from Torwood. On the morning of the 17th they began a fast advance towards Falkirk Hill. Hawley, who had dined extremely well the night before, could not believe that the Highlanders would dare to attack him. Even when warning of their approach was brought at one o'clock and confirmed by his own officers, Hawley refused to take any precautions beyond telling his informant to let the men put on their equipment.

When the Highlanders were about to ford the Carron at Dunipace Steps further warning reached Hawley's camp. At this stage, close on two o'clock, Hawley arrived at last to take command. His army was led past Bantaskin House up the steep hill face, which had a number of gullies in it. A storm of heavy rain lashing in the troops' faces damped both their ardour and their powder, so that most of their guns subsequently misfired.

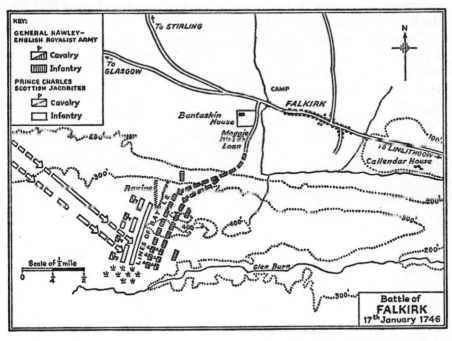

While the foot slipped and sweated along behind, the dragoons made their way successfully to the top of the hill to confront the approaching Highlanders. Despite Hawley's fond belief that the Highlanders would not stand a cavalry charge, the Macdonalds under Lord George Murray completely repelled and broke the cavalry advance with well-aimed volleys of close-quarter fire. Thereafter the Highlanders charged the foot with steel and caused all but three regiments to break and run. Hawley himself completely lost control of the situation, joining the disorderly retreat, but the three right-wing regiments, protected by a ravine in front of them and by Cobham's dragoons, who had rallied, were able to withdraw in good order, covering the rest of their army. The Hanoverian forces then hastily set fire to their tents and in pouring rain retreated towards Linlithgow in very poor order apart from their rearguard.

The Jacobite army, a little surprised to find themselves the victors, advanced on Falkirk and set about looting the enemy camp. On the Hanoverian side the dead were estimated at 16 officers and between 200–300 men, as well as about 300 prisoners. On the Jacobite side there were only 50 killed, 7 being junior officers, and between 60–80 wounded. As at Prestonpans the battle had not lasted long. It was estimated afterwards that only about twenty minutes elapsed between the first shot and the start of the rout.

The following ballad is taken from Hogg's *Jacobite Relics*. It mirrors the Jacobite surprise at finding themselves masters of the field and of Falkirk. Not surprisingly it also mirrors a growing hate for the Hanoverian forces and a certain defiant despair.

Up and rin awa', Hawley,
Up and rin awa', Hawley:
The philabegs* are coming down   *kilts i.e. Highlanders
To gie your lugs* a claw, Hawley.   *ears
Young Charlie's face at Dunipace,
Has gi'en your mou'* a throw, Hawley: *mouth
A blasting sight for bastard wight,
The warst* that e'er he saw, Hawley.   *worst
Up and rin, etc.

Gar dight* your face and turn the chace,   *hide
For fierce the wind does blow, Hawley,
And Highland Geordie's at your tail,
Wi' Drummond, Perth and a', Hawley.
Had ye but staid wi' lady's maid,
An hour or maybe twa, Hawley,
Your bacon bouk* and bastard snout,**   *body **nose
Ye might hae sav'd them a' Hawley.
Up and rin, etc.

When'er you saw the bonnets blue
Down frae the Torwood draw, Hawley,
A wisp* in need did you bestead,**   *straw wisp used as
         toilet paper
         **gather

Perhaps you needed twa, Hawley.
And General Huck, that battle busk,*   *adorned
The prime o' warriors a', Hawley,
With whip and spur he cross'd the furr,
As fast as he could ca', Hawley.
Up and rin awa, etc.

I hae but just ae word to say,
And ye maun hear it a', Hawley:
We came to charge with sword and targe,
And nae to hunt ava', Hawley.
When we came down aboun the town,
An' saw nae faes* at a', Hawley,   *foes

We couldna, sooth! believe the truth,
That ye had left us a', Hawley.
Up and rin, etc.

Nae man bedeen believe'd his een,
Till your brave back he saw, Hawley.
That bastard brat o' foreign cat,
Had neither pluck nor paw, Hawley.
We didna ken, but ye were men
Wha fight for foreign law, Hawley.
Gae fill your wame* wi' brose** at hame,   *belly **porridge
It fits ye best of a', Hawley.
Up and rin, etc.

The very frown o' Highland loon,
It gart* you drop the jaw, Hawley;   *made
It happ'd the face of a' disgrace,
And sicken'd southrown maw,* Hawley.   *mouths
The very gleam of Highland flame,
It pat* you in a thaw,* Hawley: *put **fright
Gae back and kiss your daddie's miss:
Yer naught but cowards a' Hawley.

Up and scour* awa', Hawley   *scamper
Up and scour awa', Hawley.
The Highland dirk is at your doup,*   *bottom
And that's the Highland law, Hawley.

After Falkirk the Jacobite army continued a futile siege of Stirling Castle. On the Hanoverian side, although Hawley surprisingly escaped serious reprimand, the Duke of Cumberland was sent north to take over complete control of the Hanoverian armies in Scotland. He arrived on 30 January. Young and energetic, he was also an experienced commander in the field. These attributes, together with his ability to inspire confidence in his men, made up for his somewhat limited military capabilities. The day after his arrival to take command, on 1 February, the Jacobite retreat to the Highlands began. Thereafter it was only a matter of time until the end.

The Jacobite army withdrew to Inverness and spent the next few weeks attacking Fort Augustus, which was captured, and Fort William, which was not. Meanwhile Cumberland moved to Aberdeenshire and stationed himself in a Jacobite stronghold until April. He then began his advance and by the 12th had crossed the Spey without opposition. By the 14th he was encamped by Nairn. The speed of his advance had taken the Jacobites by surprise, but they had already chosen ground for a battle at Drummossie Moor, near Culloden House. In fact it seems Lord George Murray had chosen ground near Dalcross Castle where there was a strong defensive position, but O'Sullivan, the Prince's Irish favourite and evil genius, had countermanded this choice, proposing instead the almost indefensible and highly unsuitable position at Culloden, which was the eventual battle ground.

With an empty pay chest, lacking arms and ammunition, their leaders quarrelling and openly distrustful of each other, the Jacobite army had reached the end of the road, even if the morale of the Highland troops was as yet unaffected. The Prince himself had shown decreasing interest in matters since the retreat from Derby, but Lord George Murray's position, which had often been intolerable, was now virtually impossible. O'Sullivan's open jealousy had begun to make any attempt at command a mockery. Through sheer mismanagement on the quartermaster's side the troops were without provisions. Reinforcements were expected in the next day or two and, quite understandably, the Highlanders did not wish to fight until they arrived.

It was at this stage that the Prince and O'Sullivan conceived the plan of attacking Cumberland's camp outside Nairn at dawn the following day. They had under 4,500 men against some 10,000 under Cumberland, but at Charles's suggestion they agreed to march. In the event, it was hopeless almost from the start. In the darkness, in two columns, without reliable guides, they were frequently bogged and made little headway, being still two miles from the Hanoverian camp at dawn. The attempt was given up in disorder and, still without provisions and now extremely weary, they retreated to the defenceless position on Culloden Moor.

It was here that Cumberland found them, exhausted and hungry. They did not even take up their correct positions, as reconnoitred the day before. They could hardly have been worse prepared to fight. On the other hand the Hanoverian troops marched slowly with the ponderous effect of a well-trained machine, taking up their battle positions opposite the enemy as they wished.

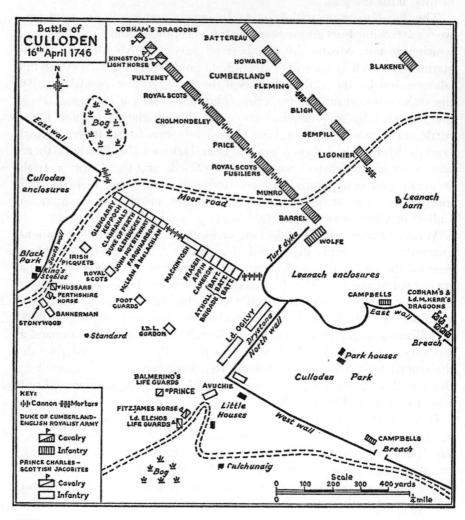

Battle of
CULLODEN
16th April 1746

KEY:
ılıl Cannon ﬀﬀﬀ Mortars
DUKE OF CUMBERLAND-
ENGLISH ROYALIST ARMY
Cavalry
Infantry
PRINCE CHARLES-
SCOTTISH JACOBITES
Cavalry
Infantry

The Hanoverian forces were drawn up in three lines. The front line was commanded by Lord Albemarle and Brigadier Sempill. The second was under General Huske. The third was under General Mordaunt. The cavalry was commanded by General Hawley and General Bland. Their total force amounted to nearly 9,000, with notably good artillery.

On the right wing of the Jacobite army was the Atholl Brigade under Lord George Murray amounting to about 1,200 men. In the centre were the Frasers, the Clan Chattan or Mackintosh, and the Farquharsons commanded by Lord John Drummond. The left wing under Keppoch, Glengarry and Clanranald, consisted of the Macdonalds and with them were the Grants of Invermoriston. In the second line were the Ogilvies, the Gordons and the Grants along with 200 French troops and 150 Irish. A squadron of horse and twelve guns under somewhat inexperienced gunners made up a total which was certainly under 5,000.

Tired, hungry and dispirited, half the number of their experienced opponents, they were forced to suffer a lengthy bombardment of well-aimed cannon fire. The rain and wind were in their faces. The smoke from their own guns blinded them. Everything that day conspired against them. Yet still they charged and against all odds drove their charges home. That they were repulsed and beaten was no dishonour. There were many acts of heroism, but all was wasted. Despite their gallantry, cannon, tactics and superior numbers decided the day.

Prince Charles's year was almost over. Ahead lay only the years of disillusion for the Highlanders and their Prince. The curtain was about to ring down on the clan system and the last battle fought on British soil. It was only regrettable that it should have been marred by the excesses of the victorious general. 'Butcher' Cumberland earned his nickname and the notoriety which still clings to his memory.

Instead of dying courageously on the field the Prince was persuaded to fly for his life in the heather and the legend of his escape wove a magic round his name which was largely undeserved. It was the poverty-stricken Highlanders whose honour and gallantry forbade them to betray him whose memory we must applaud. Ahead of them lay the Clearances and the empty glens, the sorrows and persecutions of the century to come, which resulted in the sturdy Highland stock of Canada, New Zealand and Australia as well as the United States of America.

It is significant that after Culloden, as after Flodden, there were no ballads or songs written. The years had to pass and the memory be allowed to grow dim before the feelings the day inspired could be put into song. The example included in the appendix is from James Hogg's *Jacobite Relics* and must therefore be dated earlier than 1819, but still suffers from the high-flown moral feeling that 'epic' poetry was at that time felt to require, thanks to the influence of Scott.

Translation from the Gaelic is always difficult, but two verses at least of a Gaelic poem about Culloden also included in the *Jacobite Relics*, Vol II, seem to show something of the depth of feeling the event inspired in the Highlands:

> What is there now in thee, Scotland,
> For us can pleasure give?
> What is there now in thee, Scotland,
> For which we ought to live?
> Since we have stood, and stood in vain,
> For all that we hold dear,
> Still have we left a sacrifice
> To offer on our bier.
>
> A foreign and fanatic sway
> Our southern foes may gall;
> The cup is fill'd, they yet shall drink,
> And they deserve it all.
> But there is nought for us and ours,
> In which to hope or trust,
> But hide us in our fathers' graves,
> Amid our fathers' dust.

Ballads

HARDYKNUTE OR THE BATTLE OF LARGS
THE FIELD OF BANNOCKBURN
THE HUNTING OF THE CHEVIOT *or* CHEVY CHASE
THE RAID OF THE REIDSWIRE
THE BONNY EARL OF MURRAY
THE BATTLE OF BALRINNES *or* GLENLIVET
THE DEATH OF PARCY REED
ARCHIE O' CAWFIELD
THE BATTLE OF KILLICRANKIE
THE BATTLE OF SHERIFFMUIR
THE BATTLE OF PRESTONPANS
CULLODEN

Stately stepp'd he east the wall.
  And stately stepp'd he west;
Full seventy years he now had seen,
  With scarce seven years of rest.
He lived when Britons' breach of faith
  Wrought Scotland meikle wae;
And aye his sword tauld, to their cost,
  He was their deadly fae.

High on a hill his castle stood,
  With halls and tow'rs a height.
And goodly chambers fair to see,
  Where he lodged many a knight.
His dame, sae peerless ance and fair,
  For chaste and beauty deem'd,
Nae marrow had in all the land,
  Save Elenor, the queen.

Full thirteen sons to him she bare,
  All men of valour stout;
In bluidy fight, with sword in hand,
  Nine lost their lives bust doubt.
Four yet remain; long may they live
  To stand by liege and land!
High was their fame, high was their might,
  And high was their command.

Great love they bare to Fairly fair,
  Their sister saft and dear;
Here girdle show'd her middle jimp,
  And gowden glist here hair.
What waefu' wae her beauty bred!
  Waefu' to young and auld;
Waefu', I trow, to kith and kin,
  As story ever tauld.

The king of Norse, in summer tide,
  Puff'd up with pow'r and might,

Landed in fair Scotland the isle,
  With mony a hardy knight.
The tidings to our gude Scots king,
  Came, as he sat at dine,
With noble chiefs, in brave array,
  Drinking the bluid-red wine.

'To horse! To horse! my royal liege!
  Your faes stand on the strand;
Full twenty thousand glitt'ring spears
  The king of Norse commands.'
'Bring me my steed Madge, dapple gray,'
  Our gude king rose and cry'd;
'A trustier beast in all the land
  A Scots king never try'd.

'Go, little page, tell Hardyknute,
  That lives on hill so hie,
To draw his sword, the dread of faes,
  And haste and follow me.'
The little page flew swift as dart
  Flung by his master's arm;
'Come down, come down, Lord Hardyknute,
  And rid your king frae harm.'

Then red, red grew his dark-brown cheeks,
  Sae did his dark-brown brow;
His looks grew keen, as they were wont,
  In dangers great to do.
He's ta'en a horn as green as grass,
  And gi'en five sounds sae shrill,
That trees in greenwood shook thereat,
  Sae loud rang ilka hill.

His sons in manly sport and glee
  Had pass'd that summer's morn,
When lo! down in a grassy dale,
  They heard their father's horn.
'That horn,' quo' they, 'ne'er sounds in peace —
  We've other sport to bide';

And soon they hied them up the hill,
　And soon were at his side.

Late, late yestreen I ween'd in peace
　To end my lengthen'd life;
My age might well excuse my arm
　Frae manly feats of strife;
But now that Norse do proudly boast
　Fair Scotland to enthrall,
It's ne'er be said of Hardyknute,
　He fear'd to fight or fall.

'Robin of Rothsay, bend thy bow;
　Thy arrows shoot sae leel,
That mony a comely countenance
　They've turned to deadly pale.
Brade Thomas, take ye but your lance;
　Ye need nae weapons mair,
If you fight wi't as you did ance,
　'Gainst Westmoreland's fierce heir.

'And Malcolm, light of foot as stag,
　That runs in forest wild,
Get me my thousands three of men
　Well bred to sword and shield.
Bring me my horse and harnesine,
　My blade of metal clear;
If faes but kenn'd the hand it bare,
　They soon had fled for fear.

'Farewell, my dame, sae peerless gude,' —
　And took her by the hand, —
'Fairer to me in age you seem,
　Than maids for beauty fam'd.
My youngest son shall here remain,
　To guard these stately towers,
And shut the silver bolt that keeps,
　Sae fast your painted bowers.'

And first she wet her comely cheeks,
　And then her boddice green;

Her silken cords of twirtle twist,
    Well plett with silver sheen;
And apron set with mony a dice
    Of needle work sae rare,
Wove by nae hand, as ye may guess,
    Save that of Fairly fair.

And he has ridden o'er muir and moss,
    O'er hills and mony a glen.
When he came to a wounded knight,
    Making a heavy mane:
'Here must I lie, here must I die,
    By treachery's false guiles;
Witless I was, that e'er gave faith,
    To wicked woman's smiles.'

'Sir Knight, if ye were in my bow'r,
    To lean on silken seat,
My ladye's kindly care you'd prove,
    Who ne'er kenn'd deadly hate.
Herself wou'd watch you all the day;
    Her maids watch all the night;
And Fairly fair your heart wou'd cheer,
    As she stands in your sight.'

'Arise, young knight, and mount your steed,
    Full lowns the shining day;
Choose frae my men whom you do please,
    To lead you on the way.'
With smileless look, and visage wan,
    The wound'd knight reply'd —
'Kind chieftain, your intent pursue,
    For here I maun abide.

'To me nae after day nor night
    Can e'er be sweet or fair;
But soon beneath some drapping tree,
    Cauld death shall end my care.'
With him nae pleading might prevail;
    Brave Hardyknute to gain,

224

With fairest words and reason strong,
  Strave courteously in vain.

Syne he has gone far hynd out o'er
  Lord Chattan's land sae wide:
That Lord a worthy wight was aye,
  When faes his courage try'd:
Of Pictish race, by mother's side,
  When Picts rul'd Caledon,
Lord Chattan claim'd the princely maid,
  When he sav'd Pictish Crown.

Now with his fierce and stalwart train,
  He reach'd a rising height,
Where, braid encampit on the dale,
  The Norsemen lay in sight,
'Yonder, my valiant sons and feirs,
  Our raging reivers wait
On the unconquer'd Scottish sward,
  To try with us their fate.

'Make orisons to Him that sav'd
  Our souls upon the rood,
Syne bravely show your veins are fill'd,
  With Caledonian bluid.'
Then forth he drew his trusty glave,
  While thousands all around,
Drawn frae their sheaths, glanc'd in the sun,
  And loud the bugles sound.

To join his king adown the hill
  In haste his march he made,
While, playin' pibrochs, minstrels meet,
  Before him stately strade.
'Thrice welcome, valiant stoop ot weir,
  Thy nation's shield and pride;
Thy king nae reason has to fear,
  When thou art by his side.'

When bows were bent and darts were thrown
  For thrang scarce could they flee,

The darts clove arrows as they met,
　The arrows dart the tree.
Lang did they rage and fight full fierce,
　With bloody scaith to man;
But bluidy, bluidy was the field,
　Ere that lang day was done.

The king of Scots that sindle brook'd
　The war that look'd like play,
Drew his braid sword, and brake his bow,
　Since bows seem'd but delay.
Quoth noble Rothsay—'Mine I'll keep,
　I wot it's bled a score.'
'Haste up, my merry men,' cried the king,
　As he rode on before.

The king of Norse he sought to find,
　With him to 'mence the faught;
But on his forehead there did light
　A sharp unsonsie shaft.
As he his hand put up to find
　The wound, an arrow keen,
Oh, waeful chance! there pinn'd his hand
　In midst between his een.

'Revenge! revenge!' cried Rothsay's heir,
　'Your mail-coat shall not bide
The strength and sharpness of my dart';
　Then sent in through his side.
Another arrow well he mark'd,
　It pierc'd his neck in twa;
His hands then qhat the silver reins—
　He low as earth did fa'.

'Sair bleeds my liege, sair, sair he bleeds!'
　Again with might he drew,
And gesture dread his sturdy bow,
　Fast the braid arrow flew.
Wae to the knight he ettled at!
　Lament now, queen Elgreid!

226

High dames, too, wail your darling's fall,
　　His youth and comely meid.

'Take aff, take aff, his costly jupe,'
　　(Of gold well was it twin'd,
Knit like the fowler's net, through which
　　His steely harness shin'd.)
'Take Norse that gift frae me, and bid
　　Him venge the bluid it bears;
Say, if he face my bended bow,
　　He sure naw weapon fears.'

Proud Norse, with giant body tall,
　　Braid shoulder, and arms strong,
Cried — 'Where is Hardyknute, sae fam'd
　　And fear'd at Britain's throne?
Tho' Britons tremble at his name,
　　I soon shall make him wail
That e'er my sword was made sae sharp,
　　Sae saft his coat of mail.'

That brag his stout heart couldn'a bide,
　　It lent him youthful might;
'I'm Hardyknute this day,' he cried,
　　'To Scotland's king I heght
To lay the low as horse's hoof;
　　My word I mean to keep:'
Syne, with the first stroke e'er he strake,
　　He gar'd his body bleed.

Norse e'en like gray gos-hawks stair'd wild,
　　He sigh'd with shame and spite;
'Disgrac'd is now my far-fam'd arm,
　　That left the power to smite.'
Then gave his head a blow sae fell,
　　It made him down to stoop,
As low as he to ladies us'd
　　In courtly guise to lout.

Full soon he rais'd his bent body,
　　His bow he marvell'd sair,

227

Since blows till then on him but darr'd
  As touch of Fairly fair.
Norse maevell'd too as sair as he,
  To see his staely look:
Sae soon as e'er he strake a fae,
  Sae soon his life he took.

Where, like a fire to heather set,
  Bauld Thomas did advance,
A sturdy fae, with look enrag'd,
  Up towards him did prance.
He spurr'd his steed throw thickest ranks,
  The hardy youth to quell,
Who stood unmov'd at his approach,
  His fury to repel.

'That short brown shaft, sae meanly trimm'd,
  Looks like poor Scotland's geae;
But dreadful seems the rusty point!'
  And loud he leugh in jeer.
'Oft Britons' blood has dimm'd its shin,
  This point cut short their vaunt':
Syne pierc'd boaster's bearded cheek,
  Nae time he took to taunt.

Short while he in his saddle swang,
  His stirrup was nae stay;
Sae feeble hang his unbent knee,
  Sure token he was fey.
Swith on the harden'd clay he fell,
  Right far was heard the thud;
But Thomas look'd not as he lay,
  All weltering in his bluid.

With careless gesture, mind unmov'd,
  On rode he north the plain;
His seem in throng of fiercest strife
  When winner aye the same.
Nor yet his heart-dame's dimpl'd cheek,
  Cou'd mease saft love to brook,

228

Till vengeful Ann return'd his scorn,
　　Then languid grew his look.

In thraws of death, with wallow'd cheek,
　　All panting on the plain,
The fainting corps of warriors lay,
　　Ne'er to arise again:
Ne'er to return to native lan,
　　Nae mair, with blythsome sounds,
To boast the glories of the day,
　　And show their shining wounds.

On Norway's coast the widow'd dame
　　May wash the rocks with tears —
May land look o'er the shipless seas
　　Before her mate appears.
Cease, Emma, cease to hope in vain,
　　Thy lord lies in the clay;
The valiant Scots nae reivers thole
　　To carry life away.

There on a lee, where stands a cross,
　　Set up for monument,
Thousands full fierce that summer's day
　　Fill'd keen war's black intent.
Let Scots, while Scots, praise Hardyknute,
　　Let Norse the name aye dread;
Ay, how he faught oft how he spair'd,
　　Shall latest ages read

Loud and chill blow the westlin' wind,
　　Sair beat the heavy shower.
Mirk grew the night ere Hardyknute
　　Wan near his stately tow'r.
His tow'r, that us'd with torches blaze,
　　To shine sae far at night,
Seem'd now as black as mourning weed,
　　Nae marvel sair he sigh'd.

'There's nae light in my lady's bower,
　　There's nae light in my hall;

Nae blink shines round my Fairly fair,
  Nor ward stands on my wall.
What bodes it? Robert, Thomas, say!' —
  Nae answer fits their dread.
Stand back, my sons, I'll be your guide';
  But by they pass'd with speed.

'As fast I've sped o'er Scotland's faes,' —
  There ceas'd his brag of weir;
Sair sham'd to mind ought but his dame,
  And maiden Fairly fair.
Black fear he felt; but what to fear,
  He wist not yet with dread;
Sair shook his body, sair his limbs,
  And all the warrior fled.

THE FIELD OF BANNOCKBURN

from *The Lyric gems of Scotland*

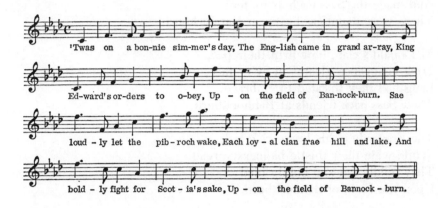

'Twas on a bon-nie sim-mer's day, The Eng-lish came in grand ar-ray, King Ed-ward's or-ders to o-bey, Up - on the field of Ban-nock-burn. Sae loud - ly let the pib - roch wake, Each loy - al clan frae hill and lake, And bold - ly fight for Scot - ia's sake, Up - on the field of Bannock - burn.

THE FIELD OF BANNOCKBURN*
(See page 33)

'Twas on a bonnie simmer's day,
The English came in grand array
King Edward's orders to obey
Upon the Field of Bannockburn.

Sae loudly let the Pibroch wake
Each loyal Clan frae hill and lake
And boldly fight for Scotia's sake
Upon the Field of Bannockburn.

King Edward raised his standard high,
Bruce shook his banners in reply —
Each army shouts for victory
Upon the Field of Bannockburn.

The English horse wi' deadly aim
Upon the Scottish army came;

* From *The Lyric Gems of Scotland*: McG. Simpson.

231

But hundreds in our pits were slain
Upon the Field of Bannockburn.

Loud rose the war cry of M'Neil,
Who flew like tigers to the field,
And made the Sass'nach army feel
There were dauntless hearts at Bannockburn.

M'Donald's clan, how firm their pace —
Dark vengeance gleams in ev'ry face,
Lang had they thirsted to embrace
Their Sass'nach friends at Bannockburn.

The Fraser bold his brave clan led,
While wide their thistle banners spread —
They boldly fell and boldly bled
Upon the Field of Bannockburn.

The ne'er behind* brave Douglas came,　*The Douglas Family motto
And also with him Donald Graham,
Their blood-red painted swords did stain
The glorious Field of Bannockburn.

That day King Edward's heart did mourn,
With joy each Scottish heart did burn,
In mem'ry now let us return
Our thanks to Bruce at Bannockburn.

Chorus

For loudly did the Pibroch wake
Our loyal clans frae hill and lake
Wha fell and bled for Scotia's sake
Upon the Field of Bannockburn.

The Hunting of The Cheviot or Chevy Chase

(See page 42)

God prosper long our noble king,
our liffes and saftyes all!
A woefull hunting once there did
in Cheuy Chase befall.

To driue the deere with hound and horne
Erle Pearcy took the way:
The child may rue that is vnborne
the hunting of that day!

The stout Erle of Northumberland
a vow to God did make
His pleasure in the Scottish woods
three sommers days to take,

The cheefest harts in Cheuy Chase
to kill and beare away:
These tydings to Erle Douglas came
in Scottland, where he lay.

Who sent Erle Pearcy present word
he wold prevent his sport;
The English erle, not fearing that,
did to the woods resort,

With fifteen hundred bowmen bold,
all chosen men of might,
Who knew ffull well in time of neede
to ayme their shafts arright.

The gallant greyhounds swiftly ran
to chase the fallow deere;
On Munday they began to hunt,
ere daylight did appeare.

And long before high noone the had
a hundred fat buckes slaine;

Then hauing dined, the drouyers went
to rouze the deare againe.

The bowmen mustered on the hills,
well able to endure;
Theire backsids all with speciall care
that day were guarded sure.

The hounds ran swiftly through the woods
the nimble deere to take,
That with their cryes the hills and dales
an eccho shrill did make.

Lord Pearcy to the querry went
to view the tender deere;
Quoth he, Erle Douglas promised once
this day to meete me heere;

But if I thought he wold not come,
noe longer wold I stay.
with that a braue younge gentlman
thus to the erle did say:

'Loe, yonder doth Erle Douglas come,
hys men in armour bright;
Full twenty hundred Scottish speres
all marching in our sight.

'All men of pleasant Tiudale,
fast by the riuer Tweede':
'O ceaze your sportts!' Erle Pearcy said,
'and take your bowes with speede.

'And now with me, my countrymen,
your courage forth advance!
For there was neuer champion yett
in Scottland nor in Ffrance,

'That euer did on horsbacke come,
but, and if my hap it were,

I durst encounter man for man,
with him to breake a spere.'

Erle Douglas on his milke-white steede,
most like a baron bold,
Rode formost of his company,
whose armor shone like gold.

'Shew me,' sayd hee, 'whose men you bee
that hunt soe boldly heere,
That without my consent doe chase
and kill my fallow deere.'

The first man that did answer make
was noble Pearcy hee,
who sayd, wee list not to declare
nor shew whose men wee bee;

'Yett wee will spend our deerest blood
thy cheefest harts to slay.'
Then Douglas swore a solempne oathe,
and thus in rage did say:

'Ere thus I will outbraued bee,
one of vs tow shall dye;
I know thee well, an erle thou art
Lord Pearcy, soe am I.

'But trust me, Pearcye, pittye it were,
and great offence, to kill
Then any of these our guiltlesse men,
for they haue done none ill.

'Let thou and I the battell trye,
and set our men aside':
'Accurst bee he' Erle Pearcye sayd,
'by whome it is denyed.'

Then stept a gallant squire forth —
Witherington was his name —

who said, 'I wold not haue it told
to Henery our king, for shame,

That ere my captaine fought on foote,
and I stand looking on.
You bee two Erles,' quoth Witherington,
and I a squier alone;

'I'le doe the best that doe I may,
while I haue power to stand;
While I haue power to weeld my sword,
I'le fight with hart and hand.'

Our English archers bent their bowes;
their harts were good and trew;
Att the first flight of arrowes sent,
full foure score Scotts the slew.

To driue the deere with hound and horne,
Douglas bade on the bent;
Two captaines moued with mickle might,
their speres to shiuers went.

They closed full fast on euerye side,
noe slacknes there was found,
But many a gallant gentleman
lay gasping on the ground.

O Christ! it was great greeue to see
how eche man chose his spere,
And how the blood out of their brests
did gush like water cleare.

At last these two stout erles did meet,
like captaines of great might;
Like lyons woode they layd on lode;
the made a cruell fight.

The fought vntill they both did sweat,
with swords of tempered steele,

236

Till blood downe their cheekes like raine
the trickling downe did feele.

'O yeeld thee, Pearcye!' Douglas sayd,
'and in faith I will thee bring
where thou shall high advanced bee
by Iames our Scottish king.

'Thy ransome I will freely giue,
and this report of thee,
Thou art the most couragious knight
that ever I did see.'

'Noe, Douglas!' quoth Erle Percy then,
'thy profer I doe scorne;
I will not yeelde to any Scott
that euer yett was borne!'

With that there came an arrow keene,
out of an English bow,
which stroke Erle Douglas on the brest
a deepe and deadlye blow.

Who neuer sayd more words than these:
Fight on, my merry men all!
For why, my life is att an end,
lord Pearcy sees my fall.

Then leauing liffe, Erle Pearcy tooke
the dead man by the hand;
Who said, 'Erle Dowglas, for thy life,
wold I had lost my land!

'O Christ! my very hart doth bleed
for sorrow for thy sake,
For sure, a more redoubted knight
mischance cold neuer take.'

A knight amongst the Scotts there was
which saw Erle Douglas dye,

who streight in hart did vow revenge
vpon the Lord Pearcye.

Sir Hugh Mountgomerye was he called,
who, with a spere full bright,
Well mounted on a gallant steed,
ran feircely through the fight,

And past the English archers all,
without all dread or feare,
And through Erle Percyes body then
he thrust his hatfull spere.

With such a vehement force and might
his body he did gore,
The staff ran through the other side
a large cloth-yard and more.

Thus did both these nobles dye,
whose courage none cold staine;
An English archer then perceiued
the noble erle was slaine.

He had a good bow in his hand,
made of a trusty tree;
An arrow of a cloth-yard long
to the hard head haled hee.

Against Sir Hugh Mountgomerye
his shaft full right he sett;
The grey-goose-winge that was there-on
in his harts bloode was wett.

This fight from breake of day did last
till setting of the sun,
For when the rung the euening-bell
the battele scarse was done.

With stout Erle Percy there was slaine
Sir John of Egerton,

Sir Robert Harcliffe and Sir William,
Sir Iames, that bold barron.

And with Sir George and Sir Iames,
both knights of good account,
Good Sir Raphe Rebbye there was slaine,
whose prowesse did surmount.

For Witherington needs must I wayle
as one in dolefull dumpes
For when his legs were smitten of,
he fought vpon his stumpes.

And with Erle Dowglas there was slaine
Sir Hugh Mountgomerye,
And Sir Charles Morrell, that from feelde
one foote wold neuer flee;

Sir Roger Heuer of Harcliffe tow,
his sisters sonne was hee;
Sir David Lambwell, well esteemed,
but saved he cold not bee.

And the Lord Maxwell, in like case,
with Douglas he did dye:
Of twenty hundred Scottish speeres,
scarce fifty-fiue did flye.

Of fifteen hundred Englishmen
went home but fifty-three;
The rest in Cheuy Chase were slaine,
vnder the greenwoode tree.

Next day did many widdowes come
their husbands to bewayle;
They washt their wounds in brinish teares,
but all wold not prevayle.

Theyr bodyes, bathed in purple blood,
the bore with them away;

They kist them dead a thousand taimes
ere the were cladd in clay.

The newes was brought to Eddenborrow,
where Scottlands king did rayne,
That brave Erle Douglas soddainlye
was with an arrow slaine.

'O heauy newes!' King Iames can say;
'Scottland may wittenesse bee
I haue not any captaine more
of such account as hee.'

Like tydings to King Henery came,
within as short a space,
That Pearcy of Northumberland
was slaine in Cheuy Chase.

'Now God be with him!' said our king,
'sith it will noe better bee;
I trust I haue within my realme
fiue hundred as good as hee.

'Yett shall not Scotts nor Scottland say
but I will vengeance take,
And be revenged on them all
for braue Erle Percyes sake.'

This vow the king did well performe
after on Humble-downe;
In one day fifty knights were slayne,
with lords of great renowne.

And of the rest, of small account,
did many hundreds dye:
Thus endeth the hunting in Cheuy Chase,
made by the Erle Pearcye.

God saue our king, and blesse this land
with plentye, joy, and peace,
And grant henceforth that foule debate
twixt noble men may ceaze!

240

THE RAID OF THE REIDSWIRE
(See page 93)

The seventh of July, the suith to say,
At the Reidswire the tryst was set;
Our wardens they affixed the day,
And, as they promised, so they met.
Alas! that day I'll ne'er forgett!
Was sure sae feard, and then sae faine —
They came theare justice for to gett,
Will never green to come again.

Carmichael was our warden then,
He caused the country to conveen;
And the Laird's Wat, that worthie man,
Brought in that sirname weil beseen:
The Armestranges that aye hae been
A hardie house, but not a hail,
The Elliots' honours to maintaine,
Brought down the lave o' Liddesdale.

Then Tividale came to wi' speid;
The Sheriffe brought the Douglas down,
Wi' Cranstone, Gladstain, good at need,
Baith Rewle water, and Hawick town.
Beanjeddart bauldy made him bound,
Wi' a' the Trumbills, stronge and stout;
The Rutherfoords, with grit renown,
Convoyed the town of Jedburgh out.

Of other clans I cannot tell,
Because our warning was not wide. —
Be this our folks hae ta'en the fell,
And planted down pallions there to hide.
We looked down the other side,
And saw come breasting ower the brae,
Wi' Sir John Foster for their guyde,
Full fifteen hundred men and mae.

It grieved him sair that day, I trow,
Wi' Sir George Hearoune of Schipsydehouse;

241

Because we were not men enow,
They counted us not worth a louse.
Sir George was gentle, meek, and douse,
But *he* was hail and het as fire;
And yet, for all his cracking crouse,
He rewd the raid o' the Reidswire.

To deal with proud men is but pain;
For either must ye fight or flee,
Or else no answer make again,
But play the beast, and let them be.
It was no wonder he was hie,
Had Tindaill, Reedsdaill, at his hand,
Wi' Cukdaill, Gladsdaill on the lee,
And Hebsrime, and Northumberland.

Yett was our meeting meek eneugh,
Begun wi' merriement and mowes,
And at the brae, aboon the heugh,
The clark sate down to call the rowes.
And some for kyne, and some for ewes,
Called in of Dandrie, Hob, and Jock —
We saw, come marching ower the knows,
Five hundred Fennicks in a flock.

With jack and speir, and bows all bent,
And warlike weapons at their will:
Although we were na weel content,
Yet, by my trouth, we feared no ill.
Some gaed to drink, and some stude still,
And some to cards and dice them sped;
Till on ane Farnstein they fyled a bill.
And he was fugitive and fled.

Carmichael bade them speik out plainlie,
And cloke no cause for ill nor good;
The other, answering him as vainlie,
Began to reckon kin and blood:
He raise, and raxed him where he stood.
And bade him match him with his marrows;

242

Then Tindaill heard them reasun rude,
And they loot off a flight of arrows.

Then was there nought but bow and speir,
And every man pull'd out a brand;
'A Schafton and a Fenwick' thare:
Gude Symington was slain frae hand.
The Scotsmen cried on other to stand,
Frae time they saw John Robson slain —
What should they cry? the King's command
Could cause no cowards turn again.

Up rose the laird to red the cumber,
Which would not be for all his boast; —
What could we doe with sic a number?
Fyve thousand men into a host,
Then Henry Purdie proved his cost,
And very narrowlie had mischiefed him,
And there we had our warden lost,
Wert not the grit God he relieved him.

Another throw the breiks him bair,
Whill flatlies to the ground he fell;
Than thought I weel we had lost him there,
Into my stomach it struck a knell!
Yet up he raise, the treuth to tell ye,
And laid about him dints full dour;
His horsemen they raid sturdilie,
And stude about him in the stoure.

Then raise the slogan with ane shout —
'Fy Tindaill, to it! Jedbrugh's here!'
I trow he was not half sae stout,
But anis his stomach was asteir,
With gun and genzie, bow and speir,
Men might see mony a cracked crown!
But up amang the merchant geir,
They are as busy as we were down.

The swallow tail frae tackles flew,
Five hundred flain into a flight,

But we had pestelets enew,
And shot among them as we might,
With help of God the game gaed right,
Fra time the foremost of them fell;
Then ower the know without goodnight,
They ran with mony a shout and yell.

But after they had turned backs,
Yet Tindaill men they turn'd again;
And had not been the merchant packs,
There had been mae of Scotland slain.
But, Jesu! if the folks were fain
To put the bussing on their thies!
And so they fled, wi' a' their main,
Down ower the brae, like clogged bees.

Sir Francis Russell ta'en was there,
And hurt, as we hear men rehearse;
Proud Wallinton was wounded sair,
Albeit he be a Fennick fierce.
But if ye wald a souldier search,
Among them a' were ta'en that night,
Was nane sae wordie to put in verse,
As Collingwood, that courteous knight.

Young Henry Schafton, he is hurt;
A souldier shot him with a bow:
Scotland has cause to mak great sturt,
For laiming of the Laird of Mow,
The Laird's Wat did weel, indeed;
His friends stood stoutlie by himsel',
With little Gladstain, gude in need,
For Gretein kend na gude be ill.

The Sheriffe wanted not gude will,
Howbeit he might not fight so fast;
Beanjeddart, Hundlie, and Hunthill,
Three, on they laid weel at the last.
Except the horsemen of the guard,
If I could put men to availe,

None stoutlier stood out for their laird,
Nor did the lads of Liddisdail.

But little harness had we there;
But auld Badreule had on a jack,
And did right weel, I you declare,
With all his Trumbills at his back.
Gude Edderstane was not to lack,
Nor Kirktoun, Newton, noble men!
Thir's all the specials I of speake,
By others that I could not ken.

Who did invent that day of play,
We need not fear to find him soon;
For Sir John Forster, I dare well say,
Made us this noisome afternoon.
Not that I speak preceislie out,
That he supposed it would be perril;
But pride, and breaking out of feuid,
Garr'd Tindaill lads begin the quarrel.

'Open the gates,
and let him come in;
He is my brother Huntly,
he'll do him nae harm.'

The gates they were opent,
they let him come in,
But fause traitor Huntly,
he did him great harm.

He's ben and ben,
and ben to his bed,
And with a sharp rapier
he stabbed him dead.

The lady came down the stair,
wringing her hands:
'He has slain the Earl o Murray,
the flower o Scotland.'

But Huntly lap on his horse,
rade to the king:
'Ye're welcome hame, Huntly,
and whare hae ye been?

'Whare hae ye been?
and how hae ye sped?'
'I've killed the Earl o Murray,
dead in his bed.'

'Foul fa you, Huntly!
and why did ye so?
You might have taen the Earl o Murray,
and saved his life too.'

'Her bread it's to bake,
her yill is to brew;

246

My sister's a widow,
and sair do I rue.

'Her corn grows ripe,
her meadows grow green,
But in bonny Dinnibristle
I darena be seen.'

Frae Dunnoter to Aberdeen,
  I raise and took the way,
Believing weel that it had been
  Not half ane hour to day.
The lift was clad with cloudis gray,
  And ower maskit was the moon,
Which me deceived where I lay,
  And made me rise ower soon.

On Towie Mount I met a man
  Well graithed in his gear;
Quoth I—'What news?' then he began
  To tell a fitt of weir
Quoth he—'The ministers, I fear,
  A bloody browst have brewn;
For yesterday, withouten mair,
  On ane hill at Stradown.

'I saw three lords in battle fight
  Right furiously awhile,
Huntlie and Errol, as they hight,
  Were both against Argyle.
Turn back with me and ride a mile,
  And I shall make it kenn'd,
How they began the form and style,
  And of the battle's end.'

Then I, as any man would be,
  Desirous was to know
Mair of that tale he told to me,
  The which, he said, he saw.
By then the day began to daw,
  And back with him I rade;
Then he began the sooth to show,
  And on this wise he said:—

MacCallen More came frae the West,
  With mony a bow and brand;

To waste the Rhinnes he thought best,
    The Earl of Huntlie's land.
He swore that none should him gainstand,
    Except that he were fey,
But all shou'd be at his command,
    That dwelt be north of Tay.

Then Huntlie, to prevent that peril,
    Directit hastilie,
Unto the noble Earl of Errol,
    Besought him for supplie.
Wha said — 'It is my dutie
    For to give Huntlie support,
For if he loses Strathbogie,*   *The Earl of Huntlie's Castle
    My Slaines* will be ill hurt   *The Earl of Errol's Castle

'Therefore I hald the subject vain,
    Wou'd reave us of our right,
First shall one of us be slain,
    The other tak the flight.
Suppose Argyle be much of might,
    By force of Hielandmen;
We's be a mote into his sight,
    Or he pass hame again.

'Be blithe, my merry men, be blithe,
    Argyle shall have the worse,
Gif he into this country kythe,*   *is found
    I houp in God his cross!'
Then leap'd this lord upon his horse,
    And with warlike troop frae Turray,* *Turriff in Aberdeenshire
To meet with Huntlie and his force,
    Rade to Elgin in the Murray.

The same night that those two lords met,
    I wot t'wou'd be thought long;
To tell you all, (I have forgot)
    The mirth was them among.
Then pipers play'd, and songsters sang,
    To glad the merry host;

249

Wha fear'd not the foemen strong,
　　Nor yet Argyle his boast.

They for two days wou'd not remove,
　　But blithely drank the wine;
Some to his lass, some to his love,
　　Some to his ladye fine.
And he that thought not for to blyne,* 　　*shrink from battle (lit. stop)
　　His mistress' token tak's,
They kiss'd it first, and set it syne
　　Upon their helmes or jacks.

They pass'd their time right wantonlie,
　　Till word came at the last,
Argyle with ane great armie,
　　Approached wond'rous fast.
Then frae the toun those Barons pass'd,
　　And Huntlie to them said, —
'Gude gentlemen, we will us cast
　　To Strathbogie, but beed.* 　　　　　　*without delay

When they unto Strathbogie came,
　　To council soon they gaed:
There to see how things might frame,* 　*take form
　　For they had meikle need.
They vowed them unto a deed,
　　As kirmen cou'd devise.
Syne pray'd that they might find good speed
　　Of their gude enterprise.

Then every man himself did arm,
　　To meet MacCallen More,
Unto Strathdoun, who did great harm
　　The Wedensday before.
As lions do poor lambs devour,
　　With bluidie teeth and nails,
They brent the biggings, took the store,
　　Syne slew the people's sells.

Beside all this hie crueltie,
　　He said, ere he should cease,

250

The standing-stones of Strathbogie
  Should be his pallion's place.
But Huntlie said—'With God his grace,
  First shall we fight them ones,
Perchance that they may tak' the chase,
  Ere they come to the stones!'

Those Lords kept on at afternoon
  With all their weirmen wight,
Then sped up to the Cabrach soon,
  Where they bad all that night.
Upon the morn, when day was light,
  They raise and made them boune,
Intil ane castle that stood on height;
  They called it Auchindoun.

Beside that castle, on a croft,
  They stended pallions there:
Then spak' a man that had been oft
  In jeopardie of weir:
'My Lords, your foes they are to fear,
  Though we were never so stout,
Therefore command some men of weir
  To watch the rest about.'

By this was done, some gentlemen,
  Of noble kin and bluid,
To council with these Lords began,
  Of matters to conclude:
For weel eneugh they understood
  The matter was of weight,
They hadna so manie men of good,
  In battle for to fight

The firstin man in council spak',
  Good Errol, it was he:
Who says—'I will the vanguard tak',
  And leading upon me.
My Lord Huntlie, come succour me,
  When ye see me opprest:

For frae the field I will not flee,
  So lang as I may last.'

Thereat some Gordons waxed wraith,
  And said he did them wrong:
To let this lord then they were laith,
  First to the battle gang.
The meeting that was them among,
  Was no man that it heard:
But Huntlie, with a troop full strong,
  Bade into the rear-guard.

This was the number of their force,
  Those Lords to battle led:
Ane thousand gentlemen on horse,
  And some footmen they had:
Three hundred that shot arrows braid,
  Four score that hagbuts bore:
This was the number that they had,
  Of footmen with them sure.

Thus with their noble chivalry
  They marched into the field:
Argyle, with ane great armie,
  Upon ane hill ta'en bield;
Abiding them with spear and shield,
  With bullets, darts, and bows:
The men could weel their weapons wield,
  To meet them was nae mows.

When they so near other were come,
  That ilk man saw his foe,
'Go to, essay the game,' said some;
  But Captain Ker said, 'No:
First let the guns before us go,
  That they may break the order.'
Quoth baith the Lords—'Let it be so,
  Or ever we gae farder.'

Then Andrew Gray, upon ane horse,
  Betwixt the battles rade,

Making the sign of hally cross,
  'In manus tuas,' he said.
He lighted there the guns to lead,
  Till they came to the rest:
Then Captain Ker unto him sped,
  And bade him shoot in haste.

'I will not shoot,' quoth Andrew Gray,
  'Till they come o'er yon hill:
We ha'e an ower gude cause this day,
  Thro' misguidings to spill.
Go back, and bid our men bide still,
  Till they come to the plain:
Then shall my shooting do them ill;
  I will not shoot in vain.'

'Shoot up, shoot up ' quoth Captain Ker,
  'Shoot up to our comfort!'
The firstin shot (it) was too near,
  It lighted all too short.
The nextin shot their foes (it) hurt,
  It lighted wond'rous weel:
Quoth Andrew Gray—'I see ane sport,
  When they begin to reel!

'Go to, good mates, and 'say the game,
  Yon folks are in a fray:
Let see how we can mell with them,
  Into their disarray:
Go, go, it is not time to stay,
  All for my benison:
Save none this day, ye may gar die,
  Till we the field ha'e won!'

(Then awful Errol he 'gan say:
  'Good fellows, follow me:
I hope it shall be ours this day,
  Or else therefore to dee.
Tho' they in number many be,
  Set on withouten words:

Let ilk brave fellow brake his tree,
   And then pursue with swords.')

Then Errol hasted to the height
   Where he did battle bide,
With him went Auchindoun and Gight,
   And Bonnitoun by his side:
Where many gentlemen did with him bide,   *suppressed
   Whose praise should not be smoor'd:*
But Captain Ker, that was their guide,
   Rade aye before my Lord.

They were not many men of weir,
   But they were wondrous true:
With hagbuts, pistols, bow and spear,
   They did their foes pursue:
Where bullets, darts and arrows flew,
   As thick as hail or rain,
Whilk many hurt; and some they slew,
   Of horse and gentlemen.

Huntlie made haste to succour him,
   And charged furiouslie,
Where many (ane) man's sight grew dim,
   The shots so thick did flee:
Whilk gar'd right many doughty dee,
   Of some on every side:
Argyle with his tald* host did flee,   *aforesaid
   But MacLean did still abide.

MacLean had on a habergeon,
   Ilk Lord had on ane jack,
Together fiercely are they run,
   With many a gun's crack.
The splinters of their spears they brak'
   Flew up into the air,
And bore doun many on their back,
   Again raise never mair.

'Alace, I see ane sorry sight!'
  Said the Laird of MacLean:
'Our feeble folks have ta'en the flight,
  And left me mine alane.
Now maun I flee or else be slain,
  Since they will not return:'
With that he ran out o'er ane den,
  Alongside ane little burn.

(Then some men said—'We will be sure
  And tak' MacLean by course.'*   *run him down
'Go to! for we are men anew
  To bear him down by force.'
But noble Errol had remorse,
  And said—'It is not best;
For the Argyle has got the worst,
  Let him gang with the rest.'

'What greater honour cou'd ye wish,
  In deeds of chivalry,
Or braver victory than this,
  Where one has chased thrice three?
Therefore, good fellows, let him be:
  He'll dee before he yield:
For he with his small company
  Bade longest in the field.')

Then, after great Argyle his host,
  Some horsemen took the chase:
They turn'd their backs, for all their boast,
  Contrair their foes to face.
They cried out, 'Oh!' and some, 'Alace!'
  But never for mercy sought:
Therefore the Gordons gave no grace,
  Because they crav'd it not.

Then some good man pursued sharp,
  With Errol and Huntlie,
And they with ane captain did carp,
  Whose name was Ogilvie.

He says — 'Gentlemen, let's see
   Who maniest slain (hast) slaid:
Save nane this day ye may gar dee,
   For pleadis nor ransom paid.'

Like harts, up howes and hills they ran,
   Where horsemen might not win:
'Retire again,' quoth Huntlie then,
   'Where we did first begin.
Here lies many carved skins,
   And many ane bloody beard,
For any help, with little din,
Shall rot abune the yeard.'*   *earth

When they came to the hill again,
   They set doun on their knees:
Syne thanked God that they had slain
   So many enemies.
They rose before Argyle his eyes,
   Made Captain Ker ane knight,
Syne bade amang the dead bodies
   Till they were out of sight.

(Now I have you already told,
   Huntly and Arrol's men
Could scarce ne thirteen hundred call'd,
   The truth if ye wou'd ken.
And yet Argyle and his thousands ten
   Were they that took the race:
And tho' that they were nine to ane,
   They caused (them) tak' the chase.

So Argyle's boast it was in vain
   (He thocht sure not to tyne)*   *lose
That if he durst come to the plain,
   He would gar every nine
Of his lay hold upon ilk man
   Huntly and Errol had:
And yet for all his odds he ran,
   To tell how ill he sped.)

This deed sae doughtilie was done,
    As I heard true men tell,
Upon a Thursday afternoon,
    Sanct Francis' eve befell.
Good Auchindoun was slain himsel',
    With seven mair in battell,
So was the laird of Lochenzell,
    Great pitie was to tell.

God send the land deliverance
Frae every reaving, riding Scot;
We'll sune hae neither cow nor ewe,
We'll sune hae neither staig nor stot.

The outlaws come frae Liddesdale,
They herry Redesdale far and near;
The rich man's gelding it maun gang,
They canna pass the puir man's mear.

Sure it were weel, had ilka thief
Around his neck a halter strang;
And curses heavy may they light
On traitors vile oursels amang.

Now Parcy Reed has Crosier taen,
He has delivered him to the law;
But Crosier says he'll do waur than that,
He'll make the tower o' Troughend fa.

And Crosier says he will do waur,
He will do waur if waur can be;
He'll make the bairns a' fatherless.
And then, the land it may lie lee.

'To the hunting, ho!' cried Parcy Reed,
'The morning sun is on the dew;
The cauler breeze frae off the fells
Will lead the dogs to the quarry true.

'To the hunting, ho!' cried Parcy Reed,
And to the hunting he has gane;
And the three fause Ha's o Girsonsfield
Alang wi him he has them taen.

They hunted high, they hunted low,
By heathery hill and birken shaw;

They raised a buck on Rooken Edge,
And blew the mort at fair Ealylawe.

They hunted high, they hunted low,
They made the echoes ring amain;
With music sweet o horn and hound,
They merry made fair Redesdale glen.

They hunted high, they hunted low,
They hunted up, they hunted down,
Until the day was past the prime,
And it grew late in the afternoon.

They hunted high in Batinghope,
When as the sun was sinking low;
Says Parcy then, Ca off the dogs,
We'll bair our steeds and homeward go.

They lighted high in Batinghope,
Atween the brown and benty ground:
They had but rested a little while
Till Parcy Reed was sleeping sound.

There's nane may lean on a rotten staff,
But him that risks to get a fa;
There's nane may in a traitor trust,
And traitors black were every Ha.

They've otown the bridle off his steed,
And they've put water in his lang gun;
They've fixed his sword within the sheath
That out again it winna come.

'Awaken ye, waken ye, Parcy Reed,
Or by your enemies be taen;
For yonder are the five Crosiers
A-coming owre the Hingin-stane.'

'If they be five, and we be four,
Sae that ye stand alang wi me,

Then every man ye will take one,
And only leave but two to me:
We will them meet as brave men ought,
And make them either fight or flee.'

'We mayna stand, we canna stand,
We daurna stand alang wi thee;
The Crosiers haud thee at a feud,
And they wad kill baith thee and we.'

'O turn thee, turn thee, Johnie Ha,
O turn thee, man and fight wi me;
When ye come to Troughend again,
My gude black naig I will gie thee;
He cost full twenty pound o gowd,
Atween my brother John and me.'

'I mayna turn, I canna turn,
I daurna turn and fight wi thee;
The Crosiers haud thee at a feud,
And they wad kill baith thee and me.'

'O turn thee, turn thee, Willie Ha,
O turn thee, man, and fight wi me;
When ye come to Troughend again,
A yoke o owsen I'll gie thee.'

'I mayna turn, I canna turn,
I daurna turn and fight wi thee;
The Crosiers haud thee at a feud,
And they wad kill baith thee and me.'

'O turn thee, turn thee, Tommy Ha,
I turn now, man, and fight wi me;
If ever we come to Troughend again,
My daughter Jean I'll gie to thee.'

'I mayna turn, I canna turn,
I daurna turn and fight wi thee;
The Crosiers haud thee at a feud,
And they wad kill baith thee and me.'

260

'O shame upon ye, traitors a'!
I wish your hames ye may never see;
Ye've stown the bridle off my naig,
And I can neither fight nor flee.

'Ye've stown the bridle off my naig,
And ye've put water i my lang gun;
Ye've fixed my sword within the sheath
That out again it winna come.'

He had but time to cross himsel,
A prayer he hadna time to say,
Till round him came the Crosiers keen,
All riding graithed and in array.

'Weel met, weel met, now, Parcy Reed,
Thou art the very man we sought;
Owre lang hae we been in your debt,
Now will we pay you as we ought.

'We'll pay thee at the nearest tree,
Where we shall hang thee like a hound;'
Brave Parcy raisd his fankit sword,
And felld the foremost to the ground.

Alake and wae for Parcy Reed,
Alake, he was an unarmed man;
Four weapons pierced him all at once,
As they assailed him there and than.

They fell upon him all at once,
They mangled him most cruellie;
The slightest wound might caused his deid,
And they hae gien him thirty-three;
They hacked off his hands and feet,
And left him lying on the lee.

'Now, Parcy Reed, we've paid our debt,
Ye canna weel dispute the tale,'
The Crosiers said, and off they rode;
They rade the airt o Liddesdale.

It was the hour o gloaming gray,
When herds come in frae fauld and pen;
A herd he saw a huntsman lie,
Says he, Can this be Laird Troughen?

'There's some will ca me Parcy Reed,
And some will ca me Laird Troughen;
It's little matter what they ca me,
My faes hae made me ill to ken.

'There's some will ca me Parcy Reed,
And speak my praise in tower and town;
It's little matter what they do now,
My life-blood rudds the heather brown.

'There's some will ca me Parcy Reed,
And a' my virtues say and sing:
I would much rather have just now
A draught o water frae the spring.'

The herd flung aff his clouted shoon
And to the nearest fountain ran;
He made his bonnet serve a cup,
And wan the blessing o the dying man.

'Now, honest herd, ye maun do mair,
Ye maun do mair, as I you tell;
Ye maun bear tidings to Troughend,
And bear likewise my last farewell.

'A farewell to my wedded wife,
A farewell to my brother John,
Wha sits into the Troughend tower
Wi heart as black as any stone.

'A farewell to my daughter Jean,
A farewell to my young sons five;
Had they been at their father's hand,
I had this night been man alive.

'A farewell to my followers a',
And a' my neighbours gude at need;
Bid them think how the treacherous Ha's
Betrayed the life o Parcy Reed.

'The laird o Clennel bears my bow,
The laird o Brandon bears my brand;
Wheneer they ride i the Border-side,
They'll mind the fate o the laird Troughend.'

As I was walking mine alane,
It was by the dawning o the day,
I heard twa brothers make their maine,
And I listned well what they did say.

The eldest to the youngest said,
'O dear brother, how can this be!
There was three brethren of us born,
And one of us is condemnd to die.'

'O chuse ye out a hundred men,
A hundred men in Christendie,
And we'll away to Dumfries town,
And set our billie Archie free.'

'A hundred men you cannot get,
Nor yet sixteen in Christendie;
For some of them will us betray.
And other some will work for fee.

'But chuse ye out eleven men,
And we ourselves thirteen will be,
And we'ill away to Dumfries town,
And borrow bony billie Archie.'

There was horsing, horsing in haste,
And there was marching upon the lee,
Untill they came to the Murraywhat,
And they lighted a' right speedylie.

'A smith, a smith!' Dickie he crys,
'A smith, a smith, right speedily,
To turn back the cakers of our horses feet!
For it is forward we would be.'

There was a horsing, horsing in haste,
There was marching on the lee,

264

Untill they came to Dumfries port,
And there they lighted right manfulie.

'There's six of us will hold the horse,
And other five watchmen will be;
But who is the man among you a'
Will go to the Tolbooth door wi me?'

O up then spake Jokie Hall
(Fra the laigh of Tiviotdale was he),
'If it should cost my life this very night,
I'll ga to the Tollbooth door wi thee.'

'O sleepst thou, wakest thow, Archie laddie?
O sleepst thou, wakest thow, dear billie?'
'I sleep but saft, I waken oft,
For the morn's the day that I man die.'

'Be o good cheer now, Archie lad,
Be o good cheer now, dear billie;
Work thou within and I without,
And the morn thou's dine at Cafield wi me.'

'O work, O work, Archie?' he cries,
'O work, O work? ther's na working for me;
For ther's fifteen stane o Spanish iron,
And it lys fow sair on my body.'

O Jokie Hall stept to the door,
And he bended it back upon his knee,
And he made the bolts that the door hang on
Jump to the wa right wantonlie.

He took the prisoner on his back,
And down the Tollbooth stairs came he;
Out then spak Dickie and said,
Let some o the weight fa on me;
'O shame a ma!' co Jokie Ha,
'For he's no the weight of a poor flee.'

The gray mare stands at the door,
And I wat neer a foot stirt she,
Till they laid the links out oer her neck,
And her girth was the gold-twist to be.

And they came down thro Dumfries town,
And O but they came bonily!
Untill they came to Lochmaben port,
And they leugh a' the night manfulie.

There was horsing, horsing in haste,
And there was marching on the lee,
Untill they came to the Murraywhat,
And they lighted a' right speedilie.

'A smith, a smith!' Dickie he cries,
'A smith, a smith, right speedilie,
To file off the shakles fra my dear brother!
For it is forward we wad be.'

They had not filtt a shakle of iron,
A shakle of iron but barely three,
Till out then spake young Simon brave.
'Ye do na see what I do see.

'Lo yonder comes Liewtenant Gordon,
And a hundred men in his company:'
'O wo is me!' then Archie cries,
'For I'm the prisoner, and I must die.'

O there was horsing, horsing in haste,
And there was marching upon the lee,
Untill they came to Annan side,
And it was flowing like the sea.

'I have a colt, and he's four years old,
And he can amble like the wind,
But when he comes to the belly deep,
He lays himself down on the ground.'

'But I have a mare, and they call her Meg,
And she's the best in Christendie;
Set ye the prisoner me behind;
Ther'll na man die but he that's fae!'

Now they did swim that wan water,
And O but they swam bonilie!
Untill they came to the other side,
And they wrang their clothes right drunkilie.

'Come through, come through, Lieutenant Gordon!
Come through, and drink some wine wi me!
For ther's a ale-house neer hard by,
And it shall not cost thee one penny.'

'Throw me my irons, Dickie!' he cries,
'For I wat they cost me right dear;'
'O shame a ma!' cries Jokie Ha,
'For they'll be good shoon to my gray mare.'

'Surely thy minnie has been some witch,
Or thy dad some warlock has been;
Else thow had never attempted such,
Or to the bottom thow had gone.

'Throw me my irons, Dickie!' he cries,
'For I wot thcy cost me dear enough;'
'O shame a ma!' cries Jokie Ha,
'They'll be good shakles to my plough.'

'Come through, come through, Liewtenant Gordon!
Come throw, and drink some wine wi me!
For ycoterday I was your prisoner,
But now the night I am set free.'

Clavers and his Highlandmen
Came down upon the raw, man,
Who, being stout, gave mony a clout,
The lads began to claw, then.
Wi' sword and targe into their hand,
Wi' which they were na slaw, man,
Wi' mony a fearfu' heavy sigh,
The lads began to claw, then.

O'er bush, o'er bank, o'er ditch, o'er stank,
She flang amang them a' man;
The Butter-box got mony knocks,
Their riggings* paid for a' then.   *backbones
They got their paiks,* wi' sudden straiks,   *blows
Which to their grief they saw, man;
Wi' clinkum clankum o'er their crowns,
The lads began to fa', then.

Hur skipt about, hur leapt about,
And flang amang them a', man;
The English blades got broken heads,
Their crowns were cleav'd in twa, then;
The durk and door made their last hour,
And prov'd their final fa', man;
They thought the devil had been there,
That play'd them sic a paw,* then.   *trick

The solemn league and covenant
Came whigging up the hills, man,
Thought Highland trews durst not refuse
For to subscribe their bills, then;
In Willie's name they thought nae ane
Durst stop their course at a', man;
But her nain sell, wi' mony a knock,
Cried, 'Furich,* Whigs awa', man.'   *hurry

Sir Evan Dhu, and his men true,
Came linking up the brink, man;

268

The Hogan Dutch they feared such,
They bred a horrid stink, then,
The true Maclean and his fierce men,
Came in amang them a', man;
Nane durst withstand his heavy hand,
A' fled and ran awa, then.

Oh on a ri! oh on a ri!
Why should she lose King Shames, man?
Oh rig in di! oh rig in di!
She shall break a' her banes, then;
With *furichinish*, and stay a while,
And speak a word or twa, man,
She's gie a straik out o'er the neck,
Before ye win awa, then.

O fie for shame, ye're three for ane!
Hur nain sell's won the day, man;
King Shames' red-coats should be hung up,
Because they ran away, then.
Had bent their brows, like Highland trues,
And made as lang a stay, man,
They'd sav'd their king, that sacred thing,
And Willie'd run away, then.

O cam' you her the fight to shun,
Or herd the sheep wi' me, man;
Or was ye at the Sherramuir,
And did the battle see, man?
I saw the battle, sair and teuch,
And reekin' red ran mony a sheuch,*   *furrow
My heart, for fear, ga'e sough for sough,
To hear the thuds, and see the cluds,
O' clans frae wuds, in tartan duds,
Wha glaum'd* at kingdoms three, man.   *grasped
Huh! hey dum dir-rum, hey dum dan,
Huh! hey dum dir-rum dey dan;
Huh! hey dum dir-rum, hey dum dan,
Huh! hey dum dir-rum dey dan.

The red-coat lads wi' black cockades,
To meet them were na slaw, man,
They rush'd and push'd, and bluid out gush'd,
And mony a bouk* did fa', man.   *body
The great Argyle led on his files,
I wat they glanced twenty miles,
They hough'd the clans like nine-pin kyles;
They hack'd and hash'd, while broad-swords clash'd,
And through they dash'd, and hew'd and smash'd,
Till feymen* died awa', man.   *those destined for death
Huh! hey etc.

But had you seen the philabegs,
And skyrin'* tartan trews, man,   *bright
When in the teeth they daur'd our Whigs,
And covenant true-blues, man.
In lines extended lang and large,
When bayonets opposed the targe,
And thousands hastened to the charge;
Wi' Highland wrath, they frae the sheath
Drew blades o' death, till out o' breath,
They fled like frighted do'es, man.
Huh! hey etc.

270

O' how de'il, Tam, can that be true?
The chase gaed frae the north, man;
I saw mysel' they did pursue
The horsemen back to Forth, man.
And at Dunblane, in my ain sight,
They took the brig wi' a' their might,
And straught to Stirling wing'd their flight,
But, cursed lot, the gates were shut,
And mony a huntit puir red-coat,
For fear amaist* did swarf,** man.   *almost **faint
Huh! hey etc.

My sister Kate cam' up the gate
Wi' crowdie* unto me, man;   *thick gruel
She swore she saw some rebels run
To Perth and to Dundee, man.
Their left-hand general had nae skill,
The Angus lads had nae guid-will
That day their neighbours' bluid to spill;
For fear, by foes, that they should lose
Their cogs o' brose,* they scared at blows,   *wooden bowls of
                                                porridge

And hameward fast did flee, man.
Huh! hey etc.

They've lost some gallant gentlemen
Amang the Highland clans, man;
I fear my Lord Panmure is slain,
Or in his enemies' hands, man.
Now wad ye sing this double fight,
Some fell for wrang, and some for right;
And mony bade the world guid night.
Say pell and mell, wi' musket knell,
How Tories fell, and Whigs to hell
Flew aff in frightened bands, man.
Huh! hey etc.

Adam Skirving's ballad 'The Ballad of Tranent Muir, or Prestonpans' is not so well known as his more popular 'Hey, Johnnie Cope', with its catchy tune, but in some ways it is more interesting. The reference at the start of the third verse to how the dragoons swore they would make them run, is to comments made by the officers during the march from Haddington when country people mingled with the troops. The officers were quite convinced that the Highlanders would never attack both infantry and cavalry in a combined force. They therefore assured the spectators that there would be no battle.

The reference to Menteith in the fifth verse is to the minister of Longformacus, a village in the Lammermuir Hills, who was a volunteer. The night before the battle he had encountered a Highlander relieving himself near Prestonpans and had tipped him over and taken his gun as a trophy. Simpson, in the sixth verse, was another volunteer minister, who was convinced he could persuade the rebels of the error of their ways by his pistols, of which he kept two in his pockets, two in his holsters and one in his belt. Neither of them appear to have distinguished themselves on the day of the battle.

Myrie, mentioned in the seventh verse, was a student of physic from Jamaica who had volunteered in Cope's army. According to the accounts he was 'miserably mangled by the broad swords'. Gardiner, as mentioned in the eighth verse, was killed. In fact he seems to have been mortally wounded and died the following morning tended by his servant in his own house. [Today there is a prominent memorial to his memory in the garden of the now roofless ruin.]

Lieutenant Smith of verse nine, incensed by the publication of the comments on his behaviour visited Haddington subsequently and sent Skirving a challenge to a duel. The latter pawkily replied that he was too busy on his farm. 'Gang awa back', he said 'and tell Mr Smith I havena the leisure to come to Haddington; but tell him to come here and I'll tak a look o' him and if I think I'm fit to fecht him, I'll fecht him; and if no, I'll do as he did—I'll rin awa.'

THE BATTLE OF PRESTONPANS
(See page 206)

The Chevalier, being void of fear,
Did march up Birsle brae, man,
And through Tranent, ere he did stent,
As fast as he could gae, man;
While General Cope did taunt and mock,
Wi' mony a loud huzza, man,
But ere next morn proclaim'd the cock,
We heard anither craw, man.

The brave Lochiel, as I heard tell,
Led Camerons on in clouds, man;
The morning fair, and clear the air,
They loos'd with devilish thuds, man.
Down guns they threw, and swords they drew,
And soon did chase them aff, man:
On Seaton crafts they buft* their chafts,**   *beat **jawbones
And gart them rin like daft, man.

The bluff dragoons swore, blood and oons!
They'd make the rebels run, man:
And yet they flee when them they see,
And winna fire a gun, man.
They turn'd their back, the foot they brake,
Such terror seiz'd them a', man,
Some wet their cheeks, some fyl'd their breeks,
And some for fear did fa', man.

The volunteers prick'd up their ears,
And vow gin they were crouse,* man!   *bold
But when the bairns saw't turn to earn'st,
They werena worth a louse, man.
Maist feck gade hame,* O fie for shame!   *stole off home
They'd better staid awa, man,
Than wi' cockade to make parade,
And do nae gude at a', man.

Menteith the great, when hersel shit,
Un'wares did ding him owre, man,

273

Yet wadna stand to bear a hand,
But aff fu fast did scour, man,
O'er Soutra Hill, ere he stood still,
Before he tasted meat, man.
Troth, he may brag of his swift nag,
That bore him aff sae fleet, man.

And Simpson, keen to clear the een
Of rebels far in wrang, man.
Did never strive wi' pistols five,
But gallopp'd wi' the thrang, man.
He turn'd his back, and in a crack
Was cleanly out o' sight, man,
And thought it best: it was nae jest,
Wi' Highlanders to fight, man.

'Mangst a' the gang, nane bade the bang
But twa, and ane was ta'en, man;
For Campbell rade, but Myrie staid,
And sair he paid the kane, man.
Four skelpe he got, was waur than shot,
Frae the sharp-edg'd claymore, man;
Frae mony a spout came running out
His recking het red gore, man.

But Gard'ner brave did still behave
Like to a hero bright, man;
His courage true, like him were few
That still despised flight, man.
For king, and laws, and country's cause,
In honour's bed he lay, man,
His life, but not his courage, fled,
While he had breath to draw, man.

And Major Bowle, that worthy soul,
Was brought down to the ground, man;
His horse being shot, it was his lot
For to get mony a wound, man.
Lieutenant Smith of Irish birth,
Frae whom he call'd for aid, man,

274

But full of dread, lap o'er his head,
And wadna be gainsaid, man.

He made sic haste, sae spurr'd his beast,
'Twas little there he saw, man;
To Berwick rade, and falsely said
The Scots were rebels a', man.
But let that end, for weel 'tis kend
His use and wonts to lie, man.
The Teague is naught, he never fought
When he had room to flee, man.

And Cadell, drest, amang the rest,
With gun and gude claymore, man,
On gelding gray he rode that day,
With pistols set before, man.
The cause was good, he'd spend his blood
Before that he would yield, man;
But the night before he left the core,*   *company
And never fac'd the field, man.

But gallant Roger, like a soger,
Stood and bravely fought, man;
I'm wae to tell, at last he fell,
And mae down wi' him brought, man.
At point of death, wi' his last breath,
Some standing round in ring, man,
On's back lying flat, he wav'd his hat,
And cried, 'God save the king!' man.

Some Highland rogues, like hungry dogs,
Neglecting to pursue, man.
About they fac'd, and, in great haste,
Upon the booty flew, man.
And they, as gain for all their pain,
Are deck'd wi' spoils of war, man;
Fu' bauld can tell how her nain sel
Was ne'er sae praw before, man.

At the thorn tree, which you may see
Bewest the meadow mill, man,

There mony slain lay on the plain,
The clans pursuing still, man.
Sic unco hacks, and deadly whacks,
I never saw the like, man;
Lost hands and heads cost them their deads,
That fell near Preston dyke, man.

That afternoon, when a' was done,
I gade to see the fray, man;
But I had wist what after past,
I'd better staid away, man:
On Seaton sands, wi' nimble hands,
They pick'd my pockets bare, man;
But I wish ne'er to dree sic fear,
For a' the sum and mair, man.

CULLODEN
(See page 218)

The heath-cock crawed o'er muir an' dale:
Red raise the sun o'er distant vale,
Our Norther clans wi' dinsome yell,
Around their chiefs were gath'ring.
'O, Duncan, are ye ready yet?
M'Donald, are ye ready yet?
O, Fraser, are ye ready yet?
To join the clans in the morning.'

On yonder hills our clans appear,
The sun back frae their spears shines clear;
The Southern trumps fall on my ear,
'Twill be an awfu' morning.
'O, Duncan', etc.

The Prince has come to claim his ain,
A stem o' Stuart's glorious name;
What Highlander his sword wad hain,
For Charlie's cause this morning.
'O, Duncan', etc.

Nae mair we'll chace the fleet, fleet roe,
O'er downie glen or mountain brow,
But rush like tempest on the foe,
Wi' sword an' targe this morning.
'O, Duncan', etc.

The contest lasted sair an' lang,
The pipers blew, the echoes rang,
The cannon roared the clans amang,
Culloden's awfu' morning.
'O, Duncan', etc.

Duncan now nae mair seems keen,
He's lost his dirk an' tartan sheen,
His bannet's stained that aince was clean
Foul fa' that awfu' morning.
'O, Duncan', etc.

277

But Scotland lang shall rue the day,
She saw her flag sae fiercely flee;
Culloden hills were hills o' wae,
It was an awfu' morning.
Duncan now nae mair, etc.

Fair Flora's gane her love to seek,
The midnight dew fa's on her cheek:
What Scottish heart that will not weep,
For Charlie's fate that morning?
Duncan now nae mair, etc.

The Battlefields

In order to understand any battle it is desirable to visit the battlefield and examine the ground. Points about tactics and strategy which had not been fully understood before then often fall into place without any difficulty. There is, indeed, a certain satisfaction in working out where the combatants went wrong and what they should have done in the circumstances. On occasions, of course, it is not as simple as that. Either there is insufficient information on the battle itself, or the exact position of the battlefield is uncertain. Here again, satisfaction may be had from working out the likeliest sites in accordance with the known facts.

After visiting a number of pre-1800 battlefields the least interested observer will note certain physical characteristics which begin to stand out as common to most. For instance, almost all such battlefields have a flat area of ground at least the size of a football pitch allowing reasonable room for manoeuvre and the tactical deployment of troops. There is also generally one position which is strategically suitable for defence due to natural characteristics of the ground, such as hills, gullies, rivers, bogs or similar features.

Naturally, in the case of battlefields some hundreds of years in the past, it is always necessary to visualize the ground as it was then, rather than as it is today. It is necessary to decide whether buildings, trees, even forests, were where they are today and whether what is perhaps now pastureland may then have been bog. These and similar questions the amateur battlefield enthusiast must ask himself, always remembering that his answers may be as good as anyone else's since most theories are difficult to disprove when all the witnesses have been dead several hundred years.

The descriptions of the battlefields which follow are by no means exhaustive. They merely outline what the reader may expect to find on the site and how to find it. Few of the Scottish battlefields have as good

281

an arrangement as that at Auldearn (see below), but a tour of the major battlefields is an illuminating experience, which brings Scotland and its countryside, including that of the Borders, into a new perspective.

AIRLIE CASTLE

'The Bonnie House of Airlie' near Kirriemuir in Angus was built originally in 1432 in an immensely strong natural position on a peninsula of land above the steep gorges formed by the junction of the Rivers Isla and Meldrum from where the magnificent views gave significance to the name. As the ballad relates it was destroyed by Argyll's forces in 1641. It was rebuilt in 1792 by David, Lord Ogilvy, who had been attainted for his part in the '45, but was allowed to return to Scotland in 1778 seventeen years after the death of his father the 4th Earl of Airlie. The only part of the old castle still standing was the outer apron wall across the neck of the peninsula, some thirty-five feet high and fifteen feet thick, but still to this day retaining the marks of fire caused by the Campbells in their attempts to destroy it. Using stones from the old outer walls a very comfortable family home was built on the old foundations. It is pleasant to record that despite the Campbells it remains one of the principal Airlie family homes.

ALFORD

Alford is a small village above the Don about thirty miles north-west of Aberdeen. There does not appear to be any monument or other marker on the site of the battlefield. The village itself, of course, was not in existence at the time of the battle in 1645. In those days what are now water meadows north of the village, bordering the River Don, would mostly have been bog. Taking the road westwards out of the village it is about half a mile to the hill where Montrose's troops took their stand, overlooking the ford across the Don below. The flat land beneath is where the mounted *mêlée* took place and the Covenanter army was caught with its back to the river in a hopeless strategical position. Their line of flight back towards Leslie is obvious and it is plain that the position, in a basin amid the surrounding hills, made it a natural site for Montrose's ambush.

AULDEARN

Auldearn stands out as by far the best presented battlefield in Scotland. Auldearn itself is a small village two and a half miles east of Nairn on the road to Inverness. There is a signpost to the Boath Doocat and Battlefield on the main road. The National Trust for Scotland has responsibility for the Boath Doocat set in the ruined remains of Boath Castle. Here, at a splendid vantage point, where Montrose's standard was set and Alasdair held out against greatly superior forces, is sited a coloured diagram and map of the battlefield with a well written description of the battle alongside. In a weatherproof 'Wareite' sandwich, this coloured map and diagram help one to appreciate the battle in a way that cannot be bettered. Congratulations must go to Colonel I. B. Cameron Taylor the Trust Historian for this first-class piece of imaginative visual presentation. From this vantage point with the assistance of the diagram it is easy to see how Montrose outguessed and outwitted Hurry and the Covenanter force. The National Trust for Scotland under Colonel Cameron Taylor's guidance have done an excellent job here. It is only a pity that all Scotlands battlefields do not have similar treatment.

BANNOCKBURN

Coxett Hill, where Bruce raised his standard during the battle, is a little over a mile out of Stirling on the A80 road to Glasgow. Known as the Borestone Site this is now in the care of the National Trust for Scotland. A circular palisade surrounds a large flagpole where the standard stood. Beyond this is a splendid statue of Bruce in full armour mounted on a caparisoned charger holding a battle axe and gazing forbiddingly over the nearby housing scheme. From November to March inclusive, the Information Centre next to the car park beside the road is closed and all the visitor will be able to see is C.d'O Pilkington Jackson's fine statue. This is not the fault of the National Trust for Scotland. They had an excellent weatherproof diagram and map of the battlefield along with a reinforced glass case containing fragments of the original borestone in which Bruce's standard was planted permanently on exhibition in the circular palisade, or 'rotunda'. Consistent hooliganism and destruction led to their reluctant removal. Now they are consigned during the winter months to the Information Centre. Here, except during November to March, the visitor may buy the excellent Trust booklets on the battle and battlefield by Colonel Cameron Taylor, the Trust Historian, and General Sir Philip Christison. Unfortunately the housing schemes and outgrowth of Stirling, St Ninians and the village of Bannockburn itself make it virtually impossible to see the battlefield clearly from this point today. It is necessary to turn onto the A9 at St Ninians then cross to the A905. This takes a route across the actual battlefield and it is possible to see clearly how the English were lured into a natural trap. Unlike the

'Borestone Site' the actual battlefield is probably little changed beyond the fact that it is now mostly farmland whereas it was then probably all rough pasture or heath.

CORICHIE

The Hill of Fare lies north of the B977 road between Echt and Banchory about fifteen miles west of Aberdeen. Close to the junction of the road leading to Crathes Castle on the north side of the B977 road there is a monument to the battle. This consists of a roughhewn slab of granite about sixteen feet high with a Gaelic inscription 'Remember the Day of Corichie'. A plaque announces that it was 'erected by the Deeside Field Club in 1951 to commemorate the Battle of Corichie fought on the Hill of Fare on 28th October 1562, between the forces of Mary Queen of Scots and the Earl of Huntly in which the former were victorious'. Beneath are the words 'Add Glory to the Past'.

On the hill beyond there is a flat area which looks like a suitable area for a battle, if Huntly was lying in wait for the Queen's party to pass. The fact that the hill is now planted for a considerable area makes it difficult to work out where the site of the battle could have been. The Deeside Field Club have wisely refused to commit themselves on this point.

CULLODEN

The site of the battlefield lies to the south of the B9006 road between Croy and Leanach, about seven miles east of Inverness. The graves of those killed in the battle, laid out by clans, are close beside the road to the south. A cairn to the fallen stands on the north of the road. Nearby the National Trust for Scotland, in whose care the battlefield is, have built an information centre. Anyone wishing to understand the battle cannot do better than buy their booklet on the subject and study the diagrams and maps they provide. The centre is not open from November to March, nor, at that time, is a plan of the battle set out for the visitor. The afforested areas, especially to the north, are of course comparatively recent in origin. Otherwise there has probably been little real change in the countryside, which remains mainly moor with boggy patches. Next to Bannockburn this is probably one of the most visited battlefields, but, emotional and sentimental factors aside, it is strategically of far less interest than nearby Auldearn.

DUNBAR

The site of the Battle of Dunbar is now marked by an irregularly shaped flattish boulder set in a circular base standing in front of a bus shelter on the main A1 road from Newcastle to Edinburgh on the left facing north at the junction to the large Portland Cement Works, just outside the southern turning to Dunbar. On the boulder is inscribed: '3rd September 1650. Here took place the Brunt or Essential agony of the Battle of Dunbar: Thomas Carlyle.' The road crosses the steep-sided Brox burn just beyond the signpost to Dunbar about half a mile further on. The wall on the right of the road surrounds Broxmouth Park and of course was not in existence in 1650. The modern Broxmouth House built in the eighteenth century stands on the site of an earlier building where Cromwell planned his attack. Looking south from the Brox burn on the A1, or from Broxmouth House it is easy to see how cramped the Scots left wing must have been against the slopes of Doon Hill. Although some of the trees in Broxmouth Park may have been in existence at the time of the battle the majority, especially the young plantations are, of course, completely new and change the ground where Cromwell's forces were deployed almost out of recognition. A drive round the Doon Hill and the Brunt, the hill above it, via Spott and the Brunt road is well worth while for the views it provides, as well as showing the tremendously strong strategic position held by the Scots both against Cromwell in 1650 and against Edward I in 1296.

FALKIRK

It is not easy to find the site of the Battle of Falkirk. Take the B803 Slamannan road out of Falkirk and turn right at the prominently signposted 'Hospital for Infectious Diseases' thus leaving Bantaskin Glen on the right. At the first fork of the road a monument will be seen on the right. It stands above Bantaskin House, which is not visible from this point. The monument is of the needle type in apricot coloured stone with no mark, or reference, to show what it represents or commemorates. However, it is easy to see from here how the Jacobite forces advancing from Torwood by way of Dunipace Steps took Hawley by surprise. It is not an easy line of advance and Hawley must have thought himself safe on Falkirk. Then it was, of course, a small village and needless to say the tower blocks of flats looming over the battlefield and the bulk of industrial Falkirk is entirely new. The ground near the monument is comparatively flat, but gullies intersect the hillside and it is understandable at once why the Hanoverian forces failed to withstand the Jacobites. After clawing their way up the slopes with the rain in their faces they would not have been able to withstand a charge. Although now intersected

285

with hedgerows and trees, the Falkirk 'Muir' would then have been moorland or indifferent grazing land devoid of trees or hedges.

FLODDEN

The village of Branxton is two miles south-east from Coldstream and is signposted on the A697. There is a monument a few hundred yards to the south-west of the village beside the road to the south on a small knoll. It is a plain cross on which is incised 'To the Brave of Both Nations'. It was erected in 1910. It is worth continuing on the same road along to Flodden Camp which is some two miles round by road. Viewing Branxton Edge from the site of the Scots' position it is clear that it was no threat to the Scots even if the English captured it. Equally it can be seen that the approach of Howard's forces over Twizel bridge would have been obscured. The short grass on the Cheviots would also have been very slippery. In 1513 there would have been no trees or hedges to obscure the views, but the haars, or mists, would have been quite as heavy and blinding as today.

GLENSHIEL

Beneath the shadow of the Five Sisters of Kintail and within sight of Eilean Donan Castle on its short isthmus jutting into Loch Alsh these are surely the most impressive surroundings imaginable for a battle. The National Trust for Scotland are proposing to erect one of their excellent maps produced by Colonel Cameron Taylor at their information centre here.

HARLAW

Take the B9001 out of Inverurie and turn left at the signpost pointing to Harlaw about a mile outside the town. It is a mile north of Balquhain (pronounced Bawhyne) mentioned in the ballad. At the site is erected surely the largest monument to any battle in Scotland. A hexagonal forty-five-foot-high, granite, crow-stepped erection like a miniature tower, it stands squatly on the scene of the battle. Around the top are incised the words 'To the Memory of Provost Robert Davidson and the Burgesses of Aberdeen who fell here in A.D. 1411'. A plaque on one side reads: 'Erected by the Burgh of Aberdeen A.D. 1911 Adam Maitland Lord Provost'. Another plaque reads simply: 'Harlaw July 24th A.D. 1411'. The ground is comparatively flat, sloping gently towards Inverurie and is now in part at least under the plough. Then it would certainly all have been moorland with no dry stone dykes or walls intersecting the fields. Nor, at that time, would there have been any houses in sight.

Haughs of Cromdale

From Grantown on Spey take the A95 road for Ballindalloch and turn right in Cromdale itself. From here there are superb views over the Spey Valley and the mountains beyond. It is easy to see how the Grants could have led the government forces in a surprise attack under cover of night from that direction. The effect of a thick mist at dawn would have been somewhat demoralizing. Equally it is easy to see how the Highlanders could make good their escape over the comparatively small Hills of Cromdale which are reasonably smooth heather and by Highland standards easy going. It is worth visiting the scene of this battlefield simply for the beauty of the surroundings, as with Glenshiel.

Inverlochy

The battlefield of Inverlochy is not marked. The principal fighting probably took place near to the square ruins of old Inverlochy Castle, opposite the British Aluminium Company's pipelines which sweep down the hillside steeply to Loch Linnhe. It could well have been down the line of the pipes themselves that Montrose's Highlanders charged on the encamped Campbell forces. It is easy to see that Argyll himself must have found his escape difficult despite the sweeps on his barge as the head of the loch is narrow at this point.

Pinned against the lochside his men had to fight or drown as many of them did. Although the old graveyard on the knoll above Inverlochy Castle appears to have no significance concerning the battle it is possible to view the site of the battlefield from there and make one's own assessments. Despite the main road to Inverness, Fort William looming near at hand, the petrol pumps, factories and housing, it is not difficult to visualize the battlefield as it must have been.

Killiecrankie

The Pass of Killiecrankie lies on the A9 Perth to Inverness road thirteen miles past Pitlochry on the road north. It is a narrow steep-sided, winding pass with the River Garry on one side and the hills rising steeply on the right. The plain beyond the Pass is the only flat ground in view. It is not a very large space for two armies to fight and it is plain that Claverhouse had the advantage of position and that Mackay and the government forces were hopelessly cramped and unable to manœuvre. Orrat House stands in the trees about five or six hundred yards from the road. At that time there would have been no trees. The River Garry would also have had a respectable depth of water in it, but is now almost dry due to hydro-electric schemes. The road would then have been no more than a stony track. There is no monument to the battlefield and no obvious marker beyond a standing stone in the field below Orrat House and many people must pass it without realizing that this was the battle where Claverhouse was killed. Some boulders below Orrat House may be gravestones of those killed.

LARGS

On the main A78 Largs to Fairlie coast road there is a needle type monument to the Battle of Largs. Looking at the area today it is easy to see how any fleet moored between the Cumbraes and the shore would be in a vulnerable position with a storm brewing. The countryside is now greatly changed and today the Norwegians would find themselves in danger of running ashore at the Nuclear Power Station at Hunterston.

LARRISTON

It is worth journeying from Bouchester Bridge south of Hawick via the B6357 down Liddesdale simply to appreciate the ballad 'Lock the door, Larriston'. The wild and lonely wastes of rough pastures, the mossy hags and rocky outcrops form a perfect background for the singing of this ballad. On one side Larriston and on the other Hermitage were the two castles blocking these invasion routes from the south. Standing sentinel in lonely isolation these two castles were the Scottish outposts. The atmosphere of each is still impressive and forbidding.

MUSSELBURGH FIELD, OR PINKIE

Turn off the northbound A1 at the Wallyford roundabout before Musselburgh on to the Dalkeith road A6094, then take the second turning to the right beyond Wallyford itself. The saucer-shaped depression between the railway and Falside Hill, behind Wallyford and the main road, is the scene of the battle. There is no monument visible in the neighbourhood. The best place to view the scene is from the bridge over the railway line. The Scots were encamped on Falside Hill towards Tranent the night before and could see the English near Musselburgh. Foolishly they came down from what was clearly a strong position. The ground towards Dalkeith would not then have been well-drained as it is today. Wallyford, of course, would not have existed and the area would have been rough pasture land with no dividing walls.

OTTERBURN AND SOUTHDEAN KIRK

On the main A68 Newcastle to Edinburgh road a mile beyond Otterburn

288

village on the right of the road is a monument known as the 'Percy Cross'. Fifteen-foot high it consists of a six-foot rough-hewn pillar on a circular base. 'Erected to commemorate the Battle of Otterburn fought 10 August 1388'. It would have been feasible to plan an ambush anywhere in this wild rolling moorland of Redesdale and the battle might well have ended near the inn at Otterburn itself on the flatter land, which could have been the scene of the encounter between the pursuing Scots and the relieving Bishop of Durham's forces. Prior to the arrival of the Forestry Commission in the area there would have been no trees visible anywhere.

To find Southdean Kirk turn left just beyond Carter Bar and follow the road for a little over two miles and the ruins are on the left of the road, between a farmhouse and farmyard. It was here the Scots leaders met prior to the Battle of Otterburn.

PHILIPHAUGH

The battlefield of Philiphaugh is easily found across the Ettrick Water to the east of Selkirk, between the river and the A707 road. The long flat plain is the only area around there where an army might reasonably camp. There is no monument visible near the scene and the fields have been deep ploughed within the last few years so that all traces of the trenches dug by the royalists have now vanished beyond trace. There is in fact a monument in the grounds of Philiphaugh House, the property of Sir William Strang Steel. It is an ivy-grown stone-cobbled cairn about twenty feet high and eighteen yards round the base. Inserted on one side is a plaque: 'Erected by Sir John Murray, Bart. To the Memory of the Covenanters who fought and gained the Battle of Philiphaugh on 13th September, 1645'. The ballad mentions 'Harewoodhead' which is at the west end of the plain close to the site of the cairn.

PRESTONPANS

The site of the battlefield is on the A198 road below Tranent on the A1. The battlefield is roughly bounded by Seton House on the one side and Preston on the other, then by Bankton House and the coal bings, or slag heaps, on the south of the railway line. The towering mass of Cockenzie Power Station, the railway, the main road and the colliery sites have all altered the scene considerably, but it is still easy enough to see how secure Cope must have felt his position to be. There is a twelve-foot high, crow-step, gabled, six-foot square monument marked simply '1745', on the left of the road heading east, close to Preston. Beyond lies the roofless remains of Bankton House, Colonel Gardiner's old residence. In the derelict garden stands a needle-style monument, more imposing than that to the actual battle, commemorating his death.

RAID OF THE REIDSWIRE

It is worth stopping at Carter Bar on the A68 after passing northwards through Redesdale just for the view of the Cheviots below. The reidswire is the area to the north of the road when heading for Jedburgh from Otterburn, just before the road starts to descend. There are parking places on either side of the road for, as in the days of the Meetings of the Wardens of the Marches, it is still a popular stopping place. It is easy to see where the stalls would have been placed and the meeting held. Once the Redesdale men were engaged in looting it is understandable that they might not have seen the approach of fresh Scots forces from Jedburgh ready to turn the tables on them. As elsewhere there would have been no trees visible, only moor and grass at the time of the affray.

RULLION GREEN

Nearly two miles north of Penicuik on the Edinburgh road, the site of the Battle of Rullion Green may be seen on the left of the road when heading north. A knoll of ground stands out as the strong position on which the Covenanters based their defence and which they held against two charges of Dalziel's horse. Looking at the ground it is only remarkable that the horse succeeded in taking the position, but it must be remembered that the charges were probably not driven home. They would merely have trotted within range and then discharged a volley and trotted away again. There appears to be no monument visible, but a house on the right of the road, nearby, has a cross on the gable end, which is presumably to commemorate the battle.

SHERIFFMUIR

On the A9 through Bridge of Allan towards Dunblane there is a signpost to Sheriffmuir. The road climbs up spectacularly providing sensational views over the windings of the upper Forth. The site of the battle is unmarked, but Sheriffmuir itself remains almost unchanged. It is a flat peaty moorland area with little to distinguish it. It is well worth the visit for the views in all directions, but particularly those over the Forth on the route which must have been taken by those of Argyll's forces fleeing back to the safety of Stirling.

290

Bibliography

Aytoun, W. E.: *The Ballads of Scotland:* 2 vols: 1858
Barrett, C. R. B.: *Battles and Battlefields of England:* 1896
Brown, Peter Hume: *History of Scotland:* 3 vols: 1911
Buchan, John: *Montrose:* 1928
Burns, Robert: *Complete Works:* Ed. William Scott Douglas: 1890
Burton, John Hill: *History of Scotland:* 8 vols: 1873
Campbell, Alexander: *Albyn's Anthology:* 2 vols: 1816–19
Campbell, John Lorne: *Highland Songs of the Forty-Five:* 1872
Caw, George: *The Poetical Museum:* 1784
Chambers, Robert: *The Scottish Ballads:* 1829
Child, Francis James: *English & Scottish Ballads:* 8 vols: 1856–9; *English &*
    Scottish Popular Ballads: 5 vols: 1882–98
Clarendon, Edward, Earl of: *History of the Rebellion:* Ed. Murray: 1888
Cromek, R. H.: *Select Scottish Songs:* 2 vols: 1810
Cunninghan, Allan: *Songs of Scotland:* 4 vols: 1825
Dunbar, William: *Collected Poems:* Ed. W. Mackay Mackenzie: 1932
Evans, Thomas: *Old Ballads:* 2 vols: 1777; Revised, R. H. Evans: 4 vols:
    1810
Finlay, J.: *Scottish Historical & Romantic Ballads:* 2 vols: 1808
Firth, C. H.: *Cromwell's Army:* 1902
Gardner, Alex: *The Ballad Minstrelsy of Scotland:* London: 1893
Gwynne, John: *Military Memoirs of the Civil War:* Ed. Scott: 1822
Herd, David: *Ancient & Modern Scottish Songs:* 1776
Hogg, James: *Jacobite Relics:* 2 vols: 1819
Johnson, James: *The Scots Musical Museum:* 6 vols: 1787 1803
Kerr & Richardson: *Scottish Songs, Ancient & Modern:* 2 vols: 1869
Kinloch, G. R.: *Ancient Scottish Ballads:* 1827
Laing, Alexander: *The Thistle of Scotland: Ancient Ballads:* 1823
Laing, Andrew: *History of Scotland:* 4 vols: 1900–06
Mackay Mackenzie, W: *The Battle of Bannockburn:* 1913
Maidment, James: *Scottish Ballads & Songs:* 1859; *Scottish Ballads & Songs:*
    2 vols: 1868; *A North Countrie Garland:* 1869
Morris J. E.: *Bannockburn:* 1914

291

Napier, Mark: *Memorials of Montrose*: 1848–50

Percy, Bishop: *Reliques of Ancient English Poetry*: Ed.: H. B. Wheatley; 3 vols: 1876–7

Ramsay, Allan: *The Evergreen, A Collection of Scots Poems*: 2 vols: 1724; *A New Miscellany of Scots Songs*: 1727; *The Miscellany*: 3 vols: 1733; *The Tea-Table Miscellany*: 1750

Ritson, Joseph: *Scottish Song*: 2 vols: 1794

Scott, Sir Walter: *Minstrelsy of the Scottish Border*: 3 vols: 1802; Ed.: J. G. Lockhart: 4 vols: 1833

Spottiswode, John: *History of the Church and State of Scotland*: 1203–1625: 3 vols: 1851

Smith, R. A.: *The Scottish Minstrel*: 6 vols: 1820–4

Stewart, David, Major General, of Garth, *Sketches of the Character, Manners and Present State of the Highlanders of Scotland*: Edinburgh: 2 vols: 1822

Whitelaw, Alexander: *Book of Scottish Ballads*: 1845

Wishart, George: *Memoirs of James, Marquis of Montrose*: Ed.: Murdoch and Simpson: 1893

Index

Aberdeen, 39, 49, 124, 137, 138, 141, 186, 282
Aboyne, Lord, 124
Airds Moss, 177
Airlie Castle, 9, 128, 282
Airlie, Dowager Countess of, 9
Airlie, Earl of, 128, 137, 149
Albany, 58–9
Albany, Duke of, 72
Albemarle, Lord, 217
Albyn's Anthology, Campbell's, 117
Alexander, Earl of Buchan, 49
Alexander, Lord of the Isles, 55
Alexander II, of Scotland, 21
Alexander III, 21–2, 24
Alford, 135, 145–6
Alford, ballad of battle, 148; battlefield, 282
Allan Water, 193
Alnwick, 40, 56, 60, 62
Alsh, Loch, 198, 286
America, United States of, 217
Ancient Scottish Ballads, 130
Anderson, a local man, 204
Angus, 28, 49, 100, 282
Angus, Archibald, 'Bell the Cat', 58
Angus, Earl of, 36, 56, 59, 83, 95, 99
Annandale, 72
Anne, Queen of England, 191–2
Appin, Stewarts of, 139
Arbroath, 55; Declaration of, 32
Archie o' Ca'field, 106, 117
Ardnamurchan, 185
Argyll, 28, 64, 150, 156–7, 164, 190, 192–193, 282
Argyll, Earl of, 59, 99, 100, 106, 124, 128, 132, 135, 138–9, 140, 146, 149, 290
Armada, 99
Armstrong, Johnnie, 72–3; ballad of, 74–8
Armstrong, Willie, of Kinmont, 107
Armstrongs, 80, 106
Arran, 21–2

Arran, Earl of, 83, 95, 106
Asloun, Castle of, 149
Atholl, 72, 135, 180; Highlanders, 139
Auchinbreck, Sir Duncan Campbell of, 139, 140
Auld Alliance, 24, 56
Auldearn, 143–4, 163, 186, 282–3
Australia, 217
Ayala, Pedro de, 60
Ayrshire, 165, 168–9; coast, 22
Awe, Loch, 139

Badenoch, 138; Highlanders, 146
Badenoch, Wolf of, 49
Balfour, John of Kinloch, 168, 170
Baliol, Edward, 36–8
Baliol, John, 24, 36
Ballachulish, 191
Balquhain, 286
Balrinnes, 100
Baillie, General William, 139, 141–2, 145–147, 149–50
Banchory, 284
Bankton, Estate & House, 202, 289
Bannockburn, 14, 27, 30–3, 38, 59, 64, 283
Bantaskin House, 211, 205
Baptists, 64
Batal, 28, 30
Batinghope, 101
Beauties of Gaelic Poetry, 158
Bedford, Earl of, 92
Ben Nevis, 110
Berwick, 24, 28, 37, 59, 154, 161, 204
Berwick Castle, 56
Bewcastle, 107
Birsley Brae, 204
Bishops Wars, 132
Black Agnes, 37
Black Watch, 199
Blackness, 59; Blackness; Castle, 96

Blair, 135, 139; Blair Atholl, 181; Blair Castle, 180
Bland, General, 217
Bleith, Captain, 169
Boath Doocat, 282–3
Boece's History, 49
Bohun, Sir Henry de, 29
Bonchester Bridge, 288
Bonny Dundee, 178–9
Bonny Earl of Murray, 96–8, 246–7
Bonny House o' Airlie, 123; ballad of, 130–1
Bonny John Seton, 123; ballad of, 126–7
Border Minstrelsy, Scott's, 117
Border Minstrelsy of Scotland, Alexander Gardner's, 100
Borderer's Table Book, Richardson's, 102
Borlum, Mackintosh of, 192
Borestone Site, 283–4
Bothwell, Earl of, 90, 91, 150
Bothwell Bridge, 168, 174–7
Boyds, the, 56
Braemar, 192
Braes o' Killicrankie, ballad of, 183–4
Brander, Pass of, 139
Bramstone, misnaming of Brankston in ballad, 66
Brankston, Battle of; English name for Flodden, 66
Branxholme, Sir Walter Scott, of, 106, 109
Branxton, 62–3, 286
Breadalbane, 191
Breadalbane, Earl of, 190
Brechin, 141–2
Broxburn, 161–2, 285
Broxmouth Park House, 285
Bruce, Edward, 30
Bruce, King Robert, 26–30, 32–3, 36–7, 59; statue of, 283
Brunt and Doon Hill, 161
Buccleuch, 106–9
Buchan, Earl of, 28, 49, 59
Burgh Sands, 26
Burleigh, 146
Burns, Robert, 14, 33, 193
Burnt Candlemas, 38
Bushell, Captain, 199
Bute, Island of, 21–2, 28

Caithness, 157
Calder, 165
Calvin, 123
Cameron, Donald of Lochiel, 20
Camerons of Lochiel, 180, 181, 185
Cameronians, 177, 185

Campbell, 55, 132, 139, 140, 190–1, 201, 209, 282
Campbell, Dugald, 128
Campbell, Sir Duncan, of Auchinbreck, 139–140
Campbell of Glenorchy, 190
Campbell of Lawers, 144, 163
Campbell of Lochinzell, 100
Candlemas, Burnt Feast of, 38
Cannon, Col Alexander of Galloway, 185
Cape Passaro, 198
Carbisdale, battle of, 157
Cargill, Donald, 177
Carlisle, 38–40, 209; Carlisle Castle, 106–8
Carlanrig Churchyard, 73
Carlyle, Thomas, 285
Carmichael, Sir John, 91
Carrick, 28
Carron, 211
Carse, of Bannockburn, 29–30
Carter Bar, 39, 92, 289–90
Caw's *Poetical Museum*, 117
Cessford, Kerr of, 56
Charles I, 123, 135, 156, 157
Charles II, 157, 160, 163–4, 177
Charles, Edward Stuart, 201–4, 209
Chattan, the Clan, 217
Cheviot, The Hunting of the, 42, 233
Cheviots, 92, 101, 286, 290
Chevy Chase, 42, 233
Child, Professor F. J., 11, 12, 23–4, 42–3, 49, 51, 83, 86, 100–1, 109, 117, 193
Christian, King of Norway, 56
Christison, General Sir Philip, 283
Clanranald, 139, 180, 217
Claverhouse, John Graham of, 169–70, 177–178, 180–1, 287
Clearances, 217
Cleland, Col Sir William, 185
Clyde, River, 174; Firth of, 21
Cobham's Dragoons, 212
Cochrane, favourite of James III, 58
Cockburn, Mrs Patrick, 69
Cockenzie Power Station, 289
Coldingham Abbey, 59
Coldstream, 286
Colinton, 105
Collingwood, Cuthbert, English prisoner, 92
Committee of Eastes, 124, 128
Comyns, or Cummings, 28
Connel, 139
Convention, the, 178
Cope, Sir John, 201–6, 289
Corichie, 85–6, 100, 284; ballad of, or Hill of Fare, 87–9

Corryarrack Pass, 202
Covenant, The National, 123–4, 128
Covenanters, 124, 132, 135–6, 138, 140, 142, 146, 149–51, 156–7, 160–5, 168, 174, 177
Coxett Hill, 29, 283
Crafford, Mr, Cornet to Claverhouse, 169
Crathes Castle, 284
Crawford, Earl of, 59, 156
Crawford, 55, 64
Crecy, 37
Crianlarich, 139
Crichtons, 55
Cromdale, battle of, 190
Cromwell, 146, 152, 156–7, 160–4, 285
Croy, 284
Crozier, 101
Culachy, 140
Culloden, 14, 209, 216, 218, 284
Cumberland, Duke of, 39, 64, 215, 217
Cumbraes, Great and Little, 21–2

Dacre, Lord, 64
Dalkeith, 40, 83, 92, 288
Dalnacardoch, 201
Dalzell's *Scottish Poems of the 16th Century*, 100
Dalziel, General Tam, 165, 290
Darien, Isthmus of, 192
Darnley, 91
Dauphin, 85
David II, 36, 38
David, son of Duke of Albany, 48
Davidson, Robert, Provost of Aberdeen, 49, 286
Dayholm of Kershope, 107
Death of Parcy Reed, ballad, 103–5, 258–63
Debatable land, 107
Declaration of Arbroath, 32
Deeside, 86, 142
Deeside Field Club, 284
Deloney's Pleasant History of John Winchcomb, etc., 66
Derby, 209, 215
Denmark, Margaret of, 22
Dingwall, 49
Donald, Earl of Mar, 87
Donald of the Isles, 48–9
Don, River, 145, 282
Donibristle, 96
Doon Hill, 161, 285
Douglas, 55, 72
Douglas, Archibald, Earl of Fife, 39
Douglas, Earls of, Red and Black, 36, 56

Douglas, James, Earl of, 39, 41
Douglas, Sir Archibald, 37
Douglas, Sir James, 27–8, 30
Doune, 142
Drumclog, 174, 177; ballad of, 171–3; battle of, 169
Dryburgh, 37, 39
Duddingstone, 202
Dunfermline, 22
Dunfermline, Earl of, 185
Dumfries, 28, 37, 56, 134
Dumfries, Tolbooth, 117
Dumfriesshire, 164
Dunbar, 22, 32, 37, 56, 152, 160–3, 202; battle of, 24, 284–5
Dunbar Drove, 163
Dunbar, William, 13, 55, 57–8, 60
Dunblane, 193, 290
Dundee, 141, 198
Dundee, Claverhouse, Earl of, 169
Dunipace Steps, 211, 285
Dunkeld, 141
Dupplin Moor, 37
Durham, 38, 40; Bishop of, 41, 289
Durham Cathedral, 163

Earlston, 66
Earn, the river, 37
East Lothian, 37
Echt, 284
Edinburgh, 27–9, 38–9, 59–60, 79, 123, 139, 150, 157, 165, 191, 202, 285, 288
Edward I, 24–6, 28, 33, 79, 161, 285
Edward II, 27–9, 38
Edward III, 36–7
Edward IV, 56, 58
Edward VI, 79, 83
Eilean Donan Castle, 198, 286
Elcho, Lord, 136, 146
Elgin, 28, 140, 142
Elliott, Miss Jane, 69
Elliot of Larriston, 79–80, 90
Elliots, 106
Elliot of Liddesdale, 90
Elizabeth, Queen of England, 99, 106–7, 100, 108
English & Scottish Popular Ballads, 11
Eric, King of Norway, 24
Eriskay, 200
Errol, Earl of, 59, 99–101
Esk, River, 108, 142
Etal, 61
Etive, Loch, 139
Ettrick Forest, 25, 28, 42
Ettrick Shepherd, 12

Ettrick Water, 151, 288
Ever Green, the, 49, 92

Fairlie, 288
Fairlie Roads, 21, 22
Fairnielee, 69
Falkirk, 25, 27–9, 209, 211, 215, 285–6
Falkirk Muir, ballad, 213–4
Falside Hill, 202, 288
Farnston, 92
Farquharsons, 217
Fenwick family, 92
Fife, 141
Fife, Archibald Douglas, Earl of, 39
Finlay's Scottish Ballads, 96
Firth of Forth, 192
Five Sisters of Kintail, 286
Flodden, 60–2, 65–6, 69, 217, 286
Flodden Field, ballad of, 67–8
Flowers of the Forest, 69, 70–1
Forbes, 49, 86, 145
Ford, 61
Forres, 28, 142
Forster, Sir John, 92
Fort Augustus, 139, 199, 215
Fort George, 199
Fort William, 199, 215, 287
Forthar Castle, 128
France, 24, 61
Frasers, 217

Gallows Hill, 145
Gardiner, Col, 201–2, 204, 272, 290
Gardner, Alexander, 100
Garioch, 49
Garry, River, 180, 287
Gaveston, Piers, 27
George I, of Hanover, 192
General Assembly, 124
Glasgow, 96, 199, 210, 283
Glencoe, 139
Glenfinnan, 201
Glengarry, 139, 217
Glenlivet, battle of, 100–1
Glenorchy, 139
Glen Roy, 140
Glenshiel, 198, 286–7
Glen Spean, 139
Gordon, Alexander, 174
Gordon, Earl of Huntly, 85
Gordon, Lord, 141–2, 144, 146–7, 149, 209
Gordon, Nathaniel, 137–8, 150
Gordon, Sir Patrick, 100
Gordon, William of Earlston, 174
Gordons, 66, 100, 209, 217

Graham, John of Claverhouse, 169–70, 174, 177–8
Graham, Patrick, 135
Grahams, 108
Grant, Laird of, 185
Grantown, 287
Grants, 140, 209, 217, 287; of Invermoriston, 217
Grassmarket, 199
Great Britain, 191
Great Glen, 199
Great Romancer of the Borders, 109–10
Gretna, 55
Grey, Lord, 59
Guardians, governing realm, 24
Gustavus Adolphus, 136

Hackston, of Rathillet, 168
Haddington, 85, 161, 202, 272
Hakin, King of Norway, 21–2
Halidon Hill, 37
Halket, Elizabeth, 22
Hall, Kitty, 102
Halls, 101
Hamilton, Duke of, 156–7
Hamilton, Robert, 169
Hamilton, Town of, 174
Hammer of the Scots, 26, 33
Hanover, George I of, 192
Hanoverian Succession, 191
Hardyknute, ballad of, 22; Scots hero, 23, 100
Harewoodhead, 289
Harlaw, 24, 48–9, 51–4, 286
Hastings, Colonel, 181
Haughs o' Cromdale, The, 13, 177, 185, 187–9, 287
Hawick, 288
Hawley, General Henry, 210–12, 217, 285
Haylie, the plain of, 21
Hays, 100
Henry VII, 61
Henry VIII, 61, 79, 83
Hepburn, of Hailes, 56
Hepburn's Horse, at Bannockburn, 30
Herd, David, 12
Hermitage Castle, 90, 288
Hertford, Earl of, 79
Hey Johnnie Cope, 13, 206, 272
Hey tuttie, taitie, 33
Hill of Fair, or Corichie, 86–9, 100
Hills of Cromdale, 287
Hogg, James, 12, 42, 69, 80, 181, 183, 212
Hogg, Mrs, 12
Holyrood, 79

Howard, Lord Thomas, High Admiral, 62, 79, 286
Hume, Earl of, 59, 204
Hundred Years War, 38
Hunterston, 21, 288
Hunting, of the Cheviot, 42, 233
Huntly, Earl of, 59, 83, 85–6, 95, 99, 101, 284
Hurry, Gen Sir John, 141–6, 156, 283
Huske, Gen, 217

Independence, Wars of, 38
Independent Companies of Highland Volunteers, 199
Inverkeithing, 163
Inverlochy, 140, 287
Inveraray, 139
Inverness, 22, 49, 55, 140, 199, 202, 282, 284, 287
Inverurie, 286
Isla, River, 282
Isles, Alexander, Lord of the, 55
Isles, Donald of the, 48
Isles, Macdonald of the, 28
Isthmus of Darien, 191
Italy, 61

Jack with the Feather, 66
Jacke of Newberie, 66
Jacobite Relics, 181, 193, 212, 217
Jacobites, 198, 200–2, 205, 285
Jamaica, 272
James I, 48, 55
James II, 56–7, 64
James III, 22, 56–9
James IV, 59–60, 62–6, 72
James V, 72, 79
James VI of Scotland, I of England, 90, 95, 99, 106, 107, 109, 123, 164
James VII and II, 177–8, 181, 193, 198
James VIII and III, 92–3, 98, 201
Jedburgh, 39, 79, 90, 91, 290
Jock o' the Side, 117–8, 122
Johnnie Cope's Road, 204
Johnson's Musical Museum, 34, 96
Johnston, Lt-Col, 124
Johnstone, 99, 106, 117
Julius II, Pope, 61

Keith, town of, 145
Keith, George, Earl Marischal, 198
Keith, Sir Robert, 28, 31
Keiths, 49
Kelso, 79
Kennedy, Bishop of St Andrews, 56

Keppoch, 139, 217
Kerr of Cessford, 56
Kershope, 107
Kilcumin, 139
Killicrankie, The Braes o', 177, 183–4
Killiecrankie, Pass of and battlefield, 180, 287
Kilgour, Lord, 135–6
Kilnockie, Johnnie Armstrong, Laird of, 73
Kilsyth, battle of, 149–50
Kinbuck, near Dunblane, 193
Kincardine, 132
Kinloch, John Balfour of, 168, 170
Kinmont Willie, 106–9, 111–6
Kintyre, 28
Kirremuir, 282
Knox, John, 91
Kyle, 28

Laign, Alexander, 147
Lambert, Major-Gen, 162–3
Lammermuir Hills, 272
Lanark, 28, 149, 169
Lanarkshire, 165
Lancashire, 157, 192
Lancaster, 56
Langside, battle of, 91
Largs, battle of, 14, 21, 24, 288
Larriston, 288
Larriston, Elliot of, 79, 90, see *Lock the door Larriston*
Lauder, 27, 29, 58
Lawers, Campbells of, 144, 163
Leanach, 284
Learnmonth, Major, 165
Leith, 79, 160
Lennox, 28, 64, 95
Lennox Stewarts, 36
Leslie, village of, 147, 282
Leslie, Gen Sir David, 151–2, 160–1, 163–4
Leslies, 49, 86
Leven, 135, 139, 141
Liddesdale, 102, 107
Lindsay of Pitscottie, 72
Lindsays, 55
Linlithgow, 120, 212
Lion, HMS, 200
Lion of Liddesdale, 90
Little Jock Elliot, 90
Livingston, of Airds, 165
Livingstone, Sir Thomas, 185
Livingstones, the, 55
Lochaber, 55, 192
Loch Awe, 139
Loch Eil, 140

Loch Etive, 139
Loch Fyne, 139
Loch Linnhe, 199, 287
Loch Ness, 139, 199
Loch Tay, 139
Lochiel, Cameron of, 180, 181, 185
Lochleven Castle, 91
Lockerbie Lick, 99
Lock the door Larriston, 80–2, 288
Lom, Ian, 158
London, 191, 200
Lorn, 139
Loudon Hill, 26, 168–9, 171–3
Loudon, Lord, 204
Louis XIV, 192
Lyric Gems of Scotland, 129, 183

Macdonald, Alasdair, 135–7, 144, 150, 283
Macdonald of Boisdale, 200
Macdonald of Glencoe, 190
Macdonald of Skye, 180, 209
Macdonalds, 139
Macdonells of Glengarry, 180
Macdougals, 28
MacIan, 190–1
Mackay, Gen, 180, 185, 287
Mackays, 209
Mackenzie, publisher of *Beauties of Gaelic Poetry*, 158
Mackenzies, 209
Mackintosh of Borlum, 192
Mackintosh, Lord & Lady, 209
Maclean, 99, 100
Macleans, 180–1; of Morven and Mull, 139
Macleod, Neil, of Assynt, 157–8
Macleods, 209
Magus Muir, 168
Maidment, John, 124
Maitland, Lord Provost Adam, 286
Man, Isle of, 22
Mar, 28, 49
Mar, Alexander earl of, 50–1
Mar, Donald, earl of, 37
March, Earl of, 40–1
Marches, on border, 90–1
Margaret, of Denmark, 22
Margaret, Maid of Norway, 24, 56
Margaret, Queen, 61, 66
Marischal, Earl Keith, 198
Marlborough, 192
Mary of Guise, 79
Mary, Queen of England, wife of William III, 178
Mary Stuart, Queen of Scotland, 79, 83, 85, 95, 284

Maryculter, 86
Master of Madderty, 135–6
Master of Stair, 190
Maxwell, 99, 117
Mearns, 28, 49
Meggatland, 73
Meldrum, River, 282
Menteith, district, 28
Menteith, 272
Methven, battle of, 26
Middle Shires, 123
Midsummer day 1314, 27
Mill Hill, a farm near Asloun, 147
Minstrelsy of the Scottish Border, 12, 41, 93, 109, 152, 165, 170, 174
Monk, Gen, 164
Monmouth, Duke of, 174
Montgomery, Sir Hugh, 41
Montrose, town of, 198
Montrose, James Graham, Marquis, 124–5, 128, 132, 134–40, 147, 149, 150–2, 156, 158, 160, 163, 180–1, 186, 282–3
Montrose's Campaigns, 14
Moray, the district, 28, 142
Moray, Sir Andrew of Bothwell, 37
Moray, Earl of, 27, 28, 30, 85–6
Moray, Elizabeth, 95
Moray, James, Earl of, 95
Moray, Randolph, Earl of, 37
Mordaunt, General, 217
Morton, Regent, 91–2
Morton Tower, 107
Mount Teviot, 69
Munros, 209
Murray, Andrew, 25
Murray, Bonnie Earl of, 95, 97–8, 117
Murray, Countess of, 96
Murray, Earl of, 40–1, 95–6
Murray, Lord of Gask, 136
Murray, Lord George, 202, 204, 212, 215
Murray, Sir John, Bart., of Tullibardine, 289
Musselboorrowe Field, 83
Musselburgh, 83, 160; Musselburgh Field, 79, 84
Myrie, Jamaican student at Prestonpans, 272

Nairn, 28, 142, 215, 282
Naseby, battle of, 146
National Covenant, 123
National Trust for Scotland, 283–4, 286
Ness, Loch, 139
Neville's Cross, 39
Newcastle, 40, 62, 117, 209, 285
Newcastle, Duke of, 134
Nicolson, Sheriff, 158

298

Nisbet Moor, 48
Nordreys, 22
Norfolk, Duke of, 79
Norham, 61
North Country Garland, 124
Northumberland, 25, 40, 48, 102
Northumberland, Earl Percy of, 40
Norway, 21, 24, 56
New Zealand, 217

Og, Angus, 28
Ogilvy, Alexander Stewart Earl of Mar and, 49
Ogilvy, Lord and Lady, 128
Ogilvies, 55, 149, 217
Ogle, James, 92
Orkney, 22, 56, 157
Old Pretender, 192, 198
Ormiston, 69
Ormonde, Duke of, 198
Orrat House, 181, 287–8
Otterburn, 24, 36, 40, 43–7, 48, 288
Outer Hebrides, 200
Oxford, 136
Oykel, River, 157

Parcy Reed, 95, 101
Pass of Brander, 139
Pass of Killiecrankie, 180
Penicuik, 290
Pentland Hills, Ballad of, 166–7
Percy, Bishop, 12
Percy Cross, 289
Percy, Earl of Northumberland, 40–1
Percy Ms, 42, 83
Percy's *Reliques*, 23
Perth, 26, 37–8, 55, 135–6, 142, 185, 192, 199, 202, 210, 287
Perth, Treaty of, 22
Peterhead, 198
Philip II, of Spain, 99
Philphaugh, 149, 151–6, 289
Pilkington Jackson, C. d'O, sculptor, 283
Pinkie, battle of, 202–3
Pitlochry, 287
Pitscottie, Lindsay of, 72
Plain of Pinkie, 00
Pleasant History of John Winchcomb, 66
Political Museum, Caw's, 117
Pope, Jullius II, 61
Porteous Riots, 199
Preston, East Lothian, 202
Preston House, 289
Preston, Lancs, 157
Prestonpans, 200, 202, 206, 212, 272, 289

Raid of the Reidswire, 49, 90–4, 100, 290
Ramsay, Allan, 12, 49, 73, 92, 96
Randolph, Earl of Moray, 37
Rathillet, Hackston of, 168
Red Bull of Dacre, 64
Red Harlaw, 49
Redesdale, 92, 101, 289–90
Reedwater, 101
Reformation, 123–4
Regent Morton, 91
Reliques, the Percy, 23
Remonstrants, 163
Renfrew, 28
Resolutioners, 163
Richard II, 39
Richard III, 59
Richmond, 27
Richardson, 102
Ripon, 27
Rob Roy, 193
Robert II, 39, 48, 57
Robert III, 48, 57
Rollo, Sir William, 138, 152
Roseneath Castle, 139
Ross, district, 28, 157
Ross, Earl of, 21, 56
Ross, Earldom of, 48
Rothes, 64
Roxburgh, 27, 69, 91
Roxburgh Castle, 56
Roy Bridge, 140
Rullion Green, 158, 165–8, 290
Ruthvens, 55

St Andrews, 168
St Giles Cathedral, 123
St Ninians, 29, 283
Salisbury, Earl of, 37
Salkeld, Lord Scrope's deputy, 107–8
Sanquhar Declaration, 177
Sark, River and Water of, 56, 107
Sauchie burn, 59
Schiltrons, 25–6, 28, 30–1
Scone, 26, 37
Scots Wha Hae, 14, 33–5
Scott, Robert, 107
Scott, Sir James, 136
Scott, Sir Walter, 12, 69, 93, 109, 117, 152, 165, 170, 174, 218
Scottish Minstrel, The, 51, 187
Scottish Poems of the 16th Century, 100
Scrope, Lord, 106–8
Selkirk, 25, 69, 151, 288
Sempill, Brigadier at Culloden, 217
Seton, Bonny John, 123, 126–7

Seton, John of Pitmedden, 124
Seton, Sir Alexander, 30
Sharp, Archbishop of St. Andrews, 168
Sheriff Nicolson, 158
Sheriffmuir, 190, 193–7, 210, 290
Shetland, 22, 56
Shiel, River, 198
Shortreed, Mr Thomas of Jedburgh, 117
Simpson, a minister, 272
Simpson, Macgregor, 33
Sinclairs, 41
Skirving, Mr, rhyming farmer of East
    Lothian, 206, 272
Slammanan road, 285
Smith, Lieutenant, butt of Mr Skirving, 272
Smith's *Scottish Minstrel*, 128
Solway Firth, 26
Solway Moss, 79, 152
Somerset, the Protector, 83
Songs of Scotland, 70, 129
Sorrowless Field, 66
Southdean Church, 39, 288–9
Soutra, 28–9
Spey, River, 215
Speyside, 138
Spey valley, 287
Spott, 285
Stair, Master of, Earl of, 190–1
Stewart, Alexander, Earl of Mar and
    Ogilvie, 49
Stewart, Gen David, of Garth, 205
Stewart, James, 85–6, 95
Stewart, Sir James of Doune, 95
Stewarts, 55
Stirling, 29, 30, 106, 185, 192, 201–2, 283,
    290
Stirling, Bridge, battle of, 25
Stirling Castle, 27, 29, 215
Stonehaven, the Raid of, 124
Strang, Sir William Steel, 289
Strathbogie, 142
Strathbolgie, 99
Strathearn, 28
Strathspey, 185
Stuart, Prince Charles Edward, 200, 202–4,
    209
Stuarts, 72, 124, 134, 185
Sudreys, 22
Surrey, Earl of, 62–66
Sutherlands, 209

Tay, River, 141
Taylor, I. B. Cameron, Trust Historian,
    9, 282–3, 286
Tayside, 139
Tea Table Miscellany (1750), 96
Telfer, James of Saughtree, 102
Teviotdale, 72
Thistle of Scotland, The, 147
Three Estates, The, 132
Till, River, 62
Tomintoul, 138
Torwood, 25, 29, 211, 285
Tranent, 151, 203–4, 289
Tranent Muir, ballad of, 208, 272
Trossachs, 142
Troughend, Parcy Reed, laird of, 101
Tudor, Margaret, 61
Tullibardine, Lord, 198
Turner, Sir James, a soldier of fortune, 164
Twizel Bridge, 286
Tynedale, 92

Union of the Crowns, 191
Union of the Parliaments, 191

Wade, Gen, 198, 210
Wars of the Roses, 56
Col Wallace, 165
William Wallace, Scots patriot and leader,
    25, 27
Walliford, 203, 208
Wardens of the Marches, 90–1, 101, 290
Wardlaw, Sir Henry and Lady, 22
Wareite sandwich, 283
Wark, 28, 56, 61
Warldis Instabilitie, The, 57–8
Water of Sark, 107
Western Isles, 21-2
White, Robert, his papers, 101
Wigan, 210
Wightman, Gen, 198
William III, of Orange, 178, 180, 190–1
Wills, Gen, 192
Wooler, 62
Worcester, battle of, 163–4

York, 92
Ythan, River, 138

300